AF361615

THE AMBIGUITY OF BEING

BERNARD LONERGAN
AND THE PROBLEMS
OF THE SUPERNATURAL

THE AMBIGUITY OF BEING

Bernard Lonergan and
the Problems of the Supernatural

Jonathan R. Heaps

The Catholic University of America Press
Washington, D.C.

Cataloging-in-Publication Data is available from the Library of Congress

ISBN: 978-0-8132-3804-3

eISBN: 978-0-8132-3805-0

For my father, Craig Allan Heaps,

who nurtured my questions.

CONTENTS

First and foremost, I thank my wife, Annie, for her patience, encouragement, support, and steadfast love throughout my research and writing for this project. Without her, it would have been simply impossible. Thanks to our three small children, Oskar, Josefine, and Hanna, whose mere existence proved lifeblood at the end of each day of wrestling with these questions and ideas. Thanks as well to both Annie's family and mine for providing material and emotional support throughout this entire process. Special thanks to my parents, Craig and Patti, for always fostering my curiosity and respecting my ideas.

Thanks to my teachers, Danielle Nussberger and Robert Doran, SJ, for having faith in this project and for trusting me to first begin tackling it as a doctoral student at Marquette University. Special thanks to Father Doran for his tireless efforts in editing the Collected Works of Bernard Lonergan, several volumes of which proved absolutely essential to my thinking on this project. Thanks as well to my many other teachers who helped to fertilize the intellectual soil in which this project germinated: Mark Johnson, Joseph Ogbonnaya, Andrew Tallon, Robert C. Neville, Wesley Wildman, Frederick Lawrence, Patrick Byrne, R. J. Snell, and Greg Clark.

This kind of project cannot come to life without a whole network of committed conversation partners who donate their time, their attention, their questions, and advice to it. Among such interlocutors, I would like to thank Ryan Hemmer, Anne Carpenter, Jakob Rinderknecht, Eric Mabry, Brian Bajzek, Robin Boeré, Chris Lilley, Luke Togni, Gene Schlesinger, Jeremy Blackwood, Paul Monson, John Brittingham, Jeremy Wilkins, Neil Ormerod, and no doubt others who at the moment may be slipping my mind.

I want to thank John Martino, my editor, for helping guide me through the anxious process of publishing my first scholarly monograph.

Finally, I should thank Anodyne, Wonderstate, Barrington, Ruby, Blueprint, Merit, and a handful of other specialty coffee roasters. Their products helped sustain the necessary condition of this and, indeed, any intellectual endeavor: consciousness.

INTRODUCTION

There is an old computer science joke that goes, "There are 10 kinds of people in the world: those who understand binary and those who do not." It is gauche, of course, to explain one's joke, but perhaps it will suffice to note that those who do not understand binary notation will not only miss the humor here but also the principle of division separating them from those who do. A similar problem can afflict discussions of the natural and the supernatural. When one lacks or mistakes the principle of distinction, one can swiftly lose the plot, miss the point, and begin to wander into thickets of confusion. The above joke works because it presupposes the apprehension of a single insight out of which all the various concepts of our digital world tumble. The card is punched or it is not. The circuit is open or it is not: yes or no, 0 or 1, and so on. The two basic terms originate in an alternative grasped by a single insight, a unitary understanding. Without it, I would be writing this paragraph on a typewriter instead of a laptop computer.

The problem of the supernatural is similarly anchored in a pair of terms issuing from a single insight. Bernard Lonergan called this single idea "the theorem of the supernatural."[1] This book aims to retrieve (and, in later chapters, extend) Lonergan's identification, explication, and application of this theorem to the relatively recent controversy around the natural and the supernatural. Whatever life those terms may have had before and after the emergence of this theorem, in his view (and mine) they derive their scientific meaning, their theoretical significance from an exhaustively dichotomous alternative grasped by this single insight.

This distinction and its principle are most famously associated with the fraught pair, "nature and grace." Lonergan's theorem of the supernatural names the *relationship* of entitative disproportion between the former and the latter. Lonergan notes several examples of the theorem at work in the medieval theology of grace:

---

1 Bernard Lonergan, *Grace and Freedom: Operative Grace in the Thought of St. Thomas Aquinas*, ed. Frederick E. Crowe and Robert M. Doran, CWL 1 (Toronto: Toronto University Press, 2000), 12, 15, 17, and *passim*.

But, with the thirteenth century, the dawn. Stephen Langton noted the connection between *gratuitum* and *meritum* to give significance to *gratum faciens*. Praepositinus placed the distinction between *gratuita* and *naturalia* on a solid basis by pointing out that reason is the highest thing in nature, yet faith is above reason. The final steps were taken by Philip, Chancellor of the University of Paris from 1218 to 1230. Against St Bernard and Hugh of St Victor, he reaffirmed William of Auxerre's affirmation of a natural *amor amicitiae erga Deum* quite distinct from charity, the meritorious love of God. He then presented the theory of two orders, entitatively disproportionate: not only was there the familiar series of grace, faith, charity, and merit, but also nature, reason, and the natural love of God.

However, Lonergan discovered that much as the digital binary can move beyond computational cards or tape to more plastic media (electrical circuits, lasers, etc.), this theorem's terms can be specified by any matter among which the basic relationship of disproportion obtains. In *Grace and Freedom*, Lonergan notes that the theorem of the supernatural controls not only the distinction between grace and nature but also Thomas's speculative theology of Creator and creatures.[2] In *Insight*, he carries the theorem yet further, to analogize between the absolutely supernatural (God's grace), and that which is only relatively supernatural, for instance the relation between chemical and biological processes.[3] Despite the myriad instances and variations of biological process, all relate to their underlying chemical processes according to this basic theorem. What occurs systematically in a living cell, for example, is relatively supernatural to what by the laws of chemistry occurs merely coincidentally. So it goes too between chemical and physical processes, to say nothing of the relation between intelligent, deliberative consciousness and psychosensitive consciousness.[4] All of these various metaphysical subtleties rest on the theorem of the supernatural applied in its full generality: *two terms, one hierarchically disproportionate to the other, originating in a unitary principle of distinction grasped by a single insight.*

---

2 Lonergan, *Grace and Freedom*, 81–82.

3 See Bernard Lonergan, *Insight: A Study of Human Understanding*, ed. Frederick E. Crowe and Robert M. Doran, CWL 3 (Toronto: University of Toronto Press, 1992), 657–59.

4 Lonergan, *Insight*, 144–51.

Just because something is simple does not mean it is easy. The theorem of the supernatural emerged into Roman Catholic speculative theology at the culmination of a long intellectual slog. As I will discuss in chapter 3, Lonergan argued that Philip the Chancellor, St. Albert the Great, and St. Thomas Aquinas set down their speculative accomplishments in the face of long-standing *aporia*.[5] The theorem of the supernatural arrived on the scene thanks to the combined force of their considerable intellects brought to bear upon fertile intellectual materials newly arrived on the European theological scene.[6] Such intellectual achievements are not just the products of single human minds or of single cultures but also an inheritance from one generation to the next and sometimes from one culture to another.

However, what one inherits one can squander.[7] In the course of several centuries, the mobility of the theorem of the supernatural was lost. Its subtle influence on Thomas's account of divine *concursus* ebbed as schoolmen found themselves living within a cosmos newly conceived as matter in motion. Thomas's hierarchy of coincident causes flattened and so shattered on the felt of billiards-table physics. There flared the sixteenth-century *de auxiliis* controversy about how and if human and divine freedom could operate in the world.[8] The ensuing disagreement famously proved at once so heated and so intractable that only papal intervention drew it to a close in 1598.[9] To resolve such a debate is not to pick a winner but to question its very terms. Indeed,

---

5 Lonergan, *Grace and Freedom*, 3–20, 193–251.

6 See David Burrell, *Towards a Jewish-Christian-Muslim Theology* (Malden, MA: Wiley-Blackwell, 2011).

7 "Not only is the new development accepted by some and rejected by others—there is the formation of schools—but the new schools then tend to splinter, to have periods of decay and revival. What is happening in a period of decay within a school? The words of the master are faithfully repeated, but the meaning has been devaluated and contracted to fit into a narrower horizon, a lower stage of development" (Bernard Lonergan, *Topics in Education: The Cincinnati Lectures of 1959 on the Philosophy of Education*, ed. Robert M. Doran and Frederick E. Crowe, CWL 10 [Toronto: University of Toronto Press, 1993], 95–96).

8 For a recent history of the *de auxiliis* controversy, see R. J. Matava, *Divine Causality and Human Free Choice: Domingo Báñez, Physical Premotion and the Controversy de Auxiliis Revisited* (Boston: Brill Academic, 2016).

9 The answers to such questions must be left to historians, but I find it hard to resist the suspicion that, absent an appreciation for the theorem of the supernatural applied in its full breadth, Molina and Báñez were left to construct *ad hoc* solutions to ever-multiplying conceptual problems until ultimately the enterprise seized altogether.

the failure to question the terms of the problem has rendered it intractable even still. In retrospect, those engaged in the *de auxiliis* controversy were led from the medieval problem of merit to broader cosmological problems by protomodern concerns. The challenge posed to sixteenth-century physics by Thomas's thirteenth-century metaphysics presaged a wider fissure to form between the medieval speculative mentality and modern ideals of scientific knowledge.[10] Lonergan, in both *Grace and Freedom* and some of his scholastic textbooks, sought a radical resolution to these commentarial confusions by an extensive retrieval of not only St. Thomas's theology of grace, but his philosophical account of agency in general. Lonergan presents Thomas's position on nature and grace as a specific, theological application of this general philosophical theorem. Part 2 of this book will concern itself with presenting what Lonergan was able to accomplish in that regard.

The medieval problem of grace found itself in a more completely modern horizon with the *Surnaturel* controversy of the 1940s. In a France divided between (among other parties) secular Republicanism, old-guard Catholic monarchism, and the emergence of a scattered-but-lively Social Catholicism, the quandaries of nature and grace took on a renewed relevance for contemporary fights about social and political authority in a pluralistic society.[11] Whether it was Maurice Blondel arguing with Pedro Descoqs about extrinsicism or Henri de Lubac with Reginald Garrigou-Lagrange about a natural desire to see God, Catholic philosophers and theologians argued about where and how God's redemptive agency—and so authority—can be discerned in the world. It was (and remains) tempting to tear "natural" and "supernatural" from their place in the discourse of speculative theology and, as though at the edge of Solomon's sword, to offer the former to the state and the latter to the Church. Conversely, one might suppose drawing *any* distinction between nature and grace would produce a death-dealing vivisection of an integral Christian doctrine (and, by extension, politics). In

10 See Bernard Lonergan, "Dimensions of Meaning," in *Collection*, 2nd ed., ed. Frederick E. Crowe and Robert M. Doran, CWL 4 (Toronto: University of Toronto Press, 1988), 232–45; "Belief: Today's Issue," in *A Second Collection*, 2nd ed., ed. Robert M. Doran and John D. Dadosky, CWL 13 (Toronto: University of Toronto Press, 2016), 75–85.

11 See Paul Misner, *Social Catholicism in Europe: From the Onset of Industrialization to the First World War* (New York: Crossroad, 1991); *Catholic Labor Movements in Europe: Social Thought and Action, 1914-1965* (Washington, DC: The Catholic University of America Press, 2015).

the last century, magisterial authorities themselves vacillated with regard to this alternative. They, for example, at one point condemned opponents of the *Action Française* and, at another, participation in the movement.[12] The theological controversy seemed to be resolved first in one direction by what some read as a repudiation of *Surnaturel* in the pages of *Humani Generis*, but then in the other by *Gaudium et Spes* 22 and the much discussed (but little defined) "post-Vatican II consensus" in Roman Catholic theological anthropology.[13]

Around the turn of the twenty-first century, this controversy reemerged, primarily in the anglophone context.[14] It appeared first as an intra-Thomist argument and then spilled over into the wider scene. Its basic theological and philosophical terms had not much changed since the 1940s, but the background concerns about modernity had matured. The internecine divisions of Republican France seem quaint and parochial when compared to the concerns about globalization, multiculturalism, decolonization, and pluralistic democracy shaping early twenty-first century Catholic theological anxieties. Nonetheless, on both sides of the more recent debate over the supernatural, the metaphysical strategies of the 1940s persisted. Answers to

12 See Peter Bernardi, *Maurice Blondel, Social Catholicism, and Action Française: The Clash over the Church's Role in Society during the Modernist Era* (Washington, DC: The Catholic University of America Press, 2009).

13 Compare *Humani Generis* ("It is well known how highly the Church regards human reason, for it falls to reason to demonstrate with certainty the existence of God, personal and one; to prove beyond doubt from divine signs the very foundations of the Christian faith; to express properly the law which the Creator has imprinted in the hearts of men; and finally to attain to some notion, indeed a very fruitful notion, of mysteries" [Pius XII, encyclical letter *Humani Generis*, August 12, 1950, sec. 29]) with *Gaudium et Spes* ("In reality it is only in the mystery of the Word made flesh that the mystery of man truly becomes clear.... For since Christ died for all, and since all men are in fact called to one and the same destiny, which is divine, we must hold that the Holy Spirit offers to all the possibility of being made partners, in a way known to God, in the paschal mystery" [Vatican Council II, *Gaudium et Spes*, Pastoral Constitution of the Church in the Modern World, December 7, 1965, sec. 22]). See also William L. Portier, "Twentieth-Century Catholic Theology and the Triumph of Maurice Blondel," *Communio* 38, no. 1 (Spring 2011): 103–37.

14 One significant exception is the volume assembled by Fr. Serge-Thomas Bonino, OP, *Surnaturel,* available in English translation (*Surnaturel: A Controversy at the Heart of Twentieth-Century Thomistic Thought,* trans. Robert Williams [Ave Maria, FL: Sapientia Press, 2009]).

a medieval speculative problem of the supernatural are expected to more or less directly address the modern problem of discerning God's work in the vast, but now-interconnected, world. It is little noted, in fact, the extent to which the debate has proceeded in the key of formal ontology or the respects in which it might move beyond that intellectual technique. A cadre of neo–de Lubacians put forward the categories of "gift" and philosophical paradox to liberate the supernatural from what they view as neo-scholastic captivity and secular modernist complicity. While this can appear anti-metaphysical (at least by contrast with its neo-scholastic opponents), the neo–de Lubacians—John Milbank's postmodern elision being noted below—nonetheless stake out a metaphysical position on the problem of the supernatural.[15] Indeed, Milbank is explicit that a mistaken theory of the natural/supernatural relation can render political theology impossible per se.[16] The neo–de Lubacians were opposed in this effort by a band of neo-neo-scholastics—both the straight-to-the-historical–Thomas "ressourcement Thomists" and the commentary-tradition-retrieving "Thomists of the strict observance"—who resolve the problem of the supernatural by rehabilitating the concept of "pure nature." At their vanguard is Steven A. Long who, although sympathetic to de Lubac's concern about pervasive secularization, thinks the rejection, let alone the marginalization of *natura pura,* was precisely the wrong approach.[17] Long argues that recognizing pure nature and its proportionate end reveals philosophically (and so, he implies, publicly) the "theonomic" character of our nature and all creation with it. Metaphysical anthropology set against the backdrop of an explicitly Thomist ontological hierarchy provides the basic position, known with natural certitude, from which God's legislative intentions can be discerned and—because it is a matter of philosophy and not sacred theology—then thematized in law. Long insists that this does not prevent it from serving a kind of apologetic purpose in an ostensibly

15 See John Milbank's argument that de Lubac's account consists in a "non-ontology" that is "articulated between the discourses of philosophy and theology, fracturing their respective autonomies, but tying them loosely and yet firmly together" (John Milbank, *The Suspended Middle: Henri de Lubac and the Renewed Split in Modern Catholic Theology*, 2nd ed. (Grand Rapids, MI: Eerdmans, 2014), 4–5.

16 John Milbank, *Theology and Social Theory: Beyond Secular Reason*, 2nd ed. (Malden, MA: Blackwell, 2006), 206–9.

17 Steven A. Long, *Natura Pura: On the Recovery of Nature in the Doctrine of Grace* (New York: Fordham University Press, 2010).

pluralistic society. Still, the only viable pluralism Long admits is that among natural law theists and Roman Catholics obedient to the Magisterium on all matters of faith and morals.

An assumption undergirds this debate and it is shared by both the neo–de Lubacians and the neo-neo-scholastics. Nearly every player in the contemporary anglophone controversy over the supernatural sets out constructing, retrieving, or elucidating a metaphysics of the natural/ supernatural relation, usually in a medieval or Renaissance mode, and very often implying (but only occasionally spelling out) the adequacy of these metaphysical positions to addressing modern concerns like secularism, atheism, individualism, and so forth.[18] Nearly all parties on all sides of this debate assume a basic reducibility of Christianity's neuralgic problems with modernity to whether or not the correct position on the metaphysical relation of nature to grace or of human nature to its end prevails in Christian theology.

Taking the turn of the century controversy as a jumping-off point, this book will proceed in four parts to address the problems generated by such methodological myopia. In the first part I will explore various forms of the above assumption about the adequacy of metaphysics to the problem of the supernatural and discern from among them that, on this approach, the debate is intractable (chapter 1). I will further discern that this intractability owes to the persistent presence of *two* problems of the supernatural at work in the twentieth- and twenty-first-century controversies. Though these two problems are integrally linked with one another, I will argue one is ultimately irreducible to the other (chapter 2). As I noted above, in the second part, I will turn to Lonergan's retrieval and reconstruction of the medieval problem of the supernatural in some detail, considering first his account of its diachronic development in the theology of grace (chapter 3). Still, the development of theological and philosophical problems and their solutions is a messy business, with certain necessary intellectual conditions falling into historical place only as adequate minds get hold of adequate materials. And

18 David Bentley Hart's somewhat belated intervention into the controversy is a laudable exception, insofar as he also proceeds according to a logico-metaphysical method but does not proceed to imply, let alone deduce, a theo-political arrangement from his basic position (which resembles Milbank in its broad strokes) or his more developed "chiastic" scheme of trinitarian participation. See David Bentley Hart, *You Are Gods: On Nature and Supernature* (Notre Dame, IN: University of Notre Dame Press, 2022).

so although part 2 will culminate with a presentation of Lonergan's synthetic appropriation of St. Thomas Aquinas's mature position, Thomas's specific position on grace carries with it and rests upon a set of general philosophical positions with regard to agency, human and divine. These hold together a Thomist understanding of the natural and the supernatural in manner that was once called "scientific," albeit in a "medieval" or "classical" sense (chapter 4). Only after I survey this process of development will I shift from the *via inventionis* to the *via doctrina* to provide a synthetic and synchronic presentation of Lonergan's Thomistic, medieval solution to the medieval problem of the supernatural (chapter 5).

In the third part, I will begin to shift away from medieval intellectual techniques toward modern ones. I will examine how, latent in the medieval solution to the medieval problem of the supernatural, there lurk some ambiguities that the emergence of modern methods and mentalities will bring to light (chapter 6). Indeed, I will consider two basic alternatives set out by these medieval ambiguities once they find their lights in the horizon set out by a modern philosophical mentality. These basic alternatives will be embodied for my purposes in the figures of Maurice Blondel and Jean-Paul Sartre (chapter 7). Still, even if I can resolve which of these basic alternatives will comport with Catholic faith and philosophy, readers will find that the modern problem of the supernatural is not so easily resolved. Indeed, they may be surprised by how difficult it will prove to even *articulate* the modern problem of the supernatural in a rigorous way (chapter 8). In the fourth and final part, I will return to the horizon of Thomist metaphysics to present an argument for why the modern problem is irreducible to and so irresolvable by medieval, metaphysical solutions. To accomplish this, I will look closely at Lonergan's Thomistic metaphysics of human freedom (chapters 8, 9, and 10). In the process, I will set out a number of (perhaps surprising) determinations of the modern problem that will inform how to articulate the modern problem of the supernatural but also how to set out a heuristic structure for anticipating its solution (chapter 11). What surprise my conclusions evoke may owe in no small part to how the final part of this book can be read as a traditional, Thomist argument that so-called "contextual" theologies are not only "valid," but *essential* to the future of theology if it can once again be called a science, albeit according to a modern, rather than medieval ideal.

A final introductory note about the appellations "medieval" and "modern" in this work. As in the above paragraphs, I mean to invoke by them two different ideals of "science," which is to say two different ideals for asking and answering questions in a systematic and reliable way. Thus, when I speak of medieval or modern problems, solutions, and ambiguities, I mean to fit them under what Max Weber called "ideal types" rather than into particular historical periods or epochs.[19] Indeed, in what follows, phrases like "the medieval ambiguities" and "the modern problem" become technical terms. If one takes my descriptions in a historical sense, a number of anomalies will arise, for some things I call "medieval" (like aspects of the Thomist commentary tradition) are arguably early modern and some things I call "modern" (like Sartre's philosophy) are arguably postmodern. Rest assured, I will return to and expand on my intended, methodological senses of "medieval" and "modern" again in chapter 2. For now, I will mention that, although Lonergan's earlier, overtly-Thomist works will serve as my primary guide through this book, I am here too borrowing one of his distinctions but from a later phase of his scholarship, one preoccupied with helping Catholic theology navigate its post-Conciliar transition from the "medieval" to the "modern."[20] That latter phase culminates in his 1972 work, *Method in Theology*, for which the book you are reading now might be considered a prolegomena, albeit one aimed at an audience of Thomists and other theologians for whom the natural/supernatural controversy has held some fascination.

19 See Max Weber, *The Methodology of the Social Sciences*, trans. and ed. Edward A. Schils and Henry A. Finch (New York: Free Press, 1949), 89–112.

20 See, for example, Lonergan, "Dimensions of Meaning."

PART I

PROBLEMS

CHAPTER 1

THE (NOT SO) NEW CONTROVERSY

The anglophone literature on the controversy over the supernatural is a shimmering, swirling vortex of vortices, sounding with the clattering and reclattering of Patristic, Thomistic, Renaissance, twentieth- and twenty-first-century theological and philosophical material. Article after article, book after book has tried to capitulate and recapitulate, again and again, Thomas's philosophical and theological achievements, the various clarifications and obfuscations, retrievals and misrememberings of the Renaissance commentarial tradition, early-twentieth-century transformations and reactions in theological method, the myriad appraisals of their post-Conciliar consequences (regarding which, for every three theologians, there are five opinions), and the fractal perspectives of each figure trying to at once offer his or her (but usually his) subtle refinement of any or all of the aforementioned, while at the same time defending his (usually his) pet figure from the attacks of the others. There are, in this cloud of witnesses, some truly masterful works. Still, in surveying about 20 years of scholarly writing on the topic, I cannot find a single work that *masters* the debate itself. As becomes more or less immediately evident in surveying the controversy, the scholarly community does not need one more rehearsal of the debate. They are ample.[1]

In what follows, I very briefly sketch the unfolding of the twenty-first-century controversy in the anglophone literature, before considering evidence for the intractability of the contemporary controversy over the supernatural. This latter task will proceed by comparison with a cognate

---

1 For an in-depth review of the contemporary controversy, see Christopher Smith, "*Surnaturel* Revisited: Henri de Lubac's Theology of the Supernatural in Contemporary Theology" (PhD diss., Universidad de Navarra, 2013). For a briefer but still excellent review, see Edward T. Oakes, "The Surnaturel Controversy: A Survey and a Response," *Nova et Vetera (English Edition)* 9, no. 3 (Summer 2011): 625–56.

controversy in France in the 1940s. In chapter 2 I will turn to this body of evidence to consider my contention that there are two problems at play in the controversy over the supernatural, and not just one. In brief, I believe that there are collapsed into the problem of the supernatural as commonly considered a "medieval" problem and a distinct—in fact, irreducible—"modern" problem of the supernatural. I will return in earnest to my claim that the modern version of the problem is irreducible to the medieval one in chapters 8 and 9, but here I will examine evidence of precisely such a reduction in the debate thus far.

The Recent Anglophone Controversy
Over the Supernatural

At the turn of the twenty-first century, the question of the supernatural was mostly a matter of intra-Thomist debate. In a 2000 article in *The Thomist*, Steven A. Long engaged dialectically with the work of Denis Bradley on the various *loci* of the debate: the notion of obediential potency, the reality of a purely natural end for human beings, the natural desire to see God, whether the latter is in vain, whether it is specifically in vain apart from grace, and how Christ reveals the profundity of our nature and its ends to us.[2] These are treated primarily as exegetical, hermeneutical, and logical matters internal to Thomas's writings. In 2004, Sapientia Press published the first edition of Lawrence Feingold's *The Natural Desire to See God according to St. Thomas Aquinas and His Interpreters,* which offers a compendious survey of the commentarial tradition on the question, as well as dialectical engagement with Henri de Lubac and the *Nouvelle théologie.*[3]

There is, at the same time, a parallel discussion about the reception and interpretation of Henri de Lubac among Anglo-Catholics. In the 1990s, John Milbank's *Theology and Social Theory* bracketed what he considered reactionary "integralism" to focus on the theological conditions of possibility for a genuine Christian socialism. He sought to adjudicate between ostensibly Rahnerian Liberation Theologies and the promise of a semi-Blondelian/

---

2 Steven A. Long, "On the Possibility of a Purely Natural End for Man," *The Thomist* 64, no. 1 (2000): 211–37.

3 Lawrence Feingold, *The Natural Desire to See God according to St. Thomas Aquinas and His Interpreters*, 1st ed. (Naples, FL: Sapientia Press, 2004).

de Lubacian/Balthasarian post-liberal political theology.[4] A decade later, Milbank addressed a wider range of Christian ontologies and with them a wider array of political theologies, sketching out his radicalized neo–de Lubacian position in the "suspended middle" between them. Thus, his *The Suspended Middle* appeared in 2005, revisiting his approach to the question of the supernatural in *Theology and Social Theory*. There, Milbank takes up Henri de Lubac's *Surnaturel* (and its reworked thesis in *The Mystery of the Supernatural*) to advance his postmodern troubling not only of the natural/supernatural distinction but also of formal ontology per se.[5] Milbank was not the only Anglo-Catholic theologian turning to de Lubac in the early 2000s on matters of church, politics, and church politics. Hans Boersma in 2007 published "Sacramental Ontology: Nature and the Supernatural in the Ecclesiology of Henri de Lubac" in *New Blackfriars*, noting not only the political context and questions of de Lubac's work but also avoiding dialectical discourse with de Lubac's Thomist critics.[6]

Although Guy Mansini presciently brought the neo-neo-scholastic and neo–de Lubacian approaches into conversation with his 2002 *Gregorianum* article, it was a 2007 issue of *Nova et Vetera* devoted to Lawrence Feingold's book that touched the match to the fuel of the contemporary controversy.[7] Steven A. Long and Reinhard Hütter's contributions anchored the book symposium, both taking a stand on Feingold's considerable research to intervene in the debate. Long took on de Lubac's interpretation of Thomas, and Hütter in turn criticized Milbank's radicalization of de Lubac.[8] Long and Hütter would remain at the core of the neo-neo-scholastic response

4 John Milbank, *Theology and Social Theory: Beyond Secular Theory*, 2nd ed. (Malden, MA: Blackwell, 2006), 206–56.

5 John Milbank, *The Suspended Middle: Henri de Lubac and the Debate concerning the Supernatural*, 1st ed. (Grand Rapids, MI: Eerdmans, 2005).

6 Hans Boersma, "Sacramental Ontology: Nature and the Supernatural in the Ecclesiology of Henri de Lubac," *New Blackfriars* 88, no. 1015 (2007): 242–73.

7 Guy Mansini, "Henri de Lubac, the Natural Desire to See God, and Pure Nature," *Gregorianum* 83, no. 1 (2002): 89–109.

8 Steven A. Long, "On the Loss, and the Recovery, of Nature as a Theonomic Principle: Reflections on the Nature/Grace Controversy," *Nova et Vetera (English Edition)* 5, no. 1 (2007): 133-83; Reinhard Hütter, "*Desiderium Naturale Visionis Dei—Est Autem Duplex Hominis Beatitudo Sive Felicitas*: Some Observations about Lawrence Feingold's and John Milbank's Recent Interventions in the Debate over the Natural Desire to See God," *Nova et Vetera (English Edition)* 5, no. 1 (2007): 81–131.

to the "de Lubac-ian consensus." Their arguments from this symposium would reappear (in whole or in part) as chapters in their own books addressing (in whole or in part) the controversy over the supernatural in the twenty-first century.[9]

The conversation spilled over into *Communio* and *Theological Studies* in 2008. Nicholas Healy's article in *Communio* tried to resituate the discussion of de Lubac's work in a more properly theological context than the usual framing in formal ontology.[10] Raymond Moloney sought to bring Bernard Lonergan's interventions to bear on the renewed debate in the pages of *Theological Studies,* perhaps with an eye to correcting Mansini's rather narrow comparison with Feingold in *Nova et Vetera*.[11] Hütter and Mansini, in turn, would take up complementary questions in the pages of *The Thomist*, the former giving a detailed exegesis of Thomas's method and conclusions regarding the desire for God in the *Summa Contra Gentiles* (with a particular eye to isolating the properly philosophical elements of Thomas's position) and the latter underlining the ongoing significance of de Lubac's theology—for good or ill—in Roman Catholic thought.[12]

In 2010's *Natura Pura*, Steven A. Long did for Feingold what Milbank had previously done for de Lubac: briefly and polemically radicalize the basic outlook embedded in the accumulation of theological data.[13] The first chapter

---

9 Steven A. Long, *Natura Pura: On the Recovery of Nature in the Doctrine of Grace* (New York: Fordham University Press, 2010); Reinhard Hütter, *Dust Bound for Heaven: Explorations in the Theology of Thomas Aquinas* (Grand Rapids, MI: Eerdmans, 2012).

10 Nicholas J. Healy, "Henri de Lubac on Nature and Grace: A Note on Some Recent Contributions to the Debate," *Communio* 35, no. 4 (Winter 2008): 535–64.

11 Raymond Moloney, "De Lubac and Lonergan on the Supernatural," *Theological Studies* 69, no. 3 (2008): 509–27. No one has managed to make Lonergan's contributions to the controversy of the 1940s a central voice in the contemporary debate. Lonergan's interventions were at some remove from the heart of the original controversy and some of the relevant texts were not widely available until the publication of "De ente supernaturali" and "De scientia atque voluntate Dei" in translation in 2011 (Bernard Lonergan, *Early Latin Theology*, ed. Robert M. Doran and H. Daniel Monsour, trans. Michael Shields, CWL 19 [Toronto: University of Toronto Press, 2011], 52–255; 256–411).

12 Reinhard Hütter, "Aquinas on the Natural Desire for the Vision of God: A Relecture of *Summa contra Gentiles* III, c. 25, *après* Henri de Lubac," *The Thomist* 73, no. 4 (2009): 523–91; Guy Mansini, "The Abiding Theological Significance of Henri de Lubac's *Surnaturel*," *The Thomist* 73, no. 4 (2009): 593–619.

13 "[The] first chapter [is] an essay written on the occasion of a symposium

offers a lightly edited version of his *Nova et Vetera* defense of *natura pura*. Then Long widened his scope to criticize Hans Urs von Balthasar's treatment and criticism of *natura pura*. Long also considers the moral and political theological proposals of three fellow Roman Catholic thinkers in light of his thesis about the centrality of *natura pura*. Against Jacques Maritain, Long argues that a practical consensus cannot be made with those who reject the "theonomic" character of reality both undergirded and made manifest by the philosophical discernment of *natura pura* in "precision from grace." Against Jean Porter, he argues for the perennial nature of this theonomicity's content, such that any effort to historicize moral reasoning as a capacity must run aground on its stubborn teleological structure and so, again, its determinate content. Long finds that David Schindler Sr. "underemphasizes the realization that the core and architectonic elements in sociopolitical, legal, and cultural life, when they have been healthy in the West and particularly in North America, have comprised a strong subset of the theoretic inheritance of Christendom (the *praembula fidea* and the truths of the natural law)."[14] In the words of D. Stephen Long, for Steven A. Long, "The Catholic doctrine of pure nature fulfills Protestantism and America."[15] Long's argument, that *natura pura* funds a) the thick conception of the natural law required for the moral life and b) a return to the confessional state required for justice to flourish, presents with admirable clarity the moral, social, and political theological questions that are always waiting in the wings of the debate about the supernatural. I will return to these in chapter 2.

While Long tried to drag the controversy closer to the center of Thomist philosophy, others aimed to widen the idiom of the debate. Conor Cunningham satirized the hypothetical logic of *natura pura* in the pages of

---

honoring the distinguished and profound contribution of Dr. Lawrence Feingold's *The Natural Desire to See God According to St. Thomas Aquinas and His Interpreters*. I have deliberately retained the character of this essay as part of the symposium largely verbatim (with two significant exceptions), both because Dr. Feingold merits that his original and lengthy manuscript be read in its entirety by every soul interested in this question, and because this essay presents arguments that are virtually unknown by many who are accustomed to the rhetoric surrounding the nature/grace dispute but not the profound and clear teaching of St. Thomas Aquinas" (Long, *Natura Pura*, 3).

14 Long, *Natura Pura*, 197.

15 D. Stephen Long, review of *Natura Pura: On the Recovery of Nature in the Doctrine of Grace*, by Steven A. Long, *Modern Theology* 27, no. 4 (2011): 695–98.

Communio, indicating that it implies a world alien to Christian doctrine.[16] Kathryn Tanner recalled the biblical link between human nature and the *imago Dei* to suggest that we recognize the relevant analogue for the divine in our unlimited plasticity. She argued that this malleable historicity is a kind of ontological poverty that accords better with the gratuity of both creation and grace.[17] Servais Pinkaers brought in a phenomenology of friendship to modulate the account of desire implied in a "natural desire to see God."[18] Edward T. Oakes made a valiant play to transpose the debate into the existential key of Balthasarian theo-dramatics, speaking of an overlooked "natural hostility to God."[19] Sean Larsen's article in *Modern Theology* was perhaps the most impressive foray, going to great lengths to enter into the mentality of both Milbank and Hütter, then measuring them both against the challenge posed by Walter Mignolo's decolonial renarration of modernity.[20] Even Larsen, who made the most responsible report on these two major figures in the debate and also the most radical challenge from beyond the controversy's usual bounds, ultimately sides with Hütter on metaphysical and epistemic grounds and only gestures in conclusion to the idea that perhaps de Lubac's central point was never really metaphysical after all.[21]

Still, others have been content to continue hashing out the problem in strictly Thomist terms. Bernard Mulcahy's book, *Aquinas's Notion of Pure Nature and the Christian Integralism of Henri de Lubac,* took an unapologetically

16 Conor Cunningham, "*Natura Pura*, the Invention of the Anti-Christ: A Week with No Sabbath," *Communio* 37, no. 2 (2010): 243–54.

17 Kathryn Tanner, "Grace without Nature," in *Without Nature?: A New Condition for Theology*, ed. David Albertson and Cabell King (New York: Fordham University Press, 2010), 363–75.

18 Servais Pinckaers, "The Natural Desire to See God," *Nova et Vetera (English Edition)* 8, no. 3 (Summer 2010): 627–46.

19 Oakes, "The Surnaturel Controversy."

20 Sean Larsen, "The Politics of Desire: Two Readings of Henri de Lubac on Nature and Grace," *Modern Theology* 29, no. 3 (July 2013): 279–310.

21 "My proposal—only a very brief suggestion here—is that a post-metaphysical reading that does not see de Lubac primarily through what he received from Blondel or Maréchal but rather as cobbling together a theological response to mid-twentieth-century politics may be a fruitful way forward in current debates about nature and grace. In this way, I have tried to provide a prolegomena for a constructive reading of de Lubac as neither a Jansenist, nor a Thomist, nor a radical Bulgakovian Origenist neoplatonist, but rather as an Augustinian" (Larsen, 310).

Thomist line.[22] Thomas Joseph White entered the fray in 2010 as well, engaging admirably with the problem of historicity and historicism, though still offering a basically Aristotelian response to Foucault and Nietzsche: nature is the intelligibility of substance, and so is required to even recognize historical transformation as change per se.[23] As mentioned above, Hütter's *Dustbound for Heaven* returned to the topic after three chapters on Thomist political theology. However, as I will discuss below, the tendency remains, even among those who venture beyond merely exegetical questions, to settle the challenges of history, morality, society, and polity in exclusively metaphysical terms.[24] Of late, the parties have retreated to their corners. Articles by Thomists are increasingly exegetical and historical.[25] The debate, though hardly settled, seemed in remission.

There have been some promising, if somewhat orthogonal, approaches to the problem using other figures and loci in more recent years. An interesting issue of *Nova et Vetera* considered the legacy of Matthias Scheeben through the lens of the nature and grace debate. Unfortunately, many of the speculative avenues suggested by Scheeben's work are, as of now, still waiting to be taken up.[26] On the other side of the debate,

---

22 It ultimately did not make much of an impression on the debate, save a review alongside Long's *Natura Pura* in *Nova et Vetera*. See Bernard Mulcahy, *Aquinas's Notion of Pure Nature and the Christian Integralism of Henri de Lubac: Not Everything Is Grace* (New York: Peter Lang, 2011); Thomas M. Osborne, "Natura Pura: Two Recent Works," *Nova et Vetera (English Edition)* 11, no. 1 (Winter 2013): 265–79.

23 Thomas Joseph White, "The 'Pure Nature' of Christology: Human Nature and *Gaudium et Spes* 22," *Nova et Vetera (English Edition)* 8, no. 2 (Spring 2010): 283–322.

24 Christopher J. Malloy, "De Lubac on Natural Desire: Difficulties and Antitheses," *Nova et Vetera (English Edition)* 9, no. 3 (2011): 567–624.

25 Joshua R. Brotherton, "The Integrity of Nature in the Grace-Freedom Dynamic: Lonergan's Critique of Báñezian Thomism," *Theological Studies* 75, no. 3 (2014): 537–63; Thomas Joseph White, "Imperfect Happiness and the Final End of Man: Thomas Aquinas and the Paradigm of Nature-Grace Orthodoxy," *The Thomist* 78, no. 2 (2014): 247–89; Shawn M. Colberg, "Aquinas and the Grace of Auxilium," *Modern Theology* 32, no. 2 (2016): 187–210.

26 Edward T. Oakes, "Scheeben the Reconciler: Resolving the Nature-Grace Debate," *Nova et Vetera (English Edition)* 11, no. 2 (Spring 2013): 435–53; Thomas Joseph White, "Good Extrinsicism: Matthias Scheeben and the Ideal Paradigm of Nature-Grace Orthodoxy," *Nova et Vetera (English Edition)* 11, no. 2 (Spring 2013): 537–63.

David Grumett's 2015 article carried de Lubac's thesis toward Augustinian doctrinal questions and away from metaphysical or political questions, and so also away from the conflict with interpreters of Thomas.[27] The appearance of John Betz and David Bentley Hart's translation of Erich Przywara's *Analogia Entis*, along with its excellent introductory material, provided English-speaking readers with another opportunity to consider cognate question from a different metaphysical frame, on one side conversant with Thomas Aquinas but on the other engaged (quite presciently) with German philosophical ontology.[28]

But even more recently, the wheel of debate seems to have turned all the way around, although this is not to say that no progress has been made. Jacob Wood's excellent 2019 work of historical theology digs deep into Thomas's predecessors and influences to provide a more fulsome, multifaceted picture of his position on nature and grace, teasing out the interactions of its various elements: the metaphysics of intellect and will as well as of matter and form.[29] Though it does repeat the early tendency to treat the problem as basically a matter of interpretation, the quality and sophistication of the interpretive method is, to this nonhistorian's eyes, much improved. On the other side, David Bentley Hart's 2022 book, *You Are Gods*, sets aside almost entirely questions of interpretation to take its own vociferous stand on the quasi-Milbankian premise that to deny spiritual natures necessarily have a supernatural end is not only sub-Christian but metaphysically blinkered. Hart, by contrast with Milbank, however, treats this as a primarily logical matter of following out the ontological implications of any remotely adequate definition of spiritual being.[30] And so, while the debate has not quite run round in a circle, it has taken the form of something like a cycloid: making meager progress by passing over again and again the same terrain.

---

27 David Grumett, "De Lubac, Grace, and the Pure Nature Debate," *Modern Theology* 31, no. 1 (January 2015): 123–46.

28 Erich Przywara, *Analogia Entis: Metaphysics—Original Structure and Universal Rhythm*, tran. John R. Betz and David Bentley Hart (Grand Rapids, MI: Eerdmans, 2014).

29 Jacob W. Wood, *To Stir a Restless Heart: Thomas Aquinas and Henri de Lubac on Nature, Grace, and the Desire for God* (Washington, DC: The Catholic University of America Press, 2019).

30 David Bentley Hart, *You Are Gods: On Nature and Supernature* (Notre Dame, IN: University of Notre Dame Press, 2022).

De Facto Intractability

The narrative above, insofar as it begins with and returns to scholarly siloes, implies that the twenty-first-century debate over the supernatural is intractable. I would venture that even the efforts to reposition or relocate the debate (among which this volume could well be counted) bolster rather than mitigate this sense. One obvious strategy for demonstrating (rather than merely implying) its intractability would involve showing how the controversy is *conceptually* or *logically* intractable. In other words, I could present first an analytic of the arguments on offer, then some synthesis of the opposed positions with due caveats for where this ideal type breaks with the data set, and a line of inference indicating why the positions as stated and so opposed *cannot* be brought to some final, adjudicated position. I could, in other words, labor to show that the contemporary controversy over the supernatural is per se intractable. This approach poses several serious problems. First, I am not *certain* that this conclusion follows from the facts, though neither am I certain that it does not. Second, it would require a Herculean (and, if it proved correct, Sisyphean) scholarly task that would occupy the entire length of this study, preventing me from turning to both an interpretive and constructive reframing of the problem. Third and finally, to be preoccupied with the problem as it stands, even to show that the problem is per se intractable, would cover over what, in my view, is the problem with the problem of the supernatural: that it consists in two problems and not just one. Parties concerned with this controversy need to face up to this problem with the problem in order to move the whole issue forward, rather than merely explaining why it is not moving or, more precisely, that what modest forward movement it has made, it makes by moving in circles.

To that end, I will present in the remainder of this chapter evidence that the controversy is *de facto* intractable.[31] My presentation will take the form of a comparison, holding up the present debate to the debates of the 1940s and especially those debates as they approached their near-term cessation in the promulgation of *Humani Generis*. Aidan Nichols's excellent short history of the *tête-à-tête* between the Jesuits of Lyon and the Dominicans of Toulouse from 1946 to 1949 will serve as a representative sample of our debate's

---

31 Nor am I alone in this assessment. Oakes agreed in 2013 that "this debate has now reached a kind of stalemate" ("Scheeben the Reconciler," 435).

prior instantiation.[32] This may not seem like the most relevant excerpt, when compared to the more famous (and arguably more pertinent) conflagration between Henri de Lubac and Reginald Garrigou-Lagrange subsequent to the publication of *Surnaturel* in the summer of 1946 or even the prior debates over the notion of Christian philosophy in the 1930s.[33] However, the vignette selected by Nichols serves better here. It is less narrowly preoccupied with the specific metaphysical quandary of the natural desire to see God, enveloping the wider and equally integral questions of theological method, its relationship to philosophy, and the merits of engaging with modern movements in thought.

This more capacious subject matter allows a wider range of correlations to be drawn with the contemporary debate. I find the major players in the debate of the 1940s like Garrigou-Lagrange, Marie-Michel Labourdette, Jean Daniélou, and Henri de Lubac making theological, philosophical, and methodological moves that presage the approaches taken by the likes of Steven A. Long, Reinhard Hütter, Servais Pinkaers, and John Milbank. My intention in drawing these parallels is to suggest that the twenty-first-century debate is not so much advancing its mid-century predecessor as reenacting it. This will be offered as warrant for the judgment that this debate was *de facto* intractable, resting on terms that hew so closely to those of the 1940s.

Nichols begins his history of the conflict at the 1946 publication of Labourdette's essay, *"La théologie et ses sources,"* in the *Revue Thomiste*. Labourdette takes aim at the *Source Chrétiennes* (edited by Daniélou and de Lubac) and *Théologie* monograph series, and so by extension at the Jesuits of Lyon from whom the series issue. Labourdette expresses "grave reservations" about both series and calls for a debate as to the "nature and task of Catholic theology."[34] He found them both, in Nichols's words, "animated by a spirit of disapprobation of, and even contempt for, the Scholastic and especially the Thomist achievement, and worse still by a depreciation of intelligence in its search for abiding truth."[35] The previous year and with reference to the

---

32 Aidan Nichols, "Thomism and the *Nouvelle Théologie*," *The Thomist* 64, no. 1 (2000): 1–19.

33 On the latter, see Gregory B. Sadler, *Reason Fulfilled by Revelation: The 1930s Christian Philosophy Debates in France* (Washington, DC: The Catholic University of America Press, 2011).

34 Nichols, "Thomism and the *Nouvelle Théologie*," 2–3.

35 Nichols, 3.

wider Continental culture, Charles Journet wrote to Jacques Maritain, "In this disintegration of the world, if you try to stay faithful to St. Thomas, they think you're mad."[36] This shift away from the centrality of Thomism (and Thomists) to the intellectual life of France was read by the Thomists concerned as, in Maritain's phrasing, "anti-intellectualism." It took on this cast especially insofar as, in their view, it "put between brackets the conceptual formulation of maybe even the revelation but certainly the theology and philosophy we have received from the Middle Ages."[37]

The echoes of this sentiment return, in our day, most strongly and most clearly from the work of Steven A. Long. In addition to a persistent tendency to quote from St. Thomas as though that alone settles matters both of philosophy and theology, to say nothing of interpretation, Long quite explicitly holds up the Thomist commentarial tradition as the achievement of true metaphysical knowledge in both the natural and the supernatural orders. Deviation from this tradition of Thomist thought "constitutes a veritable Rosetta stone in deciphering the intelligible causes and narrative of post-modern, pluralist theological fragmentation."[38] He claims that the very thing de Lubac aimed to accomplish in opposing secularist materialism and individualism "truly is achieved ... in the doctrine of St. Thomas Aquinas and of the Thomistic commentatorial tradition that de Lubac misapprehended."[39] But Long is not alone here. Thomas Joseph White has on more than one occasion taken up the Dominican mantle in this debate to insist that Thomas (and through him, Aristotle) is up to the task of providing not just a contemporary but indeed a perennial philosophy for the Church.[40] Reinhard Hütter noted relatively early on that Lawrence Feingold's compendious *The Natural Desire to See God according to St. Thomas Aquinas and His Interpreters* has perhaps proved so provocative to John Milbank and others because it proceeds in precision from both modern secular thought and more recent, culturally dialogical forms of Thomism.[41] Hütter does not shy away either

---

36 Nichols, 7.

37 Nichols, 7.

38 Long, "Nature as a Theonomic Principle," 157; *Natura Pura,* 27.

39 Long, "Nature as a Theonomic Principle," 182; *Natura Pura,* 50.

40 Thomas Joseph White, *Wisdom in the Face of Modernity: A Study in Thomistic Natural Theology* (Ave Maria, FL: Sapientia Press, 2009). See also his "Imperfect Happiness and the Final End of Man."

41 Hütter, *"Desiderium Naturale Visionis Dei,"* 91.

from indicating that this provocation is compounded by "operating in a mode of discourse very unfamiliar to theological readers by now largely unaccustomed to the conceptual precision and rigor once cultivated by the 'schoolmen.'"[42] Christopher Malloy echoes this accusation against modern Catholic theology.[43] In any case, one can see that there is a tendency still among the neo-neo-scholastics to repeat the neo-scholastic linkage of anti- or a-scholasticism with anti-intellectualism and decadence. More to my own purposes, one can note as well the tendency to see a medieval ideal of science (*scientia*) as the only genuine ideal in philosophy and theology.

But anti-intellectualism or decadence were not the only things, in Labourdette's estimation, that ailed the series emerging from Lyons in the 1930s and 40s. He also cites concerns about a historical and experiential relativism manifest in the *Nouvelle* works. As to the former, Nichols notes a tendency to treat truth as only true for a particular place and time. He cites Henri Bouillard, who "notoriously, had written at the conclusion of his study of St. Thomas's theology of grace that a theology that fails to be contemporary is to that extent false."[44] Labourdette was concerned that "a subjectivism of 'inner experience' or 'spirituality' could undermine the objective value of the truths of faith."[45] Long and White again most overtly echo this concern about relativism. Long takes a much harder line, voicing repeatedly his concern that a "dense" notion of nature has succumbed to what he vaguely refers to as "Hegelian dialectic" and so been evacuated of meaning.[46] White takes the more balanced (and, indeed, more metaphysical) view that in order for there to be any kind of intelligible historical process, there must be (*pace* Nietzsche and Foucault) some identifiable, universal, and stable human nature to undergo the changes proper thereto. This is a philosophical corollary to his theological contention that "pure nature" is needed in order to anchor the medieval theorem of the states of human nature (what he calls "states of grace").[47] Still for both Long and White and for those of their school, there is an unwillingness "to follow the representatives of these alien philosophers onto their own home ground," and a sense that those who play, in Journet's

---

42 Hütter, 91–92.

43 Malloy, "De Lubac on Natural Desire."

44 Nichols, "Thomism and the *Nouvelle Théologie*," 3.

45 Nichols, 4.

46 Long, *Natura Pura*, 2, 4, and *passim*.

47 White, "The 'Pure Nature' of Christology."

words, "on a conceptual keyboard borrowed from Hegel and Existentialism" are allowing obviously mistaken methods to derail their theologies.[48]

Though Labourdette named a number of figures in what would come to be known as the *Nouvelle théologie* (including Boullard, Balthasar, Fessard, de Lubac, and de Chardin), it was Daniélou's essay, "*Les orientations présentes de la pensée religieuse,*" in *Études* that he took as the "key" to the movement and its pernicious if subterranean agenda. Daniélou, in Nichols's appraisal, does make a strong argument that neither scholasticism nor even *ressourcement* are adequate "by themselves (to) guarantee the renewal of Catholic thought" demanded in the post-war world. Neo-Thomism, Daniélou thought, could serve as a barrier (*un garde-fau*) against Marxism, existentialism, and other modern philosophies antithetical to Catholic faith. But he thought one must *reply,* and to reply requires dialogue and dialogue requires some engagement.[49] For this task, Daniélou thought scholasticism obsolete. Rather, he proposes a phenomenological approach to "religious realities in their concrete form."[50]

Kathryn Tanner's essay, "Grace without Nature," is perhaps the contemporary contribution to the natural/supernatural debate that resonates most radically with Daniélou's vision. She argues that, because the deepest meaning of humanity is (as per Genesis 1) to bear the image of God, an infinite openness and "plasticity" of human beings is our most salient feature.[51] Moreover, this feature is salient not because it is our own but because it is God's. In whatever state we find ourselves as humans, it cannot be made sense of by distinguishing that which is specifically natural or supernatural to us, but rather always in terms of a radical gift that we receive in our unlimited plasticity. She argues that once this fact, in deep agreement with both Patristic and contemporary thought, is established, Daniélou's phenomenological approach (coupled, of course, with a doctrinal *ressourcement*) would seem the only appropriate method for investigating that which is human. The truest metaphysical word that can be said about human life at any moment is that it is, in its relation to God as origin or as end, pure gift. Beyond that, you would have to go investigate what state we find ourselves in according to the temporal unfolding of our gifted openness. Theological investigation would

---

48 Nichols, "Thomism and the *Nouvelle Théologie*," 4, 7.
49 Nichols, 4.
50 Nichols, 5.
51 Tanner, "Grace without Nature," 364.

be no different in this respect. Theology must stay close, her theology without nature implies, to our plastic concreteness.

John Milbank's approach does not excise nature so cleanly as Tanner's, content instead to trouble the notion of nature in a post-structuralist way. In *Theology and Social Theory,* Milbank fights running skirmishes against post-modern social philosophies on their own ground, aiming to show that this ground was always already Christian. At the risk of overextending the metaphor, Milbank's strategem requires one trust that the excision of the theological from modern and postmodern thought made of those thinkers poor cartographers, such that they fundamentally mistake the character of these regions of life and politics they have all-too-recently colonized. Thus, Milbank very much wants Christian theology to engage with material and existential matters and perhaps even according to modern and postmodern methods, but always according to a kind of Renaissance Augustinian theological program. Thus, when reflecting in a radical (and revisionist) way about the legacy of Henri de Lubac's *Surnaturel* in *The Suspended Middle,* Milbank asks readers to take up a radical de Lubacian "(non)ontology" that sees the microcosm of human culture as itself participating in a groundless economy of reception and return of "gift."[52] Precisely how culture should appropriately receive and return this (non)ontological gift, in both *TST* and *The Suspended Middle,* is a matter of concrete, practical, and especially *aesthetic* judgment (informed by devotion to the *tradere* of Christian practice).

Returning to Nichols, de Lubac had no intention of responding to Labourdette's suspicious accusations and call for debate, but the disagreement spilled beyond the borders of France. An ambiguous reference to the "new theology" appeared on the lips of Pius XII in de Lubac's hearing. Apparently, in the preceding months, Reginald Garrigou-Lagrange briefed the pontiff on Labourdette's forthcoming article in censorious terms.[53] In July of 1946, Garrigou-Lagrange had written to Labourdette that the opinion in Rome was that the works issuing from Lyons "are a return to Modernism."[54] Thus, the Continental politics of the Church put pressure on leadership in the Society of Jesus to produce a response. De Lubac would be its main author.[55] Published in the French Jesuit journal *Recherches de science religieuse,*

---

52 Milbank, *Suspended Middle,* 53–61.
53 Nichols, "Thomism and the *Nouvelle Théologie,*" 9.
54 Nichols, 9.
55 As to the external politics, Nichols writes, "In part, if we are to look at the

the reply was occasionally polemical ("If the evil days of Modernism are now, thank God, far from us, the evil days of integralism may be coming back"), but in the main it sought to reverse the charges of historicism and relativism. Scholasticism was to be held in reproach, on Nichols's recounting, for its historical insensitivity. The accusation of "anti-intellectualism" could, according to the Jesuit response, only be maintained from the perspective of a perverse intellectualism.[56]

This angle of response could well have appeared in *Theological Studies, Modern Theology, Communio,* or even occasionally as a minority report in the pages of *Nova et Vetera.* Most recently, David Grumett defended de Lubac in the pages of *Modern Theology* against both neo-neo-scholastic and overly politicized or culturally theorized interpretations by insisting on the deeply Augustinian character of his theological position.[57] David Burrell's review of Thomas Joseph White's *Wisdom in the Face of Modernity* called into question White's confidence in the *preambulae fidae* as pure philosophy.[58] Servais Pinkaers argued that an exclusively metaphysical treatment of the natural desire for God overlooks the existential data on our desire for friendship with God and so misses the point.[59] Conor Cunningham makes an absurdity out of hypothesizing about *natura pura* as a speculative intellectual exercise, insisting that the world hypothesized cannot be squared with the vision of creation set down by the Church Fathers.[60] Hans Boersma presents de Lubac's ontology as inseparably tied up with his ecclesiology.[61] These are but a sample of the ways in which the Jesuit response to the Dominican accusations of 1946 have been

---

events in terms of general history, the political divisions of French Catholicism were beginning to express themselves by proxy. De Lubac, deeply committed to the Resistance, was supported by the newly empurpled pro-de Gaulle cardinal Saliège of Toulouse against attacks on his theological approach sent semi-clandestinely to Rome by the erstwhile supporters of Marshal Pétain and the régime of Vichy, or even, for that matter, by members of the nationalist-monarchist Action Française, now thirsting for some form of revenge after the years their movement had spent in the ecclesial wilderness" (Nichols, 8–9).

56 Nichols, 10.

57 Grumett, "De Lubac, Grace, and Pure Nature."

58 David B. Burrell, "On Thomas Joseph White's Wisdom in the Face of Modernity," *Nova et Vetera (English Edition)* 10, no. 2 (Spring 2012): 531.

59 Pinckaers, "Natural Desire to See God," 627.

60 Cunningham, "*Natura Pura,* the Invention."

61 Boersma, "Sacramental Ontology."

from various angles repeated in the past two decades. The neo–de Lubacians and their allies continue to argue that there is some historical (in the widest sense) element to the question of the natural and the supernatural that cannot be settled at the level of metaphysical reduction to principles. To settle for metaphysical reduction and thereby think one has said everything that needs to be said on the matter (or, at least, that what remains is a small matter of prudentially mopping up accidental particularities) leaves out something essential and, moreover, essentially Christian.

In 1947, the controversy only became hotter and more widely adverted to. In the Swiss journal *Liberté de Fribourg*, the Polish Dominican Innozent Bochenzky "spoke of the new theology as a radical evolutionism and irrationalism which would warm up the tired remains of Modernism." Garrigou-Lagrange's famous article, "*La nouvelle théologie, ou va-t-elle?*" appeared in the pages of *Angelicum*. At this, Labourdette's more hardline superior forced a further salvo, although this was in lieu of publishing Garrigou-Lagrange's article in the *Revue Thomiste* and thereby inviting "a Roman intervention."[62] Nichols summarizes their response as follows:

> They maintained that the metaphysics of St. Thomas is, quite simply, true, not just as an hypothesis or as the expression of a mentality but objectively and by the nature of things. Moreover, they claimed of Thomism that it was not only a theology of nature and essence but also a theology of event and therefore in a real sense a theology of history; they accepted that theology is not revelation, and however perfect it may be leaves open spaces that premature appeal to the magisterium ought not to foreclose; they state nonetheless that they cannot be regarded as mere partisans, for Thomism is not a party but the philosophy and theology of the Church herself—even if what is most profoundly at stake in the present quarrel is not the rights of the doctrine of St. Thomas so much as those of theology itself when considered as a veridical science of God and his relations with the world.[63]

If this identification of scholastic method with theology per se proved the final battle line for the relatively moderate Dominicans like Labourdette and his superior Nicholas, then there can be little surprise that hardliners like

---

62 Nichols, "Thomism and the *Nouvelle Théologie*," 11–12.
63 Nichols, 12–13.

Bochenzky and Garrigou-Lagrange saw any departure therefrom as necessarily a return to Modernist error. Within this Thomist foundationalism, there was room to integrate new knowledge. But, in their view, "better than anyone before him Thomas grasped the foundational truths of metaphysics and how to build on them a synthesis which would be all the more hospitable to every truth precisely because dependent on a true metaphysic."[64] Because the ideal of theological science was settled in his synthesis, any departure in method could be at best a regression to prescholastic approaches or, at worst, a poisonous collaboration with the perverse mentalities of alien, indeed hostile parties.[65] But all this controversy was making the French episcopacy nervous, and so in 1947 "Labourdette wrote an irenic piece conceding the liberty of the various theological schools but not their parity," which was faint praise to the ears of the Jesuits and rather too conciliatory for his fellow Dominicans. Still, there was not much more to be said. In 1950, *Humani Generis* seemed to settle the matter and in the Dominican's favor—at least for a while.[66]

It is worth noting how much the ecclesial situation was, in the main, inverted by Vatican II and the apparent vindication of de Lubac in *Gaudium et Spes* 22. As I noted above, neo-neo-scholastics will still appeal to a medieval notion of *scientia* and its rigor to defend their positions against more phenomenological, historiographic, and sociological approaches to Catholic theology. But they were at pains to note how few in the wider Catholic theological audience are willing or (they suspect) able to engage with this mode of theologizing. Whether this evaluation is accurate or not (and some of the more recent developments suggest it is less so than it once was), it is certainly the case that much of Catholic theology in the anglophone context has moved away from thinking of their task as medieval *scientia,* unburdened by the significance of intellectual birthdates or addresses. Daniélou's concern for a theology attentive to the proximate exigencies of its time(s) and its place(s) has been well taken since the council, even if there remain serious question about how such focus on the concrete can (or should) really be considered "scientific."

Nonetheless, it is not only Thomist neo-neo-scholastics but also their neo–de Lubacian interlocutors who continued to debate the problem of the supernatural in terms of its various metaphysical *loci*. The effort of de Lubac

64 Nichols, 13.

65 Nichols, 13–15.

66 Nichols, 16.

to bring both historical and phenomenological/existential methods to bear on the problem is only occasionally appropriated by his proponents. Even in Sean Larsen's excellent *Modern Theology* article, when it comes to de Lubac's thesis, he hardly does more than *suggest* that *perhaps* what de Lubac phrased in metaphysical terms was not meant in a properly metaphysical register at all.[67] Thus there remains a certain irony: although neo-neo-scholastics sense that between *Humani Generis* and *Gaudium et Spes* they were pushed up the theological stage and into the background, so now to hold the minority position (as White calls it), the debate has been largely framed according to their native theological method.[68]

The reduction of the twenty-first century debate to this nexus of medieval, metaphysical questions will be the primary concern of the next chapter. Though I have waited until then to exposit the distinction between the medieval and modern ideals of science in more detail, I hope readers will have noted the perhaps surprising fault line running through the parallel controversies narrated above. Beneath the topside issues around nature and grace, reason and revelation, or the natural and the supernatural, there is an undergirding question of theological method, of how the techniques of theological inquiry that guided the putative medieval synthesis, the commentarial tradition, and the post–*Aeterni Patris* revival in Thomist thought should (or should not) collaborate with a relatively new constellation of modern techniques and ideals. I will argue that the long-standing intractability of the debate rests on a failure to adequately differentiate and then coordinate the medieval from the modern elements in the problem of the supernatural.

---

67 Larsen, "Politics of Desire," 310.
68 White, "The 'Pure Nature' of Christology," 322.

CHAPTER 2

THE PROBLEM(S) OF THE SUPERNATURAL

should begin by fulfilling my promise to say more about how, following Bernard Lonergan, I am distinguishing the medieval from the modern ideals of science. I have so far indicated two elements at work in the controversy over the supernatural, one "medieval" and the other "modern." The first, predominating element is metaphysical, concerned with ends, natures, powers, and orders. It proceeds according to a medieval ideal of science (albeit rooted in classical antiquity), one that proved sufficiently powerful to fund the medieval synthesis of Christian doctrine and philosophical speculation. This synthesis has an enduring relevance and each generation of Christian theologians in its wake faces the challenge of appropriating its achievements and discerning its respective applications and limitations vis-à-vis contemporary questions. But there has been another element at work in the twenty-first-century debate about the supernatural. This element is recognizably modern in its culture, its methods, and its ideals. Bernard Lonergan characterizes a modern culture in this way:

> Modern culture is the culture that knows about itself and other cultures. It is aware that they are man-made. It is aware that the cultural may sustain or destroy or refashion the social. So it is that modern man not only individually is responsible for the life he leads but also collectively is responsible for the world in which he leads it. So modern culture is culture on the move. It is not dedicated to perpetuating the wisdom of ancestors, to handing on the traditions it has inherited. The past is just the springboard to the future. It is the set of good things to be improved and of evils to be eliminated. The future will belong to those who think about it, who grasp real possibilities, who project a coherent sequence of cumulative

realizations, who speak to man's longing for achievement more wisely than the liberal apostles of automatic progress and more humanly than the liquidating Marxists.[1]

Modern scientific methods and ideals, accordingly, are not so concerned to reduce effects to their principal causes as to make sense of this human microcosm on its own terms. If the ancient ideal of science foremost aims at the synchronic structures of nature (with human nature and the nature of society and culture included), this modern element terminates in a diachronic account of historical process in its myriad contexts and a forward-looking eye to its application. Nor is this historical process reduced to ontological causes or an unfolding sequence of "ages," but is basically contingent on the human spirit and, more specifically, on human *action*.

Now, classical anthropology was metaphysical, where "one was to know acts by their objects, habits by their acts, potencies by habits, and the essences of souls by their potencies," and so "in his *De anima* Aristotle employed one and the same method for the study of plants, animals, and men."[2] Along cognate lines, modern science aimed to extend its successes in the natural world to the human one. After all (as Lonergan was fond of quoting), Herbert Butterfield had surmised that its advent "outshines everything since the rise of Christianity and reduces the Renaissance and Reformation to the rank of mere episodes, mere internal displacements, within the system of medieval Christendom."[3] "It was inevitable," Lonergan asserts, "that the success of the new idea of science should profoundly affect the rest of the cultural superstructure."[4] It can seem natural, then, that human sciences should be "conducted on the same lines as the natural sciences."[5]

1 Bernard Lonergan, "The Absence of God in Modern Culture," in *A Second Collection*, 2nd ed., ed. Robert M. Doran and John D. Dadosky, CWL 13 (Toronto: University of Toronto Press, 2016), 97.

2 Bernard Lonergan, "The Future of Thomism," in *A Second Collection*, 43.

3 Herbert Butterfield, *The Origins of Modern Science 1300–1800*, rev. ed. (New York: Free Press, 1965), 7 (as quoted in Lonergan, "Absence," 88).

4 Lonergan, "Absence," 89.

5 Bernard Lonergan, "The Response of the Jesuit as Priest and Apostle in the Modern World," in *A Second Collection*, 157. Lonergan thinks this is laudable to the extent that, as Lonergan characterizes then-contemporary American approaches, "one observes performance, proposes hypothetical correlations, and endeavors to verify one's hypothesis as probably true" ("Absence," 89). However, if this point of analogy between the natural and the human sciences is overemphasized, as in positivist,

We may commonly (if somewhat imprecisely) speak of the epoch established by the above transition as the Enlightenment. "That movement," Lonergan points out, "has lasted into our own day and still enjoys a dominant position." The Enlightenment, he explains, "was carried socially and culturally. Socially by the movement that would sweep away the remnants of feudalism and a lingering absolutism by proclaiming liberty, fraternity, equality. Culturally by the triumph of Newton, who did for mechanics what Euclid had done for geometry and whose success led philosophers to desert rationalism and swell the ranks of empiricists."[6] But Lonergan also made note of a perhaps complementary, perhaps countervailing, but in any case, distinct social and cultural movement that has emerged from the Enlightenment and has come to live alongside it. On his account, it has for its soil destabilizing developments in mathematics, in physics, in biology, and even economics, whereby "a deductivist world of mechanist determinism was making way for the probability schedules of a world in process."[7] For its seed, there is a philosophical centering of human autonomy that runs from Kant to Ricoeur through the work of Schopenhauer, Kierkegaard, Newman, Dilthey, Nietzsche, and Blondel. If one saw in this soil and seed only its rejection of certain rationalist tendencies in modern thought, one might merely call it "postmodernism." But Lonergan saw its intellectual fecundity and adopted Frederick Lawrence's coinage to label it "the Second Enlightenment."[8]

The Second Enlightenment's intellectual fecundity has shown itself, on Lonergan's view, through what in 1975 he would call the department of "human studies," but in the previous decade he would usually refer to as "the human sciences." However, this appellation involved him in an ambiguity, since it could refer to the reductionist, positivist "behavioral

---

naturalist, behaviorist, and some pragmatist approaches, "distortion occurs in man's apprehension of man," producing a human self-understanding that "if not mechanistic, is theriomorphic" and consequently omits "advertence to human dignity and respect for human morality" ("Response," 157). It can produce, in other words, a human science that is dehumanizing.

6 Bernard Lonergan, "Prolegomena to the Study of the Emerging Religious Consciousness of Our Time," in *A Third Collection*, 2nd ed., ed. Robert M. Doran and John D. Dadosky, CWL 16 (Toronto: University of Toronto Press, 2017), 60–61.

7 Lonergan, "Prolegomena," 61.

8 Frederick Lawrence, "'The Modern Philosophic Differentiation of Consciousness' or What Is the Enlightenment?," in *Lonergan Workshop*, vol. 2, ed. Fred Lawrence (Chico, CA: Scholars Press, 1981), 231–79.

sciences" of the anglophone scene or to what, until then anyway, had been a predominantly German approach under Dilthey's heading: *Geisteswissenschaften*. Where the former had stressed (over-extended, really) the analogy with the natural sciences, the latter "stresses the basic difference between natural and human science" that lies "in the very data of the two types." For, in the human sciences, the data are constituted *as data at all* by human acts of meaning. Thus,

> one could send into a law-court as many physicists, chemists, and biologists as one pleased with as much equipment as they desired. They could count, measure, weigh, describe, record, analyse, dissect to their hearts' content. But it would be only by going beyond what is just given and by attending to the meaning of the proceedings that they could discover they were dealing with a court of law; and it is only in so far as the court of law is recognized as such and the appropriate meanings are attached to the sounds and actions that the data for a human science emerge.[9]

Thus it is with the Second Enlightenment that the modern human sciences, insofar as they accept that meaning is integral to and constitutive of their objects of investigation, set out not to establish what human persons and communities are, universally and necessarily, but to give account for "all the men of every time and place, all their thoughts and words and deeds, the accidental as well as the essential, the contingent as well as the necessary, the particular as well as the universal."[10] Where the ideal of science against which scholastics, old or new, measured theology would limit itself to the abstract, essential, universal, and necessary, modern science (natural or human) accepts no such limits. The dilation of viewpoint in which this modern ideal consists has consequences both for how modern science proceeds and for the kinds of results it anticipates. "Its object," Lonergan writes, "is not necessity but verified possibility: bodies fall with a constant acceleration, but they could fall at a different rate; and similarly other natural laws aim at stating, not what cannot possibly be otherwise, but what in fact is so."[11] And when it comes to

---

9 Lonergan, "Absence," 89.

10 Bernard Lonergan, "Dimensions of Meaning," in *Collection*, 2nd ed., ed. Frederick E. Crowe and Robert M. Doran, CWL 4 (Toronto: University of Toronto Press, 1988), 241.

11 Lonergan, "Dimensions," 238–39.

the *Geisteswissenschaften,* this requires asking what in fact their objects *mean* and to whom. Consequently, the modern scientific ideal, when applied to human persons, communities, societies, and cultures, is inherently *hermeneutical.*

Medieval and Modern Elements in the 21st-Century Controversy

Both of these scientific, methodological ideals, the medieval and the modern, have been at work in the twenty-first-century controversy over the supernatural, but only occasionally have they been adverted to in their distinction from one another. The latter, modern element is, when treated at all, usually considered either as an occasion for asking the medieval metaphysical question or as the arena in which the implications of the medieval element play out. The modern problem of the supernatural guided by this modern ideal, in other words, is not recognized as a formal problem of its own. Furthermore, the reduction of modern questions to their putative causes in medieval metaphysics or other intellectual techniques is a question begging exercise that presupposes the adequacy of medieval *scientia* (in which effects are, ideally, logically reduced to their causes). Below I will point out how, even when thinkers address the modern element in a serious and sophisticated way, they commonly revert back to basically medieval, metaphysical intellectual habits to answer the questions that arise. I will wait until the chapters in part 4 to explore more precisely why this modern element is formally irreducible to its medieval counterpart, because it involves some quite technical considerations of human freedom and its rationality. For now, I will restrict myself to presenting the evidence that there are, in fact, two problems at play. But even in the longer term, I will have to make do sketching out as best I can the basic elements of the modern problem of the supernatural in its irreducible distinctness from the medieval one.

Early in the contemporary debate, Hans Boersma noted how Henri de Lubac's theology of grace followed Maurice Blondel in opposing a theological extrinsicism that, by its regional separation of nature and grace, set the stage for a philosophical immanentism. Boersma was not alone in noting how this rather academic point served de Lubac's opposition to secularization and an ecclesiology of domination.[12] Of course, contemporary secularization takes a

12 Hans Boersma, "Sacramental Ontology: Nature and the Supernatural in the Ecclesiology of Henri de Lubac," *New Blackfriars* 88, no. 1015 (2007): 249–52; see also

slightly different shape than the forms de Lubac faced, and the secularization de Lubac opposed took a different shape even than that opposed by Blondel. Blondel found himself between the anti-clerical liberalism of the French Republic and the positivist Monarchism of the *Action Française*.[13] De Lubac faced the march (both literal and figurative) of fascism and Marxism in Europe.[14] But in each of these, one finds a question about authority. Whether as an appeal to religion as otherworldly myth in mid-century fascism and its monarchist progenitors or as the material dialectic of class conflict in Marxism, Blondel's and de Lubac's centering of the supernatural aimed to undermine justifications of absolute and all-too-worldly power.

The neo-neo-scholastics share this antipathy to encroaching secularization, although—in Steven A. Long's case especially—it is not clear how they would evaluate the case of *Action Française* or its place in the genealogy of Continental authoritarianism. Long praises de Lubac for the seriousness with which he takes the problem of atheistic politics, even if he would offer a radically different prescription to treat it.[15] In case one might be tempted to think that this concern for forms of secularization in matters of politics was a quirk of de Lubac's intellectual biography or an inheritance from Blondel, it also appears in those efforts to retrieve Scheeben on the question. Oakes quotes the following from Scheeben's *Nature and Grace*:

> The crisis [of secularism] has not yet been completely settled, and it will not be settled until the supernatural order is frankly, adequately, and radically distinguished from the natural order.... Whenever these truths are not assigned their own exclusive sphere and are intermingled with truths of the natural order, they are necessarily confused with the latter, and therefore not only lose their organic union with truths of their own kind but suffer a dimming of their own light.[16]

Hans Boersma, "Accommodation to What? Univocity of Being, Pure Nature and the Anthropology of St. Irenaeus," *International Journal of Systematic Theology* 8, no. 3 (July 2006): 266–93.

13 See William L. Portier, "Twentieth-Century Catholic Theology and the Triumph of Maurice Blondel," *Communio* 38, no. 1 (Spring 2011): 103–37.

14 Raymond Moloney, "De Lubac and Lonergan on the Supernatural," *Theological Studies* 69, no. 3 (2008): 509–27.

15 Steven A. Long, *Natura Pura: On the Recovery of Nature in the Doctrine of Grace* (New York: Fordham University Press, 2010), 41–45.

16 Edward T. Oakes, "Scheeben the Reconciler: Resolving the Nature-Grace

Scheeben here distinguishes nature from the supernatural in order to unite them, rather than uniting them in order to distinguish them à la de Lubac. Whichever direction one travels between the ideas, it seems a theological concern with secularism carries along with it a concern with the nature/grace relation and, perhaps, vice versa.[17]

It is suspicious, however, that often these concerns about secularization, politics, and, ultimately, the process of history are named, only to then be abandoned. Boersma raised de Lubac's sense that the ontological, ecclesiological, and political questions are integral, but ultimately only treated the first two, at most gesturing toward the political question.[18] David Braine framed the question in terms of original sin and the logical problems relating our two-fold end, but eventually turned to the modern, existential analysis of angst and alienation considered as "empirical phenomena."[19] However, he responded to this existential, empirical, modern topic entirely in terms of metaphysics. When he gestured to ontology's implications for questions of political authority, Braine again considered only metaphysical responses and, in the end, punts on them as beyond the scope of his inquiry.[20] Nicholas Healy relegated the entire topic to a footnote.[21] Raymond Moloney noted the connection for de Lubac between his ontological project and his opposition to secularization, Nazism, and Marxism, but never returned to it after his detailed treatment of Lonergan's approach to the ontological question.[22] Mansini explicitly avoided the political question by reducing it to a theological matter of metaphysical anthropology.[23] I mentioned in the previous chapter

Debate," *Nova et Vetera (English Edition)* 11, no. 2 (Spring 2013): 446; see also Matthias Joseph Scheeben, *Nature and Grace*, trans. Cyril Vollert (St. Louis: B. Herder, 1954), 13, 15.

17 Indeed, chapters 5, 6, and 7 of Bernard Mulcahy's book *Aquinas's Notion of Pure Nature and the Christian Integralism of Henry de Lubac* are organized around different versions of this correlation in de Lubac, de Regnon, and Milbank. See Mulcahy, *Aquinas's Notion of Pure Nature and the Christian Integralism of Henri de Lubac: Not Everything Is Grace* (New York: Peter Lang, 2011), 123–200.

18 Boersma, "Sacramental Ontology," 249, 270–72.

19 David Braine, "The Debate between Henri de Lubac and His Critics," *Nova et Vetera (English Edition)* 6, no. 3 (Summer 2008): 577.

20 Braine, "The Debate," 582–83, 589.

21 Nicholas J. Healy, "Henri de Lubac on Nature and Grace: A Note on Some Recent Contributions to the Debate," *Communio* 35, no. 4 (Winter 2008): 536n3.

22 Moloney, "De Lubac and Lonergan on the Supernatural," 510.

23 "I want to consider the teaching of de Lubac, not as a counter in the relative

the way in which White responded to the challenge posed by Foucaultian historicism with an Aristotelian appeal to intelligible substance.[24] Christopher M. Cullen mentioned that the foremost implication of de Lubac's thesis is for philosophical ethics and continues to note a number of salient points about the relationship between ontology and the historical import of human autonomy, but he does not return to address the questions for moral philosophy he raised initially.[25]

There are certainly works in the contemporary debate that make no mention of those elements of the problem of the supernatural that call out for a modern, diachronic mode of response.[26] This is unobjectionable, as far as it goes, although one might be concerned that the full breadth of contemporary questions are being held in abeyance. Still, there are also several thinkers who have, in the course of the controversy, faced these questions of existential, historical, and political concern directly. I have already made note of many of them. Milbank devoted an entire chapter to the ontology of natural and supernatural in *Theology and Social Theory* with

---

fortunes of conservative and progressive agendas, but as an influence within the mind of Church. In the end, this is what must drive the 'political' for Catholics" (Guy Mansini, "The Abiding Theological Significance of Henri de Lubac's *Surnaturel*," *The Thomist* 73, no. 4 [2009]: 598).

24 Thomas Joseph White, "The 'Pure Nature' of Christology: Human Nature and *Gaudium et Spes* 22," *Nova et Vetera (English Edition)* 8, no. 2 (Spring 2010): 309–18.

25 Christopher M. Cullen, "The Natural Desire for God and Pure Nature: A Debate Renewed," *American Catholic Philosophical Quarterly* 86, no. 4 (Fall 2012): 705–30.

26 Steven A. Long, "On the Possibility of a Purely Natural End for Man," *The Thomist* 64, no. 1 (2000): 211–37; Guy Mansini, "Henri de Lubac, the Natural Desire to See God, and Pure Nature," *Gregorianum* 83, no. 1 (2002): 89–109; Mansini, "Lonergan on the Natural Desire in the Light of Feingold," *Nova et Vetera (English Edition)* 5, no. 1 (2007): 185–98; Reinhard Hütter, "Aquinas on the Natural Desire for the Vision of God: A Relecture of *Summa contra Gentiles* III, c. 25, *après* Henri de Lubac," *The Thomist* 73, no. 4 (2009): 523–91; Christopher J. Malloy, "De Lubac on Natural Desire: Difficulties and Antitheses," *Nova et Vetera (English Edition)* 9, no. 3 (2011): 567–624; Joshua R. Brotherton, "The Integrity of Nature in the Grace-Freedom Dynamic: Lonergan's Critique of Báñezian Thomism," *Theological Studies* 75, no. 3 (2014): 537–63; Thomas Joseph White, "Imperfect Happiness and the Final End of Man: Thomas Aquinas and the Paradigm of Nature-Grace Orthodoxy," *The Thomist* 78, no. 2 (2014): 247–89; Shawn M. Colberg, "Aquinas and the Grace of Auxilium," *Modern Theology* 32, no. 2 (2016): 187–210; David Bentley Hart, *You Are Gods: On Nature and Supernature* (Notre Dame, IN: University of Notre Dame Press, 2022).

an eye to discerning the theological conditions of possibility for a political theology that was not simply subordinated to secular social theory.[27] He returned to this question in *The Suspended Middle*, making a sustained attack on the idea that philosophy could maintain autonomy over the political or that (political) theology could simply be a naïve reading of grace at work in the world. But Milbank's answer at every turn, to every difficulty, is to insist again and again on the delicate maintenance of the "(non-)ontology" he attributes to de Lubac's *Surnaturel*. This (non-)ontology holds the key, he thinks, to the historical and political reiteration of a Christian culture.[28] Thus, as in *Theology and Social Theory*, one finds that for all of his wide-ranging engagement with postmodern thought, the argument of *The Suspended Middle* boils down to an *apologia* for how his politics are controlled by his ontology. An answer to the medieval question always provides the answer to modern (and postmodern) concerns.

One may detect an identical strategy in Steven A. Long's sustained *discursus* on the ontology of *natura pura* and the theocratic Catholic politics it undergirds. One of the weaknesses of Long's argument in the first chapter of *Natura Pura* is a tendency, despite his appeals to Thomas's *scientia*, to take Thomas's locutions at face value, controlling very little for context or Aquinas's theoretical controls of meaning. Much of the argument boils down to, "Thomas says ..." However, the strategy in chapter 4 proves more compelling because Long fits the "required hypothesis" of *natura pura* into a thick and well-wrought scheme for Catholic moral and political philosophy. Indeed, so systematic is this vision that *sans* some speculative account of *natura pura* (even if not precisely under that heading), a morally or politically sound social order is portrayed as fundamentally impossible. But notice here too the basic methodical assumption of the whole debate: the synchronic structure of ontology determines the shape of moral, social, and political philosophy and theology. Answers to the medieval, metaphysical question about how to relate the natural and supernatural orders more or less automatically answer diachronic modern questions by logical implication and extension.

---

27 John Milbank, *Theology and Social Theory: Beyond Secular Reason*, 2nd ed. (Malden, MA: Blackwell, 2006), 206–56.

28 John Milbank, *The Suspended Middle: Henri de Lubac and the Debate concerning the Supernatural*, 1st ed. (Grand Rapids, MI: Eerdmans, 2005), 5.

Sean Larsen's 2013 *Modern Theology* article on Milbank and Hütter comes perhaps the closest to both distinguishing the medieval and modern elements in the debate over the supernatural and addressing them as irreducible to one another. Larsen diagnoses in Milbank's approach a Renaissance romanticism whereby the medieval ontology of the natural and the supernatural is "expressed" in the ongoing repetition of aesthetically discerned Christian practices. Rather than making logical criticisms of Milbank's (non-) ontology, Larsen aims to bring the genealogical hammer of Walter Mignolo's postcolonial analysis down on what he characterizes as Milbank's nostalgia. He directly accuses Milbank of identifying the Church and the European Renaissance. Larsen shows how, *via* Mignolo, this identification has historically fit within a wider conflation of the Church and civilization per se.[29] Thus, Larsen indicates how Milbank's postliberal resistance to totalizing secular reason can be deconstructed as also and at the same time a paradigmatically colonial—and so modern—project of erasing Christianity's "others." As Lonergan pointed out, "Modern culture is the culture that knows about itself and other cultures. It is aware that they are man-made," and so there arises suspicions that the people making culture may not be doing so in good faith. In this way, Larsen brings modern methods of analysis to bear on Milbank's properly modern concerns and resists the pervasive habit of reducing them to more "fundamental" medieval, metaphysical structures.

Unfortunately, when Larsen turns to treat of Hütter's neo-neo-scholastic account of the intellect's ordering to God, he frames his positive appraisal of its implied openness to alterity exclusively in metaphysical, structural terms. From this vantage, it cannot be so decisively settled whether, relative to Long's thickly theocratic political philosophy, Hütter's implied openness is a matter of substantive differences or merely Hütter's reticence to spell out what his speculative account implies.[30] Finally, I made mention in the previous chapter of the allusive suggestion with which Larsen concludes, that de Lubac's purpose was postmetaphysical in the first place. Consequently, the sole approach to the controversy that distinguishes its medieval and modern elements and approaches them with distinct and corresponding methods still only does so halfway and, in the end, without being sustained.

29 Sean Larsen, "The Politics of Desire: Two Readings of Henri de Lubac on Nature and Grace," *Modern Theology* 29, no. 3 (July 2013): 287–91.

30 Larsen, 299–306.

Elements of the Medieval Problem

The astute reader may have noticed that, insofar as it focuses on medieval problems, ideals, and methods, the contemporary anglophone controversy orbits around twin conceptual suns: gratuity and integrity. This can be seen most clearly in a pair of complementary questions that may serve as "ideal types" in our analysis:

1) If grace is gratuitous, does it make a necessary difference?
2) If grace makes a necessary difference, is it gratuitous?

The neo-neo-scholastics respond that grace adds something of eternal importance and is necessary for the attainment of that eternal something, but it does not make a fundamental and necessary difference in our nature. If it did, then grace—so far from perfecting nature—would destroy its integrity. The neo–de Lubacians, by contrast, respond that grace makes a necessary difference. Theologies that deny this to preserve the integrity of human nature overlook the gratuity of being-a-creature itself and so, despite their protests to the contrary, violate the integrity of the unitary graced-creation that is God's unmerited gift. Now, it must be said that the neo-neo-scholastic answer implies that grace is not entirely necessary, even if that for which it is necessary is of great consequence. Grace, in other words, is not really necessary, but only "necessary for...". The neo–de Lubacian answer, however, seems to beg the question. Why, if gratuity is made the sole defining characteristic of grace, are creation and grace different? "After all," Lonergan asks, "what is there that is not a free gift of God?"[31] And certainly there are those who would exclaim, "exactly!" But both answers imply the same underlying question, albeit in different ways: "How does God's grace make a difference?" The neo-neo-scholastic answer implies it insofar as one might wonder how grace can be necessary for something like eternal life without being fundamentally necessary for our being. The neo–de Lubacian answer implies it insofar as one might wonder how grace is differentiated within creation at all. After all, if grace is simply identical with the gift of being anything at all, then it is, à la *creatio ex nihilo*, a difference only from nothing. But to be different from nothing is no difference at all.

---

31 Bernard Lonergan, *Grace and Freedom: Operative Grace in the Thought of St. Thomas Aquinas*, ed. Frederick E. Crowe and Robert M. Doran, CWL 1 (Toronto: University of Toronto Press, 2000), 15.

Still, one can ask a more general form of the question: "How does God's grace make a difference in Creation as a whole?" This more general form of the question is important and interesting, but it is not very much asked (if at all) in the contemporary anglophone debate over the supernatural. Consequently, I am going to set it aside except to note that its existence reveals that the form of the problem of the supernatural with which the debate has been concerned is a specific form of what I have been calling the medieval problem of the supernatural. If God, by granting us grace, acts in a way that makes a difference both in human beings and in creation as a whole, then there arises the question of God's action in general. But we know dogmatically that God acts in at least one other way, to create creatures, and so it becomes clear that the medieval problem of grace (as pertains to both the specific case of human beings and creation in general) is itself a specific instance of a more general problem. Thus, in addition to the specific medieval problem of the supernatural that pertains to grace, there is a generic medieval problem of the supernatural that pertains to God's *ad extra* agency in general.[32]

This generic medieval problem of the supernatural can further be expressed by a general and a specific question. The generic form of the generic medieval problem of the supernatural asks, "How does God's action make a difference in creation?" The specific form of the generic medieval problem of the supernatural asks, "How does God's action make a difference in human beings?" The answers to this generic medieval problem of the supernatural are not at all irrelevant for the specific medieval problem of the supernatural that pertains to grace. Insofar as grace is an element of God's *ad extra* agency, the determinations of God's *ad extra* agency will pertain to it. Nor does this reduce God's grace to God's general *ad extra* agency, for the determinations that pertain to the latter will not preclude, nor be adequate to reveal, that by which grace is specifically differentiated within God's *ad extra* agency as a whole.

---

32 There is a tendency to think that the appellation "supernatural" is a synonym for grace. This tendency, for example, haunts theological interpretations of Maurice Blondel's philosophy of the supernatural. But as I noted in the introduction, at least by the time of Philip the Chancellor and St. Albert, the supernatural is a controlling theorem that, as we shall see in the next chapter, demonstrates theoretical mobility and so the ability to structure solutions on more than one speculative *locus* at once.

Allow me to schematically recall the distinctions made thus far:

The Medieval Problem of the Supernatural

1) Specific Medieval Problem:
    "How does God's *grace* make a difference … ?"
    A) Generic Form: "… in Creation?"
    B) Specific Form: "… in Human Beings?"

2) Generic Medieval Problem:
    "How does God's *action* make a difference …?"
    A) Generic Form: "… in Creation?"
    B) Specific Form: "… in Human Beings?"

Now, the existence of a question implies the possibility of an answer and the existence of a problem implies the possibility of a solution. Extant specific forms of the solution to the specific medieval problem (1.B.) will be the concern of chapter 3. In brief, I am persuaded that such a solution can be found in Thomas's *Summa theologiae*, 1–2, q. 109, a. 2. As the generic form of the specific problem (1.A.) is not much at play for parties in the contemporary anglophone controversy, I will not bother addressing it here. Bernard Lonergan's *Grace and Freedom* has convinced me as well that there exist in Thomas's *corpus* generic and specific forms of a solution to the generic medieval problem of the supernatural. In brief, the answer to the generic form of the generic medieval problem (2.A) is Thomas's theory of universal causal cooperation with God. The answer, in turn, to the specific form of the generic medieval problem (2.B.) is Thomas's theory of free cooperation with God. Lonergan shows why both are integral to Thomas's position on the specific form of the specific medieval problem (1.B.), and I am arguing that all of these together constitute a medieval solution to the medieval problem overall, at least as it is raised in the contemporary debate. The elements of this wider solution, however, are rather diffuse in Thomas's *corpus*. In chapters 4 and 5, we will see how Lonergan gathered them together. I will present the position first by an analysis of its development and then synthetically.

Anticipating the Modern Problem

We do not yet possess the conceptuality we need to articulate the modern problem and why it is irreducible to its medieval counterpart. Nonetheless, it may suffice to note that the modern problem pertains to human freedom and its products. Moreover, it is a problem that fully emerges only once one has a solution to the medieval problem, because cognizance of the basic stakes of the modern problem presupposes a grip on the medieval solution. In other words, once one knows *how* God makes a difference in creation generally and in human beings specifically, it follows one can ask exactly what that difference is. But in part 2 we will see that in part the difference God makes is to make creatures to *be* in general and human beings to *be free* specifically. From this affirmation emerges the possibility of what I will call the medieval ambiguities. One might characterize these ambiguities in a preliminary way by noting that, if God causes beings to be and human beings to be free, this effect need not necessarily be read as a "difference." Or, more precisely, we might say that the "difference" God makes by making creatures to be and human beings to be free is different from nothing. The whole argument cannot be made yet, but affirming that this "difference" in fact makes a difference is a prephilosophical decision rather than conclusion of an ontological line of reasoning. But if one makes this affirmation, one also affirms that the universe of being has a sufficient reason and that human freedom has a fundamental meaning and purpose. That God makes human freedom to be means also that God makes the products of human freedom to be. Moreover, God renders both intelligible. Within the horizon established by this affirmation, it is sensible to ask *what* concretely God is making human freedom and its products to be. But, as we shall see in part 4, this is a hermeneutical question: what do human freedom and its products *mean?*

Again, a sketch of the basic elements of the modern problem of the supernatural will have to suffice for now. First, as I intimated at the beginning of this chapter, the modern problem of the supernatural is not a speculative problem, but a hermeneutical one. Moreover, it is robustly hermeneutical in that *ontological* sense brought to light by what Frederick Lawrence called "the Second Enlightenment." Consequently, the modern problem does not ask "how?" but "what?" The modern problem is not a synchronic metaphysical problem (for it presupposes the existence of a metaphysical solution) but a diachronic historical problem. In other words, instead of asking, "What difference does God make?" it asks, "What difference is God making?" The modern problem is concerned both with human freedom and the products that depend upon its exercise. Thus, the modern problem asks not only, "What difference is God making in human freedom?" but also "What difference is God making in the products of human freedom?" Since a cause and its effects are necessarily distinct, these questions pose distinct problems. The former problem I might call the "existential modern problem of the supernatural." The latter I might call the "artificial modern problem of the supernatural." The existential modern problem is "existential" in the same sense that existential philosophy is, that is, concerned with the way in which human freedom determines itself. The artificial modern problem is not artificial in the sense of being "false" or somehow fraudulent. Rather, the artificial modern problem is artificial insofar as it is concerned with the artifacts of free human making.

I can schematically summarize these anticipatory determinations of the modern problem of the supernatural as follows:

The Modern Problem of the Supernatural

>Modern Problem: "What difference is God making ...?"
>>Existential Form: "... in human freedom?"
>>Artificial Form: "... in the products of human freedom?"

A Problem of Cooperation

Thus, there are two problems, not just one. It is undeniable that something irreducibly medieval is at work in the controversy. It is, as shown above, the more evident and more developed part. When I have called this part medieval, I do not at all mean to be pejorative, but intend to name an excellence, a perfection accomplished in the Catholic intellectual tradition through the metaphysical subtlety of St. Thomas Aquinas, his predecessors, his contemporaries, and his followers. But there is also something irreducibly modern about these questions that has been suppressed in the various ways discussed above and that I have tried to make evident nonetheless. The irreducibility of this modern part demonstrates the limits of the medieval element and so of the solutions on offer. It indicates, at a minimum, the heuristic place into which an adequate theology of the supernatural would realize a modern achievement. But to settle for this merely heuristic placeholder would be too stingy an assessment of modern intellectual achievements. There are genuine modern virtues—those ideals, methods, and techniques that have facilitated the great intellectual fecundity of the Second Enlightenment—virtues that theology in general and a speculative theology of the supernatural specifically would mutilate itself by excluding.

All of this is to say that there is needed some *cooperation* between the medieval and modern philosophical and theological sciences if the medieval and modern problems of the supernatural will be addressed both in their distinct irreducibility *and* their intimate, indeed inseparable connection. This cooperation is not reducible to rendering medieval and modern approaches to the supernatural *coherent*. It is not enough to show that they are compatibly parallel descriptions of the same data, answering the same question from different perspectives, for there are two irreducible problems and not just one. Questions that really differ require really different answers. Nor is this cooperation reducible to arguing for the *continuity* of medieval and modern answers to the problem of the supernatural, for such continuity would, whether it was a formal or a merely material continuity, always only be grounded in the identity of a single question to which the Catholic intellectual tradition has labored cumulatively and progressively to answer. Such continuity may well exist, but to make it the central issue would occlude rather than solve the distinct problems of the supernatural.

Cooperation is required because there are two problems of the supernatural and not only one. Moreover, the irreducibility of these problems to one another owes to the asymmetrical bond that holds them together. Without the medieval problem and its adequate solution (in part, a theory of trans-natural cooperation between God and creatures), there can be no adequate recognition of the modern problem in its full theological scope. Still, as I will discuss in chapters 9 and 10, the integrality of the medieval problem and solution with the modern problem owes precisely to the former's inadequacy to the modern problem it reveals. Theologians and philosophers could spend lifetimes refining the medieval solution in light of intervening developments and still never adequately address the modern problem. The inadequacy of any medieval solution owes, fittingly enough, to the disproportion of the modern problem to medieval speculative techniques. In brief, the modern problem is relatively supernatural to the medieval solution, though in a sense very much to be determined. Much as our natural powers are elevated by cooperation with God's grace to habits and acts that merit what we could not without God's help, so the medieval solution finds an enlarged and enriched horizon in cooperation with the intellectual and methodological developments constitutive of the distinctly modern problem. Indeed, the horizon of the modern problem will be so much enriched and enlarged that theologians may feel it is beyond their power to address. But here too the theorem of the supernatural will be at work, reminding us that it is not just in the first-order work of our living, but also in the second-order vocation to scholarly reflection that we need God's grace to heal us from the confinement of sin, to elevate us beyond the circumscriptions of finitude, and to stitch us into the supernatural community through which God is at work in the world.

I will show that, as there is a specific obediential potency in human beings for receiving the help of grace, also there is a kind of specific obediential potency in Thomas's solution to the medieval problem. Thomas's account of rational process indicates the place that the mediation of meaning has in our knowledge of the real. When this epistemic account finds its proper place in Thomas's faculty psychology of deliberate action, one can appreciate the place that the mediation of meaning has in Thomas's account of human agency and therefore the place it has in his account of human cooperation with God. What I will call a "modern philosophical mentality" in chapter 6 offers a chance to recognize that not only does meaning mediate the fully human world of thought and action it also *constitutes* that world. The constitutive function of meaning rests both at the heart of the Second Enlightenment in general and the modern problem of the supernatural specifically, for it places human freedom beyond itself, not just in the agency by which human beings act but also in the objects about which it deliberates. Where the medieval problem asked in a metaphysical register where and how God's *ad extra* agency can be discerned in human freedom, the modern problem asks where and how God's agency can be discerned in the various nexuses of human action's products that we call, in general, "culture." The metaphysics of divine *concursus* can produce a theology telling us "that" and "how" God is at work in our cultures, but some other approach is needed to theologize in an adequately scientific (or, if you prefer, scholarly) way "what" God is up to therein. Nonetheless, a solution to the modern problem must stand on the synchronic metaphysical structure of the medieval solution in order to attempt some general heuristic for the hermeneutics of God at work in history or what I will call a "theological hermeneutics of culture." The medieval and modern theological cooperation I have in mind will consist in answering *both* the "that"/ "how" question and the "what" question in a critical and methodical way.

The relatively supernatural character of the modern problem of the supernatural with regard to its medieval counterpart should not, however, be read as an uncritical baptism of modern culture, science, scholarship, philosophy, or theology as a whole (if one could even synthesize such an aggregate in the first place). It is, instead, to engage in a bit of positive dialectic, selecting that which is authentic in two developments of the Catholic intellectual tradition and advancing them through critical, methodical inquiry and constructive cooperation. Of course, one could engage in the negative dialectics that seek to diagnose what has been inauthentic—which is to say, oblivious, obtuse, irrational, or irresponsible—in the unfolding of the Catholic speculative tradition, whether in its medieval or modern modalities.[33] One would no doubt find much to reverse. However, because facing up to the modern problem requires cooperation with the medieval synthesis, I think I am better served to discern what has been genuine and successful in both ideals and promote them for the sake of traction on this fundamental issue. Where counter-positions stand in the way, one should not shy from venturing his or her best judgment, but I will not be on the hunt for a sweeping diagnosis of all that ails either the modern or the medieval mind on this question or others.

Philosophies, Theologies, and Ambiguities

A final methodological note: what follows will pivot frequently between philosophy and theology. Moreover, it will shift between medieval and modern ideals of philosophy and theology. These transitions are significant, for a thinker's methodical frame stands to their ideas as questions stand to answers, insofar as they create a context of validating conditions and an implied criterion of relevance. Moreover, changes in the relationship between methodical frames modify their relative significance in a project of inquiry. I will argue that the separation of philosophy from its subordination to speculative theology transformed philosophy's self-understanding radically,

---

33 Bernard Lonergan, *Method in Theology*, 2nd ed., ed. Robert M. Doran and John D. Dadosky, CWL 14 (Toronto: University of Toronto Press, 2017), 22–23.

such that whole new frames of investigation became possible. If that were not complicated enough, developments in theology can occasion new questions and new answers in philosophy, just as developments in philosophy can set the stage for new advances in theology. In chapters 3 and 4 I will discuss how questions and answers in the theology of grace transformed St. Thomas's philosophy of divine transcendence and *ad extra* agency. This rebounded to allow his theology of grace to be reconfigured as a systematic account of habitual and actual grace. In some cases, these developments are sufficiently momentous that they transform not just the content of one discipline or the other but also their respective self-understandings. I will show in chapter 6 that the theorem of divine transcendence that emerged from this dialogue between medieval theology and philosophy sowed seeds of an ambiguity that at once helped to justify an autonomous and separated modern philosophy and also undermines the possibility that its autonomy can be anything more than relative.

In a similar way, the development of a modern scientific ideal for philosophy—that it should endeavor to explain the diachronic processes of history, morality, society, and politics in their concreteness—has tendered to theology a new set of questions and techniques that it still struggles to integrate within its methodical self-understanding. I will discuss how these questions and techniques apply to a new way of asking about divine *ad extra* agency in general and God's grace specifically that cannot be adequately addressed only according to medieval metaphysical techniques. Indeed, in chapter 8 I will have applied these very metaphysical techniques to the question to show that they do not dissolve the problem's force. This irreducibly modern problem of the supernatural demands a novel set of questions and techniques. But this set cannot be a mere aggregate and still aim at the unity intended in every intellectual enterprise. Thus, in chapter 11 I will suggest a heuristic that at once unifies these modern questions and thereby also sets their coordination as a criterion for the adequacy of any theology that, on the matter of the supernatural, aspires to do for the twenty-first (or twenty-second) century what Thomas Aquinas did for the thirteenth.

Still, I cannot overlook the way in which this cooperation that runs from modern philosophy to modern theology also rebounds back upon modern philosophy. In the face of the ambiguities medieval philosophy revealed, the pre-philosophical decision to pursue complete explanation by way of a modern philosophy cannot itself be completely explained within an autonomous human method of inquiry. It will always beg its own originating question. Nor can theology undo this basically undecidable decision at philosophy's beginning. Instead, theology makes explicit its heteronomy by beginning in the "yes" of faith to the created communication of God's transcendent nature. In this way, theology avows what modern philosophy must always hold in brackets, and so speaks a prophetic word to those modern philosophies that would make of their relative autonomy an absolute tyranny over both subject and object, over being itself. Modern theology can, at the same time, model for modern philosophy the practical humility required to realize the dizzying scope of its orienting aspiration to complete explanation. Finally, I would note that this vulnerable posture of intellectual risk before the ambiguity of being should, if nothing else, disabuse philosophies and theologies of the illusion that their own modernity consists in a triumph over their medieval forebears. They have carried us and we have the responsibility to, cooperatively, take our turn carrying them.

PART II

A SOLUTION

CHAPTER 3

A MEDIEVAL SOLUTION, THEOLOGICAL DEVELOPMENTS

The Medieval Problem of the Supernatural

1) Specific Medieval Problem:
"How does God's grace make a difference …?"
   A) Generic Form: "… in Creation?"
   B) Specific Form: "… in Human Beings?"

2) Generic Medieval Problem:
"How does God's action make a difference …?"
   A) Generic Form: "… in Creation?"
   B) Specific Form: "… in Human Beings?"

There is a specific medieval problem of the supernatural and it has both a generic and a specific form. It is this latter, specific form of the specific medieval problem that the twenty-first century controversy associates with the problem(s) of the supernatural. "How does God's grace make a difference in human beings?" This specific medieval problem can be framed in a more generic form that asks after the difference God's grace makes in creation as a whole. With this question I am not presently concerned. My contention, however, is that the traction Thomas Aquinas gained on the specific form of the specific medieval problem of the supernatural was due in no small part to advances he made on a more fundamental, philosophical, and generic problem of the supernatural: How does God's action make a difference in creation in general and human beings specifically? Thomas's solution to the specific form of the specific medieval problem of the supernatural consists in the application by analogy of a prior, philosophical solution to the generic problem of the supernatural. I was tipped off to this undergirding philosophical position by Bernard Lonergan's reconstruction of Thomas's theory of operative and cooperative grace, as well as his detailed treatment of divine agency, knowledge, and volition.

Bernard Lonergan made a lengthy study of Thomas Aquinas's works in the late 1930s and through the 1940s. This resulted in a number of texts. Some are exegetical works concerned with reporting what Thomas thought on the basis of what he wrote, like Lonergan's dissertation, *Gratia Operans: A Study of the Speculative Development in the Writings of Thomas Aquinas* and the heavily revised *Theological Studies* articles into which he transformed it, as well as his series of articles in the same journal on the "inner word" (to which I will give extended attention in chapters 9 and 10).[1] Others from roughly the same time period are supplementary Latin-language texts Lonergan provided to his seminary students in order to augment the assigned manuals and to aid their understanding of Thomas's synthetic positions on important theological loci, like providence, predestination, and grace.[2] What I will present below is no more than "Lonergan's Thomas." Moreover, I present the positions he retrieved, exposited, and advanced in order that they should be measured by their adequacy to the speculative problems they address, rather than by their fidelity to a reader's sense of what surely Thomas meant. I am primarily a philosopher, secondarily a speculative theologian, and not at all a historical theologian, and so I hope my readers (especially those who *are* historical theologians) will set their expectations accordingly. Nonetheless, insofar as Lonergan has been by-and-large a peripheral figure to the twenty-first century controversy, it seems to me a valuable enterprise on its own terms to retrieve at length and in detail the force of his exposition for resolving a number of persistent difficulties. But more importantly to my own purposes, the solution he articulates will set up the ambiguities with which I am concerned in the next part of the book.

According to Lonergan, the hinge between Thomas's theory of divine agency and his theory of grace is his account of divine and human

---

1 See Bernard Lonergan, *Grace and Freedom: Operative Grace in the Thought of St. Thomas Aquinas,* ed. Frederick E. Crowe and Robert M. Doran, CWL 1 (Toronto: University of Toronto Press, 2000); *Verbum: Word and Idea in Aquinas*, ed. Frederick E. Crowe and Robert M. Doran (Toronto: University of Toronto Press, 1997).

2 See especially Bernard Lonergan, "The Supernatural Order" and "God's Knowledge and Will," in *Early Latin Theology*, ed. Robert M. Doran and H. Daniel Monsour, CWL 19 (Toronto: University of Toronto Press, 2011), 53–255, 256–411.

cooperation. This second part of the book, thus, takes retrieving and representing Lonergan's exposition of Thomas's position on *concursus* as its primary purpose. In order to show this position with adequate clarity, and so manifest its character as a *solution* to the medieval problem(s) of the supernatural, I will spill a great deal of ink on the fundamental ideas that are its material. In what follows, I will first acknowledge the theological problematic that plants the notion of cooperation with God in the fertile soil of Christian speculation: the apparently contradictory dual affirmation of the need for God's grace and the reality of human freedom. Then I will follow Lonergan's reconstruction of the development in the theological material that made Thomas's synthetic solution to this problem possible. This solution, which Lonergan has organized into seven phases, rests on two foundational ideas: a theorem of the states of human nature and, most importantly for our purposes, what Lonergan calls the "theorem of the supernatural." In the next chapter, I turn from these theological materials to Lonergan's lengthy and complicated account of the philosophical material that Thomas appropriated and augmented to fund his position on divine agency. Because the development of these materials is sufficiently unwieldy, in chapter 5 I will follow up the account of their development with Lonergan's synchronic and synthetic presentation of the same notions from his supplementary textbook, *"De scientia atque voluntate Dei."*

The Dialectical Position: Grace and Freedom

Speculative theology, Lonergan posits, begins from "dialectical positions."[3] These Lonergan conceives on analogy with "methodological positions" in the natural sciences. Scientists will "maintain incompatible theories simultaneously," such as that light is both a wave and a particle, in order to both indicate what is known, but also that element which is as-yet-unknown. Lonergan's notion of a dialectical position does something similar with the doctrines of the Christian faith. Because "truth is one, and God is truth," apparently contradictory doctrines are affirmed by the speculative theologian even when the theoretical mechanics of their unity as yet escapes theological articulation. But Lonergan's notion of dialectical positions is "more radical" than the methodological positions held by the scientist. The

---

3 Lonergan, *Grace and Freedom,* 166.

theories affirmed by the scientist may be overturned in a later paradigm that clarifies the unity of the two apparently opposed accounts. The doctrines of the Christian faith, though they may develop in their expressions, are permanent in their meaning. Complete explanation of the universe is, at least in principle, a proportionate aim for the scientist. Complete positive comprehension of God is not a proportionate aim for the theologian. And so the as-yet-unknown moment in theology's dialectical positions cannot ever be entirely eliminated, even as the imperfect understanding (or, more precisely, the negative coherence of explicitly articulated noncontradiction) continues to prove intellectually fruitful. The theorems and techniques of speculative theology are instruments for achieving this imperfect but fruitful understanding, and so for discerning that element in a dialectical position that is susceptible to explanation by analogy and that element which remains mysterious and so hidden in God.

Lonergan traces the problem of the supernatural to its roots in Christian late antiquity. The conjunction of two apparently contradictory affirmations in Christian doctrine generated controversy at the end of the fourth century. St. Augustine in *De gratia et libero arbitrio* argued for both the reality of human freedom and the gratuity of God's grace. Pelagians prioritized the Christian affirmation of human freedom and moral responsibility to make the merit of human action a condition of God's grace. By contrast, there were monks at Hadrumetum who so prioritized God's grace that human freedom was denied altogether.[4] Against the Pelagians, Augustine offered an incipiently speculative distinction between operative and cooperative grace. Lonergan summarizes it as follows:

> God cooperates with good will to give it good performance; but alone he operates on bad will to make it good; so that good will itself no less than good performance is to be attributed to the divine gift of grace.... Thus God operates to initiate us in the spiritual life, and he cooperates to bring us to perfection; alone he works to give us good desires, and together with our good desires he labors to give us good performance.[5]

---

4 Lonergan, 7.

5 Lonergan, *Grace and Freedom*, 5; Augustine, *De gratia et libero arbitrio*, cc. 14–17, §§27–33, 897–901.

Whether God operates a bad will or cooperates with a good will, God's grace is always the cause of our meritorious actions. Against the opposite error, Lonergan notes Augustine's insistence that the will is just as free when God is cooperating with a good will as when God replaces a heart of stone with a heart of flesh. This is a matter of biblical witness for Augustine.[6] Still, he does not paper over this apparent difficulty. Lonergan writes,

> How, Augustine asks, can God say both *dabo vobis* and *facite vobis*? Why does he give, if man is to be the maker? Or why does he command, if he himself is to be the giver? To this the answer is the celebrated paradox: the will of man is always free but not always good: either it is free from justice, and then it is evil; or it is liberated from sin, and then it is good.[7]

I would add to Lonergan's account here that an appeal to paradox does not solve the difficulty; it only clarifies its terms. Paradox serves to acknowledge that two apparently contradictory terms are actually coincident and so the contradiction must be merely apparent. Paradox indicates that there is a dialectical position confronting the theologian. Moreover, it indicates that there must be a speculative solution to the apparent contradiction. It does not of itself provide one.

Augustine's appeal to paradox can only be considered a speculative failure if his text indicates that he had set out to provide a speculative theory of grace. Lonergan does not think *De gratia et libero arbitrio* can be considered to have such a speculative purpose. Rather, Lonergan finds Augustine argued in an essentially dogmatic manner, "marshaling such an array of [biblical and patristic] texts that the [doctrinal] claim is obviously true." In Augustine's words, "Not I, but scripture itself has argued with you."[8] That humans are free and that grace is beyond any desert of ours is something one assents to when one affirms the teaching of the Church. That affirmation need not (and for many centuries did not) include an understanding of how exactly both of those things were true without contradiction. If Augustine's readers struggled

---

6 "[God] has revealed to us through his holy scriptures that there is free choice of will in man" (Augustine, *De gratia et libero arbitrio*, c. 2, §2, 882).

7 Lonergan, *Grace and Freedom*, 6.

8 Lonergan, *Grace and Freedom*, 7; Augustine, *De gratia et libero arbitrio*, c. 20, §41, 905–6.

to understand what he put forward on the basis of what God has revealed, "They were not to dispute but to pray for light."[9]

Although the apparent antinomy of grace and freedom was shown to be no justification for straying from orthodox belief, the antinomy itself was not made to disappear. If God's grace is gratuitous and so beyond our power to merit (as the Church teaches), how does receipt of it not impinge on or even obliterate our freedom (which the Church also affirms)? How can it be that grace really changes the person who receives it, but also it does not thereby deprive that person of his or her agency? Still, these twin doctrinal commitments—to the reality of human freedom and to the absolute gratuity of God's grace—are explicitly part and parcel of the Christian endowment at least as early as St. Augustine. So began, Lonergan argues, a centuries-long effort at a coherent speculative theology that would not only affirm both, but also show how what is affirmed can be understood together.

Recall that the dialectical position on grace and freedom has its origins in Augustine's polemics against the Pelagians, where the central issue was the necessity of grace. Augustine coined the distinction between *gratia operans* and *gratia cooperans* to indicate the universal necessity of grace. Lonergan traced the development of the problem to which this distinction is an answer. He organized his inquiry into the theological development of *gratia operans* from Augustine through Aquinas around five general phases. Within these he constructed a seven-phase scheme for development on the theorem of the necessity of grace specifically. In Lonergan's view, this theorem made Thomas's final theological position on grace possible, and it is this position that I am putting forward as the solution to the specific form of the specific medieval problem of the supernatural. Tracing this development will allow me to present relevant developments in the philosophy of God as they emerge in cooperation with the theology of grace. I will show that, in the effort to answer the specific form of the specific medieval problem of the supernatural—that is, how God's grace makes a difference in human beings— Thomas will stand on his predecessors's shoulders and see clear to such developments in the philosophy of God as will make possible the position on *concursus* in which consists Thomas's solution to both the general and specific forms of the generic medieval problem of the supernatural. But I should begin at the beginning: theoretical developments on the necessity of grace.

9 Lonergan, *Grace and Freedom*, 7.

The Necessity of Grace

For Lonergan, an adequate account of the necessity of grace rests on two cognate theorems: the theorem of the supernatural and the theorem of the states of human nature. I will be concerned mainly with the theorem of the supernatural, but in the context of speculation on grace, Lonergan calls this the "generic" theorem, because it considers humans as creatures in general. The theorem of "the states of man," however, considers specifically different initial starting positions for attaining eternal life, and so Lonergan calls it the "specific" theorem. Lonergan's seven-phase scheme takes this distinction between the generic and specific theorems as a hint at the formal structure of the speculative development behind Thomas's position on grace. He notes that learning begins from the particular and then moves to the general, only to then return to the particular.[10] By underlining the place of the particular within a larger horizon, one can reveal significant features of the particular. Immediately below I will discuss how Lonergan's seven-phase scheme moves from the specific to the generic and back to the specific on the problem of grace's necessity. More broadly I aim to show how a renewed emphasis on the generic, fundamental, and philosophical problem of cooperation helps to reveal significant features of the specific medieval and modern forms of the problem of the supernatural that pertain to grace and God's redemptive work in history. But Lonergan is quite right: one needs to see how these general, philosophic positions emerged from specific, theological developments in the first place.

Phase 1

There is at hand a question, "Why is grace necessary?", but this is not yet speculative development. Development per se does not begin with the naked perplexity of a problem but only when a possible solution to the problem, a possible answer to the question, is adverted to and analyzed. Lonergan again points to Augustine as the font of development in *De correptione et gratia*. There, Augustine notes a significant difference in Adam's need for grace from our own. The first man, he notes, had been given the ability not to sin and so was "righteous in that good in which he was created."[11] By contrast,

---

10 Lonergan, 179.

11 Augustine, *De correptione et gratia*, C. 12, §34, 937.

the predestined do not have this same help that enables them to avoid sin ("perseverance"). To the extent that they do have perseverance, they have it by a different "gift" without which they could not persevere in avoiding sin.[12] Augustine also says that "a greater liberty is needed" against temptations that did not exist in the pre-lapsarian paradise. Adam was created with a free will that he "made a slave to sin," whereas the predestined have a will that "had been a slave to sin" but was liberated by Christ. This liberation, however, is not to the freedom possessed by Adam but a different freedom provided by the Second Adam, Christ—a freedom enslaved to justice and God forever.[13] The specific theorem—the theorem of the states of human nature—first sneaks onto the scene with this hunch that grace is needed because of a specific difference in our state from that possessed by our first parents after their creation and prior to their fall into sin. We need a gift they did not need and a freedom they did not have.

Phase 2

The second phase generalizes the basic tendency of the specific theorem into a full articulation of the difference between our need for grace and that of pre-lapsarian persons. The tendency in Augustine to treat grace and liberty as correlates gets taken up and extended into an account of the four states of, not human nature in general, but human liberty specifically. Lonergan follows Artur Landgraf in locating this scheme's full articulation in Lombard's

---

12 Augustine, *De correptione et gratia*, C. 12, §34, 937: "Such a help to perseverance is not given to the predestined, but such that perseverance itself is given; not only so that without that gift they are unable to persevere, but also so that by means of this gift they are actually persevering and not failing to do so."

13 Augustine, *De correptione et gratia*, C. 12, §35, 937–38: "A greater liberty is needed against so many and such strong temptations, which did not exist in paradise.... To him [Adam] therefore was given without any sin the free will with which he was created, and he [Adam] made it a slave to sin; but of these [who are predestined], when [their] will had been the slave of sin, it was liberated by him who said, If the Son has set you free, then you will be truly free [John 8:36].... To this sin [of final impenitence] they are no longer slaves, not free in that first state as he was, but by the grace of God set free through the second Adam, and in that liberation having the free will by which they are slaves to God, not that by which they are taken captive by the devil. For set free from sin they are made slaves to justice [Romans 6:18], in which they will stand to the very end."

Sentences.[14] The first state of human liberty is possessed "before sin." Nothing impedes the good, nothing impels evil, reason can proceed without error, and the will can desire what is good without difficulty. The second state is possessed "after sin without grace." We are able to sin, unable to not sin, and our concupiscence oppresses and conquers us. The third state is possessed "after reparation" by grace. Though we are still oppressed by concupiscence, we are not conquered by it, so that in our liberty and weakness we are able to sin, but in our liberty and God's grace we are once again able not to sin. The fourth state is possessed "after confirmation" in grace. We are unable to be either conquered *or* oppressed by concupiscence, and so have the inability to sin.[15] One can see, then, how when the need for grace is addressed by a fully generalized theorem of the states of man, the whole discussion proceeds in terms of liberty, but without an articulated theory of liberty itself. In other words, freedom is not considered in terms of a nature distinct from grace. That grace and freedom (and so human nature) are compatible is affirmed, but still not explained.

Phase 3

In the third phase, Lonergan notes how Augustine's tendency to treat grace and liberty as correlates becomes codified in an established theorem and this specific theorem, that of the states of nature, alone is applied to the question of the need for grace. As a result, a number of speculative inadequacies appear more clearly. The need for some further speculative

14 Some enterprising historical theologian might consider undertaking a study that evaluates the current state of scholarship on those points where Lonergan depends on Landgraf for his account of theological development in *Grace and Freedom* and evaluates in detail its continuing viability, updating it as needed.

15 Peter Lombard, *Libri IV Sententiarum,* 2, d. 25, c. 6: "And four states of free will can be noted in man. For before sin there was nothing to impede the good, and nothing to impel to evil ... then reason was able to judge without error, and will able without difficulty to desire the good. But after sin, before the reparation of grace, [man] is oppressed by concupiscence and conquered.... He is able to sin and unable not to sin, even to the incurring of damnation. But after reparation ... [man] is oppressed by concupiscence, but is not conquered ... so that because of liberty and weakness he is able to sin, and because of liberty and helping grace he is able not to sin.... But after confirmation [in grace] ... he will be unable either to be oppressed or conquered, and then he will have the inability to sin."

apparatus becomes manifest as the specific theorem raises further questions it is inadequate to answer.

First, there is inadequacy on the question of merit. In Lonergan's view, Peter Lombard states the doctrine of merit quite correctly. Adam and Eve need grace because, though they are adequate to the avoidance of sin as created, they are not adequate to merit eternal life; for that another grace besides creation is needed. The problem remains, however, why avoiding sin without further grace is not meritorious.[16] The specific theorem alone cannot explain this. A distinction between *naturalia* and *gratuita,* though commonplace, is left similarly without a supporting theory or explanation. If the specific theorem is the only available speculative scheme on hand, Lonergan argues, it is perfectly logical (as Radulphus Ardens had it) to argue that all virtues were originally natural but were lost by original sin, and are only now gratuitous for us in our present state.[17] Of course, this means that although *gratuita* are strongly affirmed, it is at the expense of *naturalia,* which Lonergan thinks are effectively denied. From this follows claims like that without charity, there are no virtues at all, that besides charity there is only cupidity, and that nature is per se crooked.[18]

From this denial or, anyway, evisceration of nature emerges a further inadequacy with regard to the definition of grace. The doctrinal definition was established. No one disagreed that "grace is what is due to God's free gift and not due to man's desert." The speculative difficulty was to say what, on that definition, was *not* grace—"after all, what is there that is not a free gift of God?"[19] While some neo–de Lubacians may cheer the collapse of the doctrines of creation and grace into indistinction, Lonergan finds the medievals were not so sanguine on the prospect. On the other hand, Cardinal Laborans, for example, variously defined grace first as "everything man either

---

16 Lombard speculates that post-lapsarian humans merit eternal life when we avoid sin, but because we have difficulty doing so. In the state of original innocence, there was no difficulty and so no merit. Lonergan attributes St. Albert's befuddlement at this position to Albert having fully absorbed the generic theorem of the supernatural without realizing it was a development not available to Lombard See Lonergan, *Grace and Freedom*, 185n51, 217.

17 Lonergan, *Grace and Freedom, 186. See also Artur Landgraf, "Studien zur Erkenntnis des Übernatürlichen in der Frühscholastik," Scholastik 4 (1929): 212; alternatively, see Dogmengeschichte der Frühscholastik* (Regensburg: Verlag Friedrich Pustet, 1952), 180.

18 Lonergan, *Grace and Freedom*, 186.

19 Lonergan, 15, 186.

has at birth or receives after birth," then more specifically, "everything that the elect have at birth or receive afterwards," finally landing on the virtues of the elect.[20] And so the tendency to resolve the question by an undifferentiated appeal to "gift" is not a uniquely modern, nor a forgotten Patristic insight.

Further, a purely psychological description of grace—as healing fallen reason and will—leaves the practice of infant baptism in a mess of controversies. Lonergan notes that forgiveness of sin and justification are in scripture attributed to conversion, faith, and charity, which do not on their face seem to be habits, but psychological acts. However, it is also said that baptism of infants "opens the gates of heaven."[21] It seems to follow, then, that the baptized infant is justified. Evidently the essence of justification could not lie in the order of acts. What it is about the "sacrament of faith" that infants receive in baptism that justifies them remained unclear, Lonergan claims, until the thirteenth century. He believed that, in part, this difficulty persisted so long because the speculative question itself went unasked by many.

More importantly, when the speculative question was asked, the requisite theoretical materials were simply unavailable. The Aristotelian theory of habit was not on the scene, but also, in the absence of the more wide-ranging theorem of the supernatural, the effort to apply only the theorem of the states of liberty/nature to the question distorted the entire enterprise. It left Lombard indecisive, for instance, about whether virtue is an act or a habit and inclined many to the view that the notion of virtue as a habit was simply inconceivable. Lonergan speculates that this may have led to the mistaken distinction between remission of sins in infants and the infusion of grace in adults.[22] It is only when Waldenses and Cathari begin to demand rebaptism of adults baptized as infants that the issue is resolved dogmatically in a condemnation of the above distinction.[23] The lack of a speculative solution remained, however. Continued correlation of liberty (in terms of reason and will) and grace (exclusively understood as the reparation of fallen reason and will) left firmly entrenched the psychological approach to grace that created the problem regarding infant baptism in the first place.[24]

---

20 Lonergan, 15–16.

21 Lonergan, 175.

22 Lonergan, 177n33.

23 Lonergan, 178.

24 "[Anselm] gave the problem of infant baptism a solution which, if brilliant and containing an essential element of the truth, nonetheless tended to postpone

The final inadequacy, then, is the decisive one: though grace is defined in terms of liberty, no adequate *philosophical* theory of liberty can emerge into the speculative theological enterprise. Thus, the theory of grace is rendered viciously circular. A philosophical theory of liberty is needed to shed analogical light upon the speculative problem of grace and generate synthetic (rather than merely analytic) approaches thereto. Lonergan speculates that the condemnation of Abelard's position on liberty ("That free will is enough by itself for [doing] some good") may have led to Lombard's definition: "free will is the faculty of reason and will by which the good, with the help of grace, is chosen, or evil [is chosen] when grace is lacking."[25] If the question, "Why is grace necessary?" stood alone, this could perhaps prove a satisfying definition. However, the foregoing has labored to show how the speculative question about the necessity of grace serves an ulterior, indeed prior aim: explaining the coherence of affirming *both* the universal need for grace and the reality of human freedom. Lombard's definition simply restates the dialectical position in its paradoxical form. St. Anselm and St. Bernard had, in Lonergan's view, the same problem.[26] This is not to say that there was no philosophical definition of liberty at hand (Lombard quotes Boethius's definition, for example), but the problem is how to deploy it in such a way that the natural element and the revealed element are affirmed coherently and not just paradoxically.[27]

Phase 4

The entrance of the notion of habitual grace onto the scene helped to crack open a number of these problems, but the more momentous advance in Lonergan's view was the theorem of the supernatural and with it a governing tendency to distinguish two different orders, one disproportionate to the other. With the advent of the theorem of the supernatural, Lonergan argues, the fourth phase of speculation on the necessity of grace could begin. He

---

indefinitely the true solution. Briefly, his position was this: the infant cannot have justice, for it elicits no act of will; but this incapacity is sinful before baptism because of Adam's sin; on the other hand, because baptism removes the culpa, the infant's incapacity becomes excusable" (Lonergan, 177).

25 Lonergan, 173–74; Lombard, *Sententiae*, 2, d. 24, c. 3.

26 Lonergan, *Grace and Freedom*, 174n15.

27 Lonergan, 174–75.

finds the first hints of its speculative efficacy when Stephen Langton links *gratum faciens, gratuitum,* and *meritum.* This linkage begins to suggest that grace is not merely a matter of healing the psychological effects of sin but also of making the created soul somehow fit for eternal life. Praepositinus makes more headway "by pointing out that reason is the highest thing in nature, yet faith is above reason."[28] This begins to make more explicit a distinction between ontological orders. But it was, in Lonergan's view, Philip the Chancellor who established the significance of the theorem of the supernatural permanently by breaking with St. Bernard and Hugh of St. Victor to affirm a distinction between a natural *amor amicitiae erga Deum* and charity as the meritorious love of God.[29] In doing so, he further distinguished two kinds of appetite, natural and rational: "[He] asserted the former to be self-regarding, the latter to tend absolutely to the *honestum*; and then subdistinguished two rational appetites, one following reason, another following faith; the former of these is *dilectio naturalis*, the latter is charity."[30] Lonergan finds that Philip gave a decisive articulation of the theorem of the supernatural, in this case applied to the question of a meritorious love of God. To the "familiar series of grace, faith, charity, and merit," Philip the Chancellor systematically correlated "nature, reason, and the natural love of God." His is a "theory of two orders, entitatively disproportionate."[31] This structure of two disproportionate orders is the generic theorem of the supernatural at work. It will, in Lonergan's estimation, crack open the question of the necessity of grace and by extension the question of *gratia operans et cooperans.* It also facilitates a more adequate articulation of divine transcendence and immanence that leads to what I am calling the solution to the generic medieval problem of the supernatural and, as in chapter 6, its attendant ambiguities.

Lonergan goes to some lengths to insist that the theorem of the supernatural is not some new doctrinal element added to the definition of grace. It does not add any data to the problem. As a theorem, it is the intelligible nexus organizing the data into a coherent unity. Thus, when Philip addresses the question of merit by delineating two orders, he is not introducing a supernatural character to grace that was not already affirmed. In phase three, I showed how *gratuitas* was never in danger, but often it was

28 Lonergan, 16–7, 185.
29 Lonergan, 17, 185.
30 Lonergan, 185; Landgraf, *Dogmengeschichte,* 197–99.
31 Lonergan, *Grace and Freedom,* 17; Landgraf, *Dogmengeschichte,* 182, 197–99.

affirmed at the expense of *naturalia*. What Philip achieved "was the creation of a mental perspective, the introduction of a set of coordinates," making it possible to intelligently affirm "the validity of a line of reference termed nature."[32] It became possible to recognize that the root inadequacy in the specific theorem of states of nature consisted in an inability to distinguish in thought what in the concrete is given all together (the gift of grace and the nature of freedom). The theorem of the supernatural made this intellectual distinction possible. The general need for *gratia elavans* and the specific need for *gratia sanans* could eventually be coordinated on firm speculative ground.

Phase 5

In the fifth phase, as in the second, there is the generalization of the newly emergent theorem to its full articulation and application. Once Philip the Chancellor introduces the theorem of the supernatural onto the speculative scene, it can (like the specific theorem before it) be generalized and so extended to a number of extant problems. Lonergan has Alexander of Hales taking it up to resolve the problem of merit in pre-lapsarian humans that Lombard had failed to address. Lonergan also has Albert the Great developing a theory of sanctifying grace to resolve the issue of infant baptism and also providing some clarity to the respect in which divine virtues were divine. Finally, Lonergan comes to Thomas Aquinas's direct statement of the need for grace in terms of the disproportion of the divine essence to the powers of any created being in the *Summa contra Gentiles*: "*Quidquid excedit limites alicuius naturae, non potest sibi advenire nisi per actionem alterius.*"[33]

Phase 6

In the sixth phase, as in the third, there is the tendency to utilize one theorem to the exclusion of any other. But now it is the generic theorem, the theorem of the supernatural that is given pride of place. Lonergan finds that the force of the theorem of the supernatural in explaining the need for grace in our first parents to merit eternal life and the efficacy of sanctifying grace in baptized infants to the same effect eclipsed the problem of moral impotence in St.

---

32 Lonergan, *Grace and Freedom*, 17.
33 Lonergan, 17–18.

Albert's *Sentence* commentary and the early works of St. Thomas.[34] According to Lonergan, "both attempt to reduce the *non posse non peccare* to the sinner's inability to obtain the remission of his sins without grace." In their historical moment, the issue was reconciling *non posse non peccare* with liberty. In that sense, a generalized application of the generic theorem to the problems that occasioned the specific theorem meant, on Lonergan's read, that a certain subterranean Pelagianism loomed. Without the specifications of our concrete situation—namely, the moral impotence proper to a fallen nature—Thomas's rather direct statement that "man is able to fulfill through free will that good which is proportionate to human nature" becomes dangerously ambiguous.[35] Even Thomas's follow-up remark, "But although man can perform good works of this kind without the grace that makes him pleasing [to God], still he cannot perform them without God," does not quite snatch the issue back from the brink. Habitual grace called out for a distinct notion of actual grace as the theological analogue to the Aristotelian pair, habit and act, but initially Thomas allows a general notion of divine providence to carry the whole issue.[36] Consequently, Lonergan thinks it is not fully clear if grace is concretely needed to perform naturally virtuous acts or merely providence. It is not clear if grace is both *operans* and *cooperans* as *elevans* and *sanans* in both habit and act.

Phase 7

In the seventh phase, Thomas is able to synthesize the generic theorem of the supernatural and the specific theorem of the states of nature into a compound theory of the necessity of grace. The relevant paragraph from the *Prima Secundae* is so clear in its application of both theorems to the question that I feel compelled to present it in its entirety here:

> Thus, then, there is one respect in which man in the state of integral nature needs a gratuitous power superadded to the power of nature, namely, (the power) to do and will a supernatural good. But in the state of fallen nature, there are two respects (in which he needs

34 Lonergan, 188n63.

35 Lonergan, 184n41; see also Thomas Aquinas, *Super II Sententiarum*, d. 28, q. i, a. 2.

36 This point will receive elaboration below when I directly consider Thomas's mature position on providence, *Deus operans*, and the question of cooperation.

something gratuitous added): namely, for healing, and further to perform a good work of supernatural power, which is meritorious. Further still, in both states man needs divine help in order to be moved by that help to act righteously.[37]

First, there is presented an answer to the question why we need grace in terms of the generic theorem of the supernatural. The powers of our human nature need a gratuitous, supernatural power added to them in order to be proportionate to desiring and performing supernatural goods. Without this elevation of our natures, they are disproportionate to the divine order in which they would participate. Second, there is the restatement of our need for grace in terms of our specified state of nature—namely, fallen. Absent grace and considered concretely, we are both disproportionate to the supernatural good but also so wounded by sin that we are morally impotent with regard to both disproportionate *and* proportionate goods. Further, in the light of the generic theorem, the blanket statement *non posse non peccare* can now be specified. In general, there are goods to which human beings are created proportionate, but, specifically, fallen humans are unable to will and do these without the help of healing (*gratia sanans*). Finally, because of this commerce between the two theorems, Thomas can identify two sets of two respects in which human beings need divine help to act righteously: both to elevate and to heal and both to do the proportionate good and the disproportionate good. Thus is laid the foundation of a distinction between the help of general providence and the help of grace, operative and cooperative, healing and elevating, habitual and actual.

But this last point gets me out ahead of myself. The theorem of the supernatural turns out to have significance beyond the questions of merit and the necessity of grace. This significance regards God's general providence, the theory of divine operation, and the question of free human cooperation with God. All of these play a role in Thomas's medieval solution to the medieval problem of the supernatural and the ambiguities that follow therefrom. But what do the generic and specific medieval problems of the supernatural share in common? Both puzzle over the integral cooperation between two disproportionate orders. Consequently, the generic medieval solution is a theory of cooperation, and Thomas applies it by analogy to the specific medieval problem, as evident in *ST* 1-2, q. 109, a. 2 above.

---

37 Thomas Aquinas, *Summa theologiae*, 1–2, q. 109, a. 2.

But before a theory of *co*-operation can be derived, there is needed a prior account of operation itself. It is fitting, then, that I turn next to Lonergan's retrieval of Thomas's theory of operation, both in general and specifically on the matter of divine operation. First, I will consider Thomas's appropriation and augmentation of Aristotle's theory of action. Second, some consideration will be given to what Lonergan considers Thomas's adaptation of Aristotle's theory of *praemotio physica* and the argument that effective action requires "application," or an order that brings agent and patient into proper disposition. Third, the notion of hierarchical degrees of causality will be explicated so that, fourth and finally, Thomas's theory of divine cooperation or "*concursus*" can at last be laid out with some clarity. Indeed, with the theorem of divine *concursus*, we are finally getting down to the business at hand: explicating the theory of divine and creaturely cooperation that at once undergirds the medieval solution to the medieval problem of the supernatural, but at the same time reveals the medieval ambiguity waiting behind an adequate philosophy of divine agency.

CHAPTER 4

A MEDIEVAL SOLUTION, PHILOSOPHICAL DEVELOPMENTS

Whether one is investigating the question of God's general *auxilium* or the specific question of God's grace, attributing agency to God can carry a problematic implication: does God, in acting, change? If so, at the very least God's simplicity, infinity, and eternity are all called into question. On the other hand, if God does not change, how can there be meaningful free cooperation between human beings and God? Would not God's unchanging agency determine the human will such that any hint of freedom is excluded? Again, the same problem appears whether one takes up the topic of providence or of grace because it is a problem that hounds talk of divine agency in general. For Lonergan, this problem haunts the theology of providence and of grace alike because it has its roots in philosophical assumptions about agency itself. This, after all, is the nature of speculative theology: "It constructs its theorems with respect to the supernatural order by appealing to the analogy of nature."[1] Thus, when Lonergan approaches the problems of divine action in his dissertation, he tackles the philosophical question of agency first out of the gate.

Action

The fundamental question is whether, in passing from *posse agere* to *actu agere*, an agent undergoes change *qua* agent. On its face, there seems good reason to think so. "Now it is evident," Lonergan writes "that the two propositions,

---

1 Bernard Lonergan, *Grace and Freedom: Operative Grace in the Thought of St. Thomas Aquinas,* ed. Frederick E. Crowe and Robert M. Doran, CWL 1 (Toronto: University of Toronto Press, 2000), 252.

potest agere, actu agere, cannot both be true with respect to the same agent and the same activity at the same time. The two, as defined, are contradictory: the first means that (one) is not acting; the second that (one) is acting." There must be, then, some real difference in the objective situations described by the respective propositions, "for contradictory propositions cannot be verified in identical situations."[2] However, to assume that a real change in the agent *qua* agent provides this difference creates a problem for any Thomistic or Aristotelian philosophy: it excludes a *motor immobilis.* If one affirms a change in the agent passing from *posse agere* to *actu agere* as a priori necessary, one has to also accept the implication that this change is a priori universal. If that is the case—if *omne movens movetur*—then there is excluded the possibility of a *motor immobilis* and so, by dint of infinite regress, neither can there be motion, nor by extension can there be action.[3]

Perhaps there is a theological reason one can affirm a real change in the agent actually acting. Did I not already follow the great lengths Lonergan took to show the mark left on Thomas's thought by the theorem of the supernatural? Perhaps there is a difference between the agency of the Creator and the agency of creatures on the question of *posse agere* and *actu agere.* Lonergan denies that Thomas thought so. True, the Creator acts in virtue of a substantial act and the creature an accidental one, as Thomas indicates in *ST* 1 q. 54, aa. 1–3, but Lonergan insists there is no evidence that he also "places in the creature a real distinction between a *posse agere* and *actu agere.*"[4] Thomas's account of agency is a completely general philosophic account. In addressing the position Thomas held, Lonergan briefly exposits the Aristotelian doctrine of agency Thomas appropriated and then turns to Thomas's commentary on Aristotle's *Physics,* which includes first a defense of the doctrine and then an important augmentation. This augmentation regards how action is predicated of an agent and it seems meant to head off the very misunderstanding with which I am concerned here—namely, the attribution of a real difference in one *actu agere.*

<hr>

2 Lonergan, 252.
3 Lonergan, 253–54.
4 Lonergan, 254.

Thomas Reads Aristotle's Position

First, then, there is Aristotle's position on motion.[5] Lonergan summarizes it as it appears in *Physics III*, boiling it down to seven definitions and a six-step exposition. Notice how Lonergan breaks down Aristotle's philosophical position into its basic terms and defines them by their relation to one another, only then fitting them into a theorematic scheme.

First, the definitions:

1) An actively moving thing (*motivum*) is that which can move something (*movere*).
2) A mover (*movens*) is that which moves something (*movet*).
3) A movable thing (*mobile*) is that which can be moved (*moveri*).
4) A moved thing (*motum*) is that which is moved (*movetur*).
5) Movement (*motus*) is the act of something existing in potency (*potentia*) insofar as it is in potency.
6) Action (*actio*) is a movement … as from the agent (*ut ab agente*).
7) Passion (*passio*) is a movement … as in the patient (*patiente*).[6]

Lonergan then exposits in six steps how these terms fit together into a single theorematic scheme to explain what motion is. The first three steps delineate which terms in the above definitions constitute what Lonergan calls "real and adequate distinctions" and which do not. First, between a mover (*movens*) and

---

5 Thomas initially sides with Avicenna against Aristotle on the question of *actio*, treating an action as an accident that must be double because it cannot reside in two different subjects at once, even if the movement itself is one. But again, Lonergan insists that, even before Thomas abandons this position of the *Sentences* and *De potentia*, he never explicitly asserts that this inherence of *actio* as an accident amounts to a real change in the agent *qua* agent. In Lonergan's estimation, however, Thomas comes around to Aristotle's position in his commentaries and in the *Summa theologiae*. The strong implication is that the later position is the mature position, and indeed the position that makes a successful analogy from the nature of agency possible in the speculative theology of grace. Though Thomas sticks to his own terminology (*actio* rather than *motus*), Lonergan shows how he presents, defends, and helpfully augments Aristotle's position in the commentaries on the *Physics*, *De anima*, and the *Metaphysics*. See Lonergan, *Grace and Freedom*, 254–60.

6 Lonergan, *Grace and Freedom*, 261; for clarity, I have slightly modified the translations provided in the lexicon of Latin and Greek phrases provided by the editors (493–514).

an actively moving thing (*motivum*) there is no real distinction. Second, there are adequate real distinctions between a mover and a movement (*motus*), between a mover and a movable thing (*mobile*), and between a moveable thing and a movement. Third, there is a real, but inadequate distinction between a moveable thing and a moved thing (*motum*) and between a movement and a moved thing.

The latter three steps of Lonergan's exposition make more explicit how the above definitions fit together into a full theory of agency. Fourth, then, the reality of a movement is common in both action (*actio*) and passion (*passio*), such that there is only one entity, but it is called an action when considered from its relation to its origin, and it is called passion from its relation to its subject. Fifth, the active potency of a thing moving (*motivum*) and the passive potency of a moveable thing *both* move from potency to act, but this transit involves *only one act*. This act is the same movement in the moveable thing (as *passio*) and from the mover (as *actio*). Sixth, and finally, the distinction between action and passion is thereby maintained even though the reality, the *motus*, is a single entity. This is because the movement has two terms: its origin and its subject. When the movement is considered from the origin, it is called action. When it is considered in the subject, it is called passion.[7]

For Aristotle, as Thomas reads him, motion is a single entity that can be considered from the vantage of its origin or from the vantage of its subject. Though both the origin (*movens*) and the subject (*motum*) transit from potency to act—actually moving and actually moved, respectively—there is only one act, the movement itself. This inheres in the moved subject, but is merely "from" the moving origin. This turns out to be the fundamental point in Aristotle's theory of agency as appropriated by Thomas. Thus, the distinction between *actio* and *passio* is maintained, but as notional rather than real. In other words, the distinction survives despite Aristotle demoting its ground from the assumed substantial difference to a difference of relation.

Thomas's Commentary on Aristotle's Physics

Thomas clarifies Aristotle's account by distinguishing between a mover moving *as* mover and a mover "*happening* to be moved when moving."[8] He insists on the theoretical control of meaning at work in Aristotle's definitions: "Still movement is not the act of the thing moving but of the movable thing

---

7 Lonergan, 261–62.
8 Lonergan, 262 (emphasis added).

insofar as it is movable."[9] To recur to definition 5 above: Movement (*motus*) is the act of something existing in potency (*potentia*) insofar as it is in potency. That the mover is concretely moving does not mean that it is moving *qua* mover, and so the abstractions of Aristotle's doctrine are liberated from the ostensible "self-evidence" of the way things appear—the very "obviousness" of which gave rise to the quandaries of physics in the first place.

Lonergan notes how Thomas also underlines what I noted above: since the movement as *passio* is in the patient and only from the agent, the act of a movement inheres in the moved because "the act of anything at all is in that to whom the act belongs."[10] Now, the movement is still *caused* by the mover or agent, even though the movement—and so the act of the movement—is in the patient. But this leads to something of a subtlety in Thomas's commentary. Because the mover is also moving, which is to say that it has movement in it in another respect (than as agent), it must also have act in some respect. Thus, the question is raised: is this movement in the mover the difference or change needed to explain the transit from *posse agere* to *actu agere*?[11] Thomas's answer is worth quoting at length:

> He (Aristotle) shows that the same act is act of the mover and the moved. For "mover" is said insofar as something acts, but "moved" insofar as it is changed; but it is the same thing which as mover causes by acting and which as moved is changed by receiving. And this is what he says (in stating) that the mover is the "active force of the movable thing," that is, it causes the act of the movable thing. And therefore it is necessary that there be just one act of the two, namely, of the mover and of the moved; for it is the same thing that is from the mover as from agent cause, and is in the patient as receiver.[12]

Lonergan wants us to see with Thomas the pay-off of Aristotle's control of theoretical terms. Movers cause by acting, but receiving this active force *changes* the moved. Thus, the act is shared in the movement from agent to patient, but only the patient is changed. What, though, about the movement in the agent? Is not that a change in the mover *qua* mover, in the agent *qua* agent? Aristotle denies this on the basis of the objection already noted above:

---

9 Lonergan, 262.
10 Lonergan, 262.
11 Lonergan, 263.
12 Thomas Aquinas, *In Aristotelis libros Physicorum*, 3, lect. 4, §306.

if it were, then every mover would also be moving and there could be no unmoved mover. As Lonergan puts it: "Parmenides would have won."[13]

Lonergan adverts to another, a posteriori argument Thomas uses to bolster the a priori argument from infinite regress. Thomas notes in his commentary on the *De anima* that the faculty or organ of hearing receives its act from sounding, but the act of both sounding and of hearing are in the organ of hearing, that which is according to its potency.[14] Were the act of sounding not received by that which has the potency of hearing, there could not be an act of hearing, and so the act of both must be in the faculty or organ as recipient or patient. This carries as a corroborating, negative implication what Thomas had stated explicitly as early as *De potentia*: the patient is related to the agent in such a way that, should the act of the patient cease or be removed, the agent is unchanged.[15] If an act of hearing ceases, the concrete sounding from which it received its act need not cease or change. It can ring on, unaffected. Indeed, to be unaffected is what it is to be the mover and not the moved.

Thomas's Augmentation

Having traversed Aristotle's basic position on motion and Thomas's clarifications, I can now consider Thomas's augmentation of Aristotle's position. His augmentation concerns how action is properly predicated of an agent and rests on a parallel between logic and metaphysics. The ten genera or "predicates" of being are not, Thomas notes, divided univocally the way that species within a genus are. Instead, he writes, they are divided "according to the diversity in (their) mode of being."[16] That is to say that they are divided in proportion to the modes of predicating. Hence, they are called "predicaments." Not all the kinds of predicament are of the same nature and Thomas distinguishes three basic kinds. There are predicaments of substance, which regard the essence of a thing. There are "inhering" predicaments, such as quantity (which regards the matter of a thing), quality (which regards the form of a thing), and relation (which regards being by reference to another). Finally, there is what he calls "extrinsic" predication, which regards a thing

13 Lonergan, *Grace and Freedom*, 264.
14 Lonergan, 265.
15 Lonergan, 258–59.
16 *In III Phys.*, lect. 5, §322.

"by way of some denomination."[17] This notion of extrinsic predication or, as Lonergan sometimes calls it, "extrinsic denomination," is crucial for avoiding the error that would assume transit from possibly acting to actually acting involves a real change in the agent. Lonergan says that extrinsic predication "attacks the very root of the error."

This third, extrinsic kind of predication is the kind of predication that pertains to agency. The predicament of passion is denominated from the agent, "for to suffer is nothing else than to receive something from the agent."[18] Contrariwise, the predicament of action is denominated from the patient, "for action is an act (going) from the agent to another."[19] Without this notion, it is too easy to assume that the "objective real difference involved by the transition from the truth of one proposition [*posse agere*] to the truth of the other [*actu agere*]" inheres in the agent.[20] But this is merely an assumption and an incorrect assumption at that. Lonergan writes: "What is overlooked is that the emergence of the effect does supply such a real difference in the objective field. And the reason why it is overlooked is that it is assumed that all predication is of exactly the same nature, that *ens* divides univocally into the ten predicaments the way a genus divides into its species. Such a blunder cannot be attributed to St. Thomas."[21] On Lonergan's read, not only does Thomas affirm Aristotle's account of *actio* and underline the core, controlling theoretical elements in his commentaries, but he also augments Aristotle's position with an explication of the unspoken element in these metaphysical problems that might lead one to reject Aristotle's doctrine. If one supposes that all predicaments are denominated of a subject in the same, inherent way, then the problem becomes insoluble. But if one recognizes the logical and metaphysical legitimacy of extrinsic predications, it becomes possible to see why not all movers are moving.

Lest Thomas's defense and augmentation of Aristotle's position leave any doubt as to whether he also appropriated this same philosophical position in his mature speculative theology, Lonergan directs us to two passages in the *Prima pars* that indicate Thomas has. On the topic of divine procession and having just mentioned Aristotle's *Physics*, Thomas summarizes the Aristotelian

---

17 *In III Phys.*, lect. 5, §322; Lonergan, *Grace and Freedom*, 266.

18 Lonergan, *Grace and Freedom*, 266.

19 Lonergan, 266.

20 Lonergan, 267.

21 Lonergan, 267.

doctrine thusly: "although action is the same as movement, and similarly passion, still it does not follow that action and passion are the same; because in action there is implied a reference 'as that from which there is movement in the movable thing,' but in passion (the reference is) 'as that which is from another.'"[22] When it comes to Thomas's account of creation, one finds the Aristotelian position (if not Aristotle's terminology) organizing the argument, such that "since *actio* is *motus ut ab hoc* and in creation there is no motion [of itself], it follows that *creatio* is simply the relation."[23]

In summary, then, the notion of extrinsic predication clarifies the logico-metaphysical relation of patient to agent. An agent is denominated as acting from the patient who receives the act of its inhering movement. The patient's receipt of the act of movement does not involve a real change in the agent and this can be seen both a posteriori in the fact that *passio* can cease without a change in the agent and a priori from the proximate implication that all movers would have to be moving and the remote and subsequent implication that there could thus be no *motor immobilis*, and so no motion at all. Agency, then, is a matter of the patient's dependence for its act upon another and so the transit from *posse agere* to *actu agere* is verified in the changed patient rather than any change in the agent. This general position on agency must be held in mind as I move through the following section. If it is lost, the subsequent accounts of application, of universal instrumentality, and of Creator/creature cooperation will fall into irretrievable incoherence and the medieval solution will be lost with it.

Action's Order

The above account of agency explicitly abstracted from a mover's own motion. The motion of the mover was noted only insofar as Thomas followed Aristotle in insisting this motion is not in the mover *qua* agent. But such an account is insufficient to explain actual motion, because to be an actually moving thing is part of the definition of what it is to be that which can actually move something.[24] Thus, the above position on agency merely

---

22 *Summa theologiae*, 1, q. 28, a. 3, ad 1m; Lonergan, *Grace and Freedom*, 268.

23 Lonergan, *Grace and Freedom*, 268.

24 This is to say that to be *posse agere* in the first place means being in act and not to contradict the above position on change in agents *qua* agents when they transit from *posse agere* to *actu agere*.

explains the form of any possible movement or change without giving a full account of actual motions. It bears, in other words, the abstractness proper to any formal explanation. For any particular possible movement to become actual there is required some situation or mutual relation or disposition of the mover and the moved. Lonergan explains how Aristotle's doctrine of physical premotion serves to provide an explanatory frame for how such situations, mutual relations, or dispositions are provided to the possibly moving and possibly moved such that the active power of the mover-as-cause can be applied to the moved-as-effect.[25]

On this point, Lonergan again adverts to Thomas's commentaries on Aristotle. Thomas says, commenting on the *Physics*, that all things that act (whether according to nature or understanding) or suffer are possible agents and patients. They cannot just move or be moved in any disposition or situation, but only in some determinate relationship or "propinquity" to one another. Only under these proper circumstances does one move and is the other moved.[26] But as we have already seen, if *omne movens movetur*, there cannot be a first motion.[27] In Aristotle's cosmology, on Thomas's read, this problem is resolved by making the first mover a *motor immobilis*. The heavenly spheres, then, are that which is primarily moved and move eternally, sustaining the earthly eternal series of *generabilia* and *corruptibilia* that are sometimes, but not always moving. The mediation of the *corpus caeleste* is required because the first mover cannot cause terrestrial *quandoque moventia*. It would have to act differently at different times and that would itself require motion, negating its very character as *motor immobilis*. Instead, "physical premotion" is sustained by the ever-wheeling *corpus caeleste*, bringing mover and moved together, with the first mover serving as final cause.[28] For change in the world to be maintained, there must be and always have been a source of constant motion bringing those situations about, changing the disposition of or relations among movers and moved. For Aristotle, the physical premotion of the *corpus caeleste* is universal, because in every coincidence of worldly mover and moved, there has to have been an ordering premotion of this kind.

Thomas, for his part, adopts this doctrine of physical premotion in his account of God's providential agency but transforms it significantly

---

25 Lonergan, *Grace and Freedom*, 278–79.
26 *In III phys.*, lect. 2, §978.
27 *In III phys.*, lect. 2, §976.
28 Lonergan, *Grace and Freedom*, 281–82n65.

by resituating its first mover to the horizon of personal theism. Lonergan underlines a hint from Thomas's commentary on the *Metaphysics* to exactly *how* he will appropriate the doctrine of premotion—under the heading "application." When the passive element in a movement or change is brought into sufficient proximity to the active element, the act of the mover/agent can be communicated to the moved/patient. For example, when something combustible is applied to an open flame, the actual combustion is communicated to the combustible material. Without this application—that is, without this spatiotemporal ordering of the combustible to that which is already burning—there cannot be any actual movement, change, action, or passion.

Thomas takes up this way of speaking (*applicatur*) with reference to how God "moves all things to their appointed end by His intellect."[29] As Thomas says in a number of places, *Deus omnia applicat.*[30] In one respect, this is a straightforward appropriation of Aristotle's teaching. Thomas quite logically affirms universal application, because for Thomas God is not less than first mover in Aristotle's sense, and the first mover causes all motion and premotion.[31] But to identify premotion with universal application by divine providence already assumes the horizon of personal theism. Strictly speaking, universal divine premotion is not yet *providence*. Aristotle's first mover acts simply as final cause and the *corpus caeleste* only ensures change continues perpetually. Thomas's God acts by His intellect, and that means God is furthermore "the *causa per se* of every coincidence of mover and

---

29 Thomas Aquinas, *De substantiis separatis*, c. 14, §129.

30 *Summa contra Gentiles*, 3, cc. 67 [§2418] and 70 [§2464]; *De potentia*, q. 3, a. 7; *Summa theologiae*, 1, q. 105, a. 5.

31 Moreover, because Thomas accepted Aristotle's cosmology, he deduces several consequences of universal application. First, though God is the sole cause of *esse*, creatures are the cause of *fieri*. Second, the execution of providence is mediated. Third, the execution of providence is a motion. Fourth, there are no motions not intended by divine providence. Fifth and finally, if God did not control the wills of angels or of human beings, there could be no providence in the spiritual or material world. On Lonergan's read, all of this follows from the affirmation of universal premotion for everything except God as first mover. God, therefore, is the cause of the action of every natural thing as moving and applying a power to its action. These deductions, then, are synthesized with Thomas's comments on the *Physics* in the *Summa contra Gentiles* (3, c. 70), where Thomas affirms that God's application is in every particular application of an active power to its action.

moved, every conjunction of causes, every combination of effects."[32] Thomas writes in the *Prima pars*, "But God is not the cause of something except as he is intelligent, for his substance is his understanding.... And everything acts through the mode of its substance. God therefore moves all things to their proper ends through his intellect. But this is to be provident."[33] In this way, God's application is Aristotelian premotion, but also rather more. God causes each particular motion in the further sense that God's mind plans and God's will intends "the endless premotions that constitute the dynamic pattern of the universe."[34] Thus, the way that Lonergan reads Thomas's theory of providence, an intellectually intended premotion simply *is* an application, such that *Deus omnia applicat.*

Thomas's appropriation and augmentation of Aristotle's theory of premotion helps to highlight an aspect of God's providential agency that is sometimes overlooked. I have focused in this section primarily on what Lonergan saw as the influence of Aristotle's philosophy on Thomas's theology, providing natural, philosophical elements as material for a theological position on grace and freedom. But Thomas's augmentation of Aristotle's theory of premotion gives us an example of that influence running the other direction in the commerce between philosophy and theology. The Christian insistence on a personal God, with a mind and a will, transforms Aristotle's theory even as it accepts its basic theorematic shape and the cosmology in which it is ensconced. Thomas's God does not simply create beings with certain natures and powers and then leave them to the exercise of these with the on-going underwriting of divine conservation. For Lonergan, Thomas understands God's providential agency as not just creating and conserving but also applying these entities to their effects within a cosmic order. It is the order that meets the conditions required for possible motions to become actual motions. God intends it eternally, but it unfolds temporally. Thus, as Lonergan reads Thomas, God's will not only creatively intends the existence of things but also the order from which they emerge over time, and so (by extension) those things *in their mode of emergence.* As I will emphasize below, in the case of human beings, this means God wills our exercise of free agency as well.

---

32 Lonergan, *Grace and Freedom*, 285; *Summa contra Gentiles*, 3, c. 94; *Summa theologiae*, 1, q. 19, a. 6; q. 103, a. 7.

33 *De substantiis separatis*, c. 14, §129; Lonergan, *Grace and Freedom*, 287.

34 Lonergan, *Grace and Freedom*, 285.

Degrees of Causality in Action's Order

To call God the *causa per se* of premotion implies that every created thing is an "instrument" of providence. Once again, Lonergan notes that Thomas appeals to a perfectly general philosophical theory (of causality, in this case) to provide the intellectual structure undergirding his speculative theological account. The trail of this implication begins with the nature of causality. Following Thomas's account in the *De Veritate*, Lonergan notes that being a cause *qua* cause has two aspects.

1) it must be something in act: *omne ens agit quatenus est actu.*
2) the something that it is must be proportionate to the effect intended: *omne agens agit sibi simile.*[35]

With regard to the second aspect, Lonergan lists four ways of being proportionate to an intended effect. First, something can be proportionate to its effect in virtue of that something's natural form and, second, in virtue of a more eminent form. Thus, fire is proportionate to causing heat by virtue of its natural form, while the *corpus caeleste*, neither hot nor cold in itself, "is the principal cause of all emergence of heat, cold, humidity, and dryness."[36] Third, something can be proportionate to its intended effect in virtue of an idea in the mind and, fourth, in virtue of an idea transitioning from a mind to the effect. Thus, an architect's intention (*vis artis*) for a building is proportionate to the building as an effect as in his or her mind, but the same idea distributed (*virtus artis*) through the division of labor (to electricians, steel workers, etc.) in the building's construction is also proportionate to this effect.[37]

This enumeration is also a hierarchy of degrees. Lonergan explains it by analogy from motion as *esse incompletum*. Motion, on this Aristotelian approach, "is not 'something' but a process 'towards something.'"[38] The analogy goes, "As a motion is the *esse incompletum* of its term ... so also the proportion of the instrument is an incomplete realization of the proportion of the principal cause." In other words, instruments rely on another, more eminent cause to complete their proportion to an effect. Thus, 1) fire is

---

35 Lonergan, 288.
36 Lonergan, 288.
37 Thomas Aquinas, *De veritate*, q. 27, a. 7.
38 Lonergan, *Grace and Freedom*, 288; *In III Phys.*, lect. 3, §296.

proportionate to producing heat *per modum naturae completae* and 2) the *corpus caeleste per modum naturae completae et eminentioris*. By its nature fire produces heat, but the premotion of the heavens is required for it to actually be in the disposition to do so, and so it is in a sense an instrument of the order of the heavens, even though its nature is in complete proportion to the effect of producing heat. Hence the *corpus caeleste* is a more eminent cause than the flame itself.

In the realm of intellectual causes, then, we have 3) the architect who is proportionate to his or her effect as an intellectual agent, *per formam apprehensam* and 4) the various instruments of his or her design that are proportionate to the effect *per modum naturae incompletae, per quoddam esse incompletum.*[39] The form of the architect's understanding is proportionate to the building as its effect, but the mediation of his or her various laborers is instrumental insofar as they are proportionate to welding, electrical work, and so forth, but not to the nature of the desired effect: a complete building. The efficacy of the artist's intentions resides in the workers as in a medium—*per modum quo colores sunt in acre, et virtus artis in instrumento artificis.*[40] And so, Lonergan says, it becomes possible to define *instrument*: "an instrument in the strict sense is a cause that is proportionate to its effect *per modum naturae incompletae.*"[41]

Hence it is that Thomas affirms God's providence as being proportionate to its effects *per modum naturae completae et eminentioris* because God is first mover, but also *per formam apprehensam* because God is an intellectual agent.[42] Not only do the forms of creatures participate in the divine ideas, but so too does the order of cosmic unfolding participate in God's providential design.[43] We also get a clearer sense of what it meant to say above that "the execution of providence is mediated."[44] Fate, this cosmic ordering, is the artistic vision

<hr>

[39] Lonergan, *Grace and Freedom*, 288.

[40] *De Potentia*, q. 3, a. 7, ad 7m.

[41] Lonergan, *Grace and Freedom*, 288.

[42] Lonergan, 290–93; see also *Super I Sententiarum*, d. 38, q. 1, a. 1: "Knowledge in its character as knowledge does not imply any causality, otherwise all knowledge would be a cause; but insofar as it is the knowledge of the artisan using things, in this way it has the character of a cause with respect to the thing used by art. And therefore as there is causality in the artisan through his art, so must be considered the causality of divine knowledge."

[43] *De veritate*, q. 5, a. 1, ad 1m.

[44] *Summa theologiae*, 1, q. 116, a. 2 c: "Divine providence executes its effects through mediate causes. That ordination of effects can therefore be considered in two

of God according to another mode of existence, one embedded in secondary causes such that they produce God's desired effects.[45] Recall, moreover, that it is embedded in the secondary causes as their "disposition or series, that is, (their) order."[46]

As I already noted, to be the patient of an action is to be in a relation of dependence upon the communicated act of the agent, and so the mediation of the secondary causes does not add anything to or change anything about God's agency. Thomas says, "The efficacy of the principal agent is found instrumentally in all the instruments ordered to the effect, as being one in a certain order."[47] Rather than something added to God's agency by arithmetic composition—that is, in a sense where "God does this much and creatures do this much"—Thomas is describing a hierarchy of *qualitative* degrees of causality, in all of which God's agency is immanently efficacious. As I turn now to consider this hierarchy explicitly, I hope it will become evident how holding both kinds of causal proportion in mind—*per modum … eminentioris* and *per formam apprehensam*—is essential to Thomas's philosophical appropriation and theological augmentation of Aristotle's theory of physical premotion.

What has not been explained yet, however, is precisely what is meant by "eminence." For if both God and a creature are proportionate by nature to some effect, why is God a "higher" cause of that effect than the creature? Lonergan adverts to Thomas's commentary on the *Liber de causis* to address this question. Lonergan notes, "It is argued that the higher cause *prius intrat, vehementius imprimit, et tardius recedit.*"[48] This locution is impressionistic, to be sure,

---

ways. In one way, as it exists in God himself, and then this ordination of effects is called providence…. But according as the aforesaid ordination is considered in mediate causes ordained for the production of some effects, in this way it has the character of fate."

45 Lonergan, *Grace and Freedom*, 295; "And therefore it has to be said that fate, from the viewpoint of secondary causes, is changeable; but as subject to divine providence, it shares in unchangeableness, not indeed that of absolute necessity but of conditioned; in the way in which we say that this conditional is true or necessary, 'If God knows this will be, it will be'" (*Summa theologiae*, 1, q. 116, a. 3 c).

46 *Summa theologiae*, 1, q. 116, a. 3, ad 1m, ad 3m: "Fate is called a disposition, not that which is had in the genus of quality, but according as disposition designates an order, which is not a substance but a relation. And that order, considered in comparison to its principle, is one; and in this way fate is called one. But if it is considered in comparison to [its] effects or to those mediate causes, then it is multiplied, in the way in which the poet said, 'Your fates draw you.'"

47 *Summa theologiae*, 3, q. 62, a. 4, ad 4m.

48 Lonergan, *Grace and Freedom,* 298; see *Super Librum De causis*, lect. 1, §13.

but Lonergan finds the context suggests a rather restrained interpretation—that "the activity of the higher cause is a presupposition of the activity of the lower"[49]—and it is an elaboration of a more general metaphysical principle. In the same commentary, Thomas writes, "If whiteness were separate, simple whiteness itself, and not something participating in whiteness, it would be the cause of all white things insofar as they are white," and so accordingly, "the Platonists held that that which is being itself is the cause of being for all things."[50]

What if there are a plurality of relevant causes for some given predicate? How then does one proceed? Lonergan directs attention to how Thomas summarizes Aristotle's answer as follows:

> We must always take the media which are nearer the subject in which we seek the cause of that common effect; and we must proceed in this way until we come to that which is immediate to the common effect. And he assigns the reason for this, namely, that that which is from the side of what is contained under something common is the cause for its being under that common (predication): for example, if D is under B, and if C is the cause for D that B is in it. And from this it follows further that C is the cause that A is in D; and B is the cause that A is in C. But A is in B itself per se and immediately.[51]

Then Lonergan helps walk through what this means:

> Here "immediate" has its etymological sense of "nonmediated," "logical first." Thus, Socrates is mortal, because he is a man; a man is mortal, because he is an animal; an animal is mortal, because its material cause is composed of contraries. The three middle terms are "man," "animal," "with material cause composed of contraries." The first of these is the least general. The last is the real cause of mortality: not only does it make "animal," "man," and "Socrates" mortal; it also is the cause of "animal" making "man" mortal, and of "man" making "Socrates" mortal.[52]

---

49 Lonergan, *Grace and Freedom*, 298.

50 Lonergan, *Grace and Freedom*, 298; *Super Librum De causis*, lect. 3, §80. Compare to *De veritate*, q. 5, a. 9, ad 7m.

51 Lonergan, *Grace and Freedom*, 300; Thomas Aquinas, *In Aristotelis libros Posteriorum analyticorum*, 2, lect. 19, §580.

52 Lonergan, *Grace and Freedom*, 300.

It becomes clear in light of the above what it means to say that a higher cause "arrives first, makes the greater impression, and leaves last." Human beings are mortal even if they are not Socrates, and animals are mortal even if they are not human, and animals are not the only beings possessed of "a material cause composed of contraries" such that they one day die. The higher cause precedes the lower as a condition. It is the difference that makes a difference. It persists even if lower media are logically excluded. To put it more briefly, its activity is the presupposition of the activity of lower causes. A cause is higher to the extent that it is a more fundamental presupposition of effect in consideration. Thus, the scale of causal eminence terminates in causal ultimacy.

This is simply good Aristotelian metaphysical analysis by which things are reduced to their causes, but it also suggests the way in which higher causes do not compete with lower causes for explanatory "space" in Thomas's theory of action. Lonergan finds this has significant pay-off for Thomas's theory of *Deus operans et cooperans* (the skeleton on which Thomas's theory of grace hangs). Another somewhat lengthy quote merits reproduction here insofar as it makes this connection explicit for us:

> Let A, B, C be three causes in an ordered series so that C is the ultimate one performing the action. It is clear that C performs the action by its own power; and the fact that it is able through its own power to (do) this, this is through the power of B and further through the power of A. And therefore if it is asked, Why does C act? the reply is, Through its own power. And why through its own power? Through the power of B. And so on till (the series) is reduced to the power of the first cause, to which the Philosopher, in book II of the *Posterior Analytics*, text. 22, and book II of the *Physics*, text. 38, teaches (us) to resolve questions. *And thus it is clear that, since God is the first cause of all things, his power is most immediate to all things.*[53]

There can appear now the conjunction between the cosmic spatiotemporal ordering effected by the eternal and universal application of God's providential intention and the *logically* ordered series of agents that constitute the hierarchy of causes. Because God's providential ordering of the cosmos and its creaturely inhabitants is a condition of the efficacy of those creatures as agents, God's providential ordering is the ultimate, "highest" cause of any

---

53 *Super I Sententiarum*, d. 37, q. 1, a. 1, ad 4m (emphasis added); Lonergan, *Grace and Freedom*, 302.

and every created effect. One can see this conjunction by the ambient light of Thomas's appropriation and augmentation of Aristotle's theory of motion and agency. Because agency is extrinsically predicated of agents, God can have this immediate relationship to the agency of creatures without Himself having to be moved. God can be at once the highest and the most immediate cause, all without displacing "lower" creaturely agents in the explanation of cosmic unfolding. Most importantly, I am now prepared to discuss Thomas's theory of cooperation, the last of the theorematic materials required for both the philosophy of divine and human agency and the theology of operative and cooperative grace in which the medieval solution to the medieval problem of the supernatural consist.

The Theory of Cooperation or *"Concursus"*

I can turn now to what Lonergan calls the "central theorem" in Thomas's theory of grace: his notion of cooperation. The general notion of cooperation is that two or more causes combine to produce a single effect. This occasions a question: if each cause has its own *actio* (which it must by definition), how do the *actiones* of these relate? Lonergan enumerates three kinds of cooperation. The first he calls "coordinate cooperation," as when two people pull a boat together. This is cooperation in the sense denied of creaturely cooperation with the Creator above: person A pulls this much and person B pulls this much and in so doing they move the boat together. In this case, the *actiones* of each cause are combined by (vectoral) addition. However one might imagine cooperation with God, Lonergan will not even briefly consider that coordinate cooperation applies here. "With it we are not concerned."[54] The second kind of cooperation Lonergan calls "accidental cooperation," in which there are two distinct *actiones* and they produce two effects, as when Abraham begat Isaac and Isaac begat Jacob. Lonergan is not going to consider this kind either. After all, what creaturely action could add anything to divine agency's *ad extra* operation?

Only what Lonergan calls "serial cooperation" pertains to the divine *concursus*. Serial cooperation involves three *actiones*, but a single product, as when (on Lonergan's example) Peter kills Paul with a sword. Here, we have three *actiones*.

----

54 Lonergan, *Grace and Freedom*, 302.

1) Peter moves his sword to strike a death blow.
2) His sword, so moved, kills Paul.
3) Peter kills Paul.

Recall again that agency is predicated extrinsically from the existence of the effect. Peter is the mover of his sword because the sword so moves. The sword is the slayer of Paul because Paul dies in receiving its *actio*. Lastly, Peter is also (and no less) the slayer of Paul because, in receiving Peter's *actio* in the medium of the sword, Paul dies. Thus it is that there can truly be distinguished three *actiones*, but only the one really distinct product (the death of poor Paul) and one notionally distinct product (a moved sword). There is, however, no third product. Indeed, if there is not only one really distinct product of more than two really distinct *actiones*, it is not an instance of serial cooperation. Finally, the third *actio* is the cooperation itself.[55]

Lonergan distinguishes this basic philosophical notion of cooperation in preparation for what he views as Thomas's central theorem on *ad extra* divine agency: *Deus operatur in omni operante*. In brief, created agents cannot have *actio* without attributing the same *actio* to God. Lonergan distinguishes in Thomas's presentation a direct and an indirect statement of the theorem. The direct statement is, as already stated, that God operates in all operation. The indirect statement, then, is that unless God moves, creatures cannot operate.[56] I will follow Lonergan in presenting a number of passages from Thomas's corpus in which these two forms of the theorem appear.

First, the direct statement of the theorem: in the *De veritate*, it appears as the general form of God's operation in the will: "as every natural action is from God, so every action of the will, insofar as it is an action, is not only from the will as acting immediately, but from God as the first agent (and the one)

---

55 Lonergan makes an important point about the two potential errors this account of cooperation invites and how they seem to have produced the opposed positions of Durandus, Báñez, and Molina. He writes, "Now these two errors [denying that there is a third *actio* and affirming a third product] correspond to the two positions between which St. Thomas steers a middle course. He does not deny a third *actio*, and so differs from Durandus, who is reputed to have held that God merely creates and conserves. He does not affirm a third product, and so he differs from Báñez, who posits a *praemotio physica*, and from Molina, who posits a *concursus simultaneus*. The point to be grasped is that to deny the position of Báñez or of Molina is not to affirm the position of Durandus" (303–4).

56 Lonergan, 304–5.

who makes a stronger impression."[57] One finds here also the impressionistic language of the commentary on the *Liber de causis* (*"vehementius imprimit"*) deployed with precisely the same theoretical control as before, insisting on the immediacy of the higher cause to the lower as its presupposition. Thus, God operates in the will as God acts in all of nature, with the plain implication that God then operates in all operation.

The *Summa contra gentiles* has an entire chapter devoted to the proposition *quod Deus est causa operandi omnibus operantibus*, and Lonergan notes that it begins with the statement, "*Deus est causa omnibus operantibus ut operantur.*" Thomas gives six reasons why this is true. First, insofar as creatures act *virtute divina*, they can of themselves be causes of being. Second, because "God is the cause of the *virtus* from which proceeds the creature's *operatio*," and thus God is its cause.[58] Third, the divine conservation of the *virtus* is necessary for the *virtus* to enable the *actio*, and so God causes the act. Fourth, divine application is required for any actual *actio* and *passio*, and so God is the cause of both. Fifth, because all lower agents act in virtue of their higher causes, "God is more the cause of any *actio* than any subordinate agent."[59] Sixth, because God ordains all things to their ends, everything acts *virtute divina*, and so God is the cause of all *actio*.

Three chapters later in the *SCG*, Thomas explicitly raises the question of cooperation. How can two agents do one producing? Here, it is reinforced that the lower agent(s) act in virtue of the higher and both produce the whole effect, though in different manners.[60] The same treatment appears in *De potentia* q. 3 a.7, in the *sed contra*, in which analogies are drawn from art, generation, and existence to show, in the end, how there is a single product produced by at least two agents. In other words, it shows that creatures and the Creator cooperate and, on Lonergan's analysis, that their cooperation is an instance of *serial* cooperation.[61] Lonergan finds that Thomas, presumably

---

57 *De Veritate*, q. 22, a. 8.

58 Lonergan, *Grace and Freedom*, 306.

59 Lonergan, 306.

60 Lonergan, 307n152.

61 "As art presupposes nature, so nature presupposes God. But nature operates in the operation of art.... Therefore God too operates in the operation of nature.... According to the Philosopher man and the sun generate a man. But as the operation of man in generating depends on the action of the sun, so also and much more fully does the action of nature depend on the action of God. Therefore God operates whatever nature operates.... Nothing can operate unless it exists. But nature cannot exist except

in his maturity, simplifies the presentation of this theorem in the *Prima pars.* Instead of constellating a number of interlocking causal reasons to affirm cooperation between Creator and creature in every *actio,* he boils things down to three active causes: final, efficient, and formal. *Deus operatur in omni operante* is affirmed in all three respects, but final cause becomes the controlling notion. Lonergan writes, "[The final cause] is the cause of the activity of the efficient cause; therefore any effect is causally related to the final cause; but any causal relation is an *actio* of some sort, and so, even on the ground of finality, God operates in all operation."[62] While the efficiency of this form of presentation is to be admired as a speculative accomplishment, it is so general as to be nearly occlusive of the metaphysical mechanics at work. The presentation in the *SCG* is perhaps less systematic, but pedagogically more helpful. For Lonergan, in any case, the point is to see that the theorem at work is identical.

Finally, Lonergan treats of the indirect statement that, unless God moves, no creature may operate. In the *De veritate,* this principle is presented only in terms of the divine operation as creating and conserving the creature.[63] "For God is the cause of a natural operation, insofar as he gives and preserves that which is the principle of natural operation in the thing, from which by necessity a determinate operation follows; as when he preserves gravitation in the earth, which is the principle of downward motion."[64] By the *Prima secundae,* Thomas has added a further element to the indirect statement of the theorem. Created causes, because they are agents *in tempore,* need the ordering of premotion in order to actually act. Thus, creatures act *both* in virtue of God's creative and conserving agency, but also *virtute motionis divinae.* See, on this point, the "general reason" that human beings need the *auxilio gratiae* in *ST* 1-2, Q. 109, A. 9.[65]

---

by the action of God.... Therefore nature cannot act except by the agency of God.... The power of God is in any natural thing whatever, because God is said to be in all things by his essence, by his power, and by his presence. But it must not be said that the divine power as it is in things is otiose. Therefore as found in nature it operates. Nor can it be said that [God] operates something different from what nature operates, since nothing is found there except the one operation. Therefore God operates in any operation whatever of nature" (*De potentia,* q. 3, a. 7, *Sed contra*).

62 Lonergan, *Grace and Freedom,* 309.

63 Lonergan, 311.

64 *De veritate,* q. 24, a. 14.

65 Lonergan, *Grace and Freedom,* 311–12.

With Lonergan's reconstruction of Thomas's theory of cooperation in hand, my aggregation of the philosophical material beneath or behind Thomas's solution to the medieval problem of the supernatural is complete. The notion of serial cooperation clarifies the manner in which the divine operation acts in all created operations. Moreover, it becomes evident how Thomas's various appropriations and augmentations of Aristotle's philosophical advances are synthesized into a position on divine agency that so far from impinging upon the agency of creatures, is explicitly the existential presupposition of any creaturely agency at all. It remains to state Thomas's synthesis on divine action and providence directly. Then I will turn to Lonergan's retrieval of Thomas's position on God's operation not in creation generally but specifically in the human will. That position, in concert with the general account of divine agency, prepares the way to the general ambiguity of created causality and the specific ambiguities pertaining to human freedom with which chapter 6 will begin.

CHAPTER 5

A MEDIEVAL SOLUTION, SYNTHESIS

God acts. Indeed, God necessarily acts. God is the infinite, eternal, pure act of existence. God's essence is God's act of existence. Thus, divine action poses no problem, per se. Even if one distinguishes within God's infinite and eternal act the action of knowing God's self or of willing the infinite good that God is, still these acts are likewise infinite, eternal, and necessary in God. The speculative problem arises when one asks whether God's infinite, eternal, and necessary act has any effects. Does God, in other words, act *ad extra*? Is God an efficient cause? These questions suggest a perhaps difficult implication: If God does have *ad extra* effects, these effects (because conditioned by God's agency) are contingent and so predicated of God contingently. How can a necessary agent cause contingent effects? The short answer is that though God acts necessarily, God's *ad extra* agency is predicated of God contingently. If God is an *ad extra* efficient cause, God is eternally the efficient cause of every being that is not God.

But there exist beings that are not God. So, we affirm that God is the efficient cause of every being that is not God. Moreover, because they are conditioned by God's efficient causality, every thing that is not God is a contingent thing. It is true, then, that being the cause of every contingent thing is predicated of God and God's agency contingently. The difficulty remains, however: how can a contingent effect be predicated of a necessary cause? If God is an efficient cause contingently, how is he such eternally and without limit? First, it is important to recall the Aristotelian nature of efficient causality in Thomas's work. Second, recall Thomas's augmentation of Aristotle's theory: the extrinsic mode of predication/denomination. Further, it will also be important to distinguish kinds or senses of necessity.

First, efficient causality is, by nature, an action that produces a passion. Action and passion are two aspects of a single reality. This entity is considered "action" as from the agent, but "passion" as in the patient. The agent, then, is the efficient cause of the effect in the patient. Its act is communicated to the patient in producing an effect. The movement, change, or difference inheres in the patient, but is only "from" the agent. In this way, the production of an effect does not produce a change in the agent, for if it did, it would in this respect be a patient instead (by definition). Moreover, if it were a metaphysical law that agents changed when they acted, then there could be no unmoved, first mover, and so no motion at all.[1] Thus, to predicate efficient causality of God and specifically efficient causality with regard to every existing, contingent thing involves no change in God, and so no threat to divine eternality, simplicity, or impassibility.

Second, agency is not predicated of a subject intrinsically, but as explained above, *extrinsically*. It is predicated by denomination from something "outside" or other to that subject—namely, its effect. Thus, in order to truly say that God is the cause of every contingent thing does not impute any contingency to God, but only predicates efficient causality of God contingently. Lonergan writes, "Whatever is predicated of God contingently has its truth-correspondence through extrinsic denomination."[2] Extrinsic predication/denomination makes it possible that contingent propositions can be true of a necessary being, because they are true by reason of something that is not God. Lonergan notes that propositions are called "simultaneous in truth" when "they are true by reason of one and the same entity."[3] Extrinsic predication makes possible propositions that are simultaneous in truth. The attribution of agency and the acknowledgement of an effect are both true by virtue of the existence of the difference produced in the thing affected. Thus, the statements that contingent beings exist and that God causes contingent beings to exist are both true by virtue of the reality of contingent beings.[4]

Third, Lonergan distinguishes three kinds or senses of necessity: 1) absolute necessity, 2) that which is necessary upon the supposition of something else, and 3) that which is necessary upon the supposition of itself. The first is the necessity proper to God's being and only to God,

---

1 Bernard Lonergan, "God's Knowledge and Will," in *Early Latin Theology*, ed. Robert M. Doran and H. Daniel Monsour, CWL 19 (Toronto: University of Toronto Press, 2011), 272–73.

2 Lonergan, 271.

3 Lonergan, 267.

4 Lonergan, 267.

that which cannot not exist. The second, "that which is necessary upon the supposition of something else," consists in the relationship of antecedents and consequents. This second necessity includes metaphysical necessity (e.g., that "finite substances cannot exist without inseparable accidents"), physical necessity (e.g., the diffusion of heat), and moral necessity (e.g., "if you speak, you tell the truth"). But it is the third kind of necessity, 'that which is necessary upon the supposition of itself,' that provides clarification on this question.[5]

Now, any and every being is necessary on the supposition of itself, because this is the minimal necessity that, as long as something is, it necessarily is. This kind of necessity pertains to any being, even if it possesses none of the other forms of necessity above. For example, Lonergan says, "[Take] an action that is both free and supererogatory. As long as it exists, it necessarily exists; and yet such an action is neither absolutely nor metaphysically nor physically nor morally necessary."[6] None of these in the second class of necessity—metaphysical, physical, or moral—or, in their absence, the correlate kinds of contingency, can be deduced or derived from the presence or possession of this third kind.

In sum, God causes (as efficient cause) contingent beings such that they receive the act of their contingent existence from the infinite, eternal act of existence that is God's being. God, then, is the agent of this action because contingent beings depend upon receiving the act of their existence from God. This contingent existence, however, inheres in the contingent being and not in God. Efficient causality is predicated of God extrinsically because it is predicated of God in virtue of an entity other than God. Consequently, the propositions "contingent beings exist" and "God causes contingent beings to exist" are simultaneously true by reason of the same entity—namely, the existent contingent beings. Finally, these contingent beings exist, at minimum, with the necessity of that which necessarily is by supposition of itself. From this necessity, no other forms of necessity can be deduced or derived.

God's Transcendent Causality

Though above I have focused on God's agency as an efficient cause, God's agency is also transcendent. This was already hinted at in a general way when I affirmed that God is the cause of every contingent being and every being

5 Lonergan, 275.
6 Lonergan, 275.

that is not God is contingent. Thus, the distinction between God as cause and everything else as effect is also a distinction between Creator and creature. The specific reasons for affirming the transcendence of God's agency come into view at the conjunction of four principles: first, the principle of priority; second, the principle of simultaneity of truth; third, the irresistibility of divine action; fourth, an inverse insight into the relation between God's causality and created causality.

First, the principle of priority simply insists that a cause is prior to its effect. God is eternal, and so the priority here obviously cannot be temporal priority. There is no "before" God created the cosmos in that temporal sense. God's causing a thing is prior to its existing, rather, in the sense that God's action is a presupposition for its being.[7] But God is the efficient cause of all things, and so whatever exists comes from God's prior action.

Second, the principle of simultaneity in the order of truth means that truths that are true through the same entity are true simultaneously. As with our first principle, however, one must here assiduously avoid attributing temporality to God and so any "simultaneity" in truths predicated of God must be on the side of the creature. Hence, such truths are, both in general and in this specifically theological case, grounded in extrinsic predication. Any statement predicated of God contingently is predicated extrinsically and so posits the existence of an extrinsic denominator—that is, a creature. Thus, the statement that God causes a universe of contingent beings is true simultaneously with the statement that there exists a universe of contingent beings.[8] "When," therefore, is God creating creatures? Whenever they exist.

Third, these two principles together imply that God's creative action is, in the traditional Thomist language, irresistible. God is the prior cause of everything that is. By extrinsic predication, the statements, "God causes something to be," and, "It is," are simultaneously true by reason of one and the same entity: the contingently existing thing. What God causes to be exists necessarily, but only with the minimal necessity that is from the supposition of itself.

Fourth, the above three points may occasion an inverse insight—indeed, an inverse insight at the heart of the medieval ambiguities presented in chapter 6. There is no contradiction between the statement that what God causes to be in God's transcendence necessarily exists and the statement that what God

7 Lonergan, 283.
8 Lonergan, 283.

causes to be is contingent. Indeed, these are convertible statements. From God, the action is necessarily effective. In the creature it is contingent because it is conditioned by God's action. Moreover, because the effect is contingent, the agency by which God's action is necessarily effective is predicated of God contingently. Though one might expect it to, this simultaneous dual affirmation of God's transcendent agency does not, on its own, tell one anything about the order of necessity and contingency, because it regards God's agency *as transcendent*. Lonergan says, "One cannot determine solely by the irresistibility of (God's) action whether what he … effects is necessary by metaphysical, physical, or moral necessity," or merely contingent in any or all of those respects. The only necessity that can be deduced or derived from God's transcendent agency is that those things that are necessary by the supposition of themselves. This kind of necessity accords equally with contingency or necessity of the metaphysical, physical, or moral kind. The affirmation of God's transcendent causality tells us that God causes the world that is, but not what kind of world God has caused. This inverse insight into the relation of all things to God as their creator will be at the heart of the medieval ambiguities explored in chapter 6. It leads us to a general form of the specific problematic of grace: what kind of difference does God's action make?

These four principles prepare the central notion governing Lonergan's account of God's transcendent causality: proportion. Agents must be proportionate to their effects, and the proportion of an efficient cause is determined by its nature. As I affirmed at the beginning, God and only God exists by nature, which is why God is the only absolutely necessary being. Not only is God the cause of every contingent being but also the only being proportionate to causing existence.[9] The act of existence is received by and inheres in creatures as patients of God's transcendent action. Moreover, it is communicated gratuitously, both because creatures are not by nature proportionate to operatively apprehending existence but more fundamentally because without its gratuitous communication, creatures do not exist to operate at all. This general disproportion between creatures and the Creator to being the cause of existence is the most general form that the theorem of the supernatural takes. The (dis)proportions between entities or their orders, after all, are at the core of the theorem of the supernatural itself and this expression of the theorem pertains to all existing entities and orders.

9 Lonergan, 319.

At this point one can see most clearly the service paid by theology to the philosophy of God. The effort to figure out why pre-lapsarian humans required God's grace produced this distinction between entitatively disproportionate orders. This distinction, then, possesses the theoretical mobility proper to a theorem, such that it can serve to control the relation of terms in the philosophy of God as well. Although the theorem of the supernatural emerged historically in the speculative theological context and so is temporally prior to any separated philosophy of God, the present project rests on the insight that its general philosophical application to the question of the cause of existence is theoretically prior to its specific speculative theological application on the *aporia* of grace. After all, the existence of creatures is logically prior to whatever state with regard to sin in which they may find themselves. But this also highlights why the theorem of the supernatural is not enough to explain our need for grace on its own. "What, after all," as Lonergan says, "is not a free gift of God?"

God's Artisanal Governance

So far, however, I have only established that God's *ad extra* agency creates and conserves the existence of beings if and when they exist. Lonergan, following Thomas, is able to derive further significance from God's action by applying the analogy of an artisan working with instruments. This analogy opens up the question of God as cause to not just the aggregate totality of existent beings, but also to the order that obtains between them, and so of God as not just operating to cause the existence of creatures but operating in and through the operation of those creatures.

The question arises, if God is the cause of every contingent thing, is the totality of created beings itself an intelligible, complete unity? Are these myriad beings, in other words, parts in a whole? Does the universe have an order? Lonergan says yes. When one asks after the totality of created beings without exception, one heuristically takes the vantage of eternity. From this heuristic vantage, not only does one anticipate that the universe possesses an order but that it has a perfect(ed) order. For Lonergan, every possible world conceived in the mind of God is a complete, intelligible unity. God acts through intellect and so possible worlds are those that God conceives in wisdom and chooses justly. But, Lonergan says, intelligence grasps unity and wisdom arranges things in order. Furthermore, perfect justice leaves nothing incomplete.[10] Thus, every possible universe, including this actual one, is not just an aggregate of beings but (from the vantage of eternity) a whole with a complete, intelligible order.[11] Thus, in every possible world and in this actual world, every being has a relation to the whole as one of its parts and is ordered within the whole as such. God causes the actual order of the universe, then, as well as the existence of the smaller wholes that make up its parts.

From the viewpoint of temporal being, however, one finds divine action causing the order of the universe in three ways: by instrumentality, by application, and so by cooperation. Because no created cause is proportionate to causing the existence of its effects, all created causes are causes only in the essential order. They cannot by nature cause their effects to be, but only to be this or that or, as Lonergan says, "such." Nonetheless, created causes *do* cause their effects to exist. Their act is communicated to the effect and inheres in the patient as affected. Such communication, after all, is that in which agency consists. As I showed above with regard to existence, every created cause acts *per modum naturae incompletae, per quoddam esse incompletum.*[12] Thus, every created cause must also be an instrument of God's creative causality insofar as it produces the existence of an existing effect.

This minimal sense of instrumentality, however, is not yet enough for created causes to be effective causes. That created beings possess an act to be communicated makes them only potentially agents. In order for them to actually produce effects, there is further required premotion. They must be brought into a proper relation or disposition with regard to that in which they would potentially produce an effect or else the potential patient is not available to receive its act from the agent. Just as from the vantage of eternity there is an order of beings as wholes in themselves, as parts of larger wholes, and each subsidiary whole as a part in the complete intelligible unity of the universe, so from the view of temporal being there is also a correlate order of the spatiotemporal relations that are presupposed in each actual instance of created efficient causality.

10 Thomas Aquinas, *Summa theologiae,* 1, q. 25, a. 5, ad 1m.

11 Bernard Lonergan, *Grace and Freedom: Operative Grace in the Thought of St. Thomas Aquinas,* ed. Frederick E. Crowe and Robert M. Doran, CWL 1 (Toronto: Toronto University Press, 2000), 297–99.

12 Lonergan, 288.

In this way, created causes are instruments of God in the further sense that they are moved into relations or dispositions for effective causation according to God's governance. Thus, God applies all causes to their effects by the instrument of premotion. The opportunities to act and be affected are as caused by God as the form and existence in which the power to act and/or the potential to be affected inhere.[13] As Lonergan puts it, "God wills B should exist because of A."[14] The dynamic spatiotemporal order of the universe is also an effect of God's action through God's intellect. In this way, God acts *ad extra per formam apprehensam,* and so God's agency is analogous to the agency of an artisan exercising his or her proportionate power and understanding through the instrument of either subcontractors or tools or both. Hence the title of this section: God's artisanal governance.

In summary, created causes, in their existence, in their movement through the universe, and in their efficacy as causes, cooperate with God's agency. They cooperate by the serial cooperation described above. Because God acts irresistibly, created causes cooperate with God insofar as they operate at all. God's action is necessary for all created action. Because of God's transcendence, the necessity of God's action for all created action tells us nothing about whether those created actions are metaphysically, physically, or morally necessary or contingent. Insofar as God acts in them, they are necessary only on the supposition of themselves. Neither does God's universal and unfailing application of every cause to its effect(s) provide the means to deduce or derive whether the cause produces its effect with metaphysical, physical, or moral necessity or contingency. Every potential cause has the occasion for its actual efficacy according to the cosmic order effected by God, and so is determined by God. But it is *completely* determined by God and so is determined both in its mode of existence *and* its mode of emergence. These include both contingent and necessary modes (to say nothing yet of the freedom that pertains to human causality).

Distinguishing the necessity for God's action in created causes and the necessity with which created causes produce their effect when God acts in them from the mundane forms of necessity and contingency (metaphysical, physical, moral) in the above fashion rests on the intellectual force of the theorem of the supernatural. Without the disproportion of creatures to the Creator, this radically determining but not *deterministic* account of God's

---

13 Lonergan, "God's Knowledge and Will," 321.
14 Lonergan, 309.

ad extra agency would not be possible at the theological or philosophical level. Though Lonergan underlines the specific difference the theorem of the supernatural makes in the speculative theology of grace, here I want to underline the general and indeed foundational difference the theorem makes in the philosophy of God and God's agency.

Divine Operation in the Human Will

A free agent is free in two respects. First, it is the cause of its own determination. Because to be free is a mode of agency, action in general is that which is determined by this determination. The source of this determination as determinate is the intellect. It makes this determination, primarily, by apprehending some good.[15] The apprehension of some good is not of itself enough to determine what a free agent will do, because the will can act or not act with regard to this or that good, no matter what the object presented to it for decision. Lonergan notes that even the infinite good may not move the will automatically, depending how one interprets *ST*, 1-2, q. 10, a. 2. Thus, the will can be determined and moved by some good apprehended, but it is not *necessarily* so determined or moved.[16]

Second, the will may or may not move itself from potency to act. When the intellect apprehends a good, the will is brought into act with respect to this good as an end, and then it may move itself from potency to act with regard to the means to that end. In this way a free agent determines what it will do by its intellect, but whether it will act at all the will determines. A will is called free primarily insofar as it may or may not move itself to act— which is to say, actually willing the means to an apprehended good as its end. Secondarily, it is called free because the means to an end are optional rather than necessary, the practical judgment that selects these means is contingent, and the *bonum apprehensum* does not move the will efficaciously but, as I have already noted, only formally.[17]

But is the free agent's contingency *qua* free in contradiction with the affirmation already established that God irresistibly acts in every created cause? Lonergan identifies several errors that might lead to such a conclusion.

---

15 Lonergan, *Grace and Freedom*, 318. I will return at length to the nature of this intellectual apprehension and determination in chapter 10.

16 Lonergan, 319.

17 Lonergan, 320.

Errors, he says, that emerge because of anthropomorphism in our thought about God and God's agency. Today, one might call these errors "cognitive defaults" and expect them to crop up regularly. First, there is a tendency to think of God's agency as temporal instead of eternal, and so to mistake the priority of God's action for sequential, rather than causal, priority. Because God is eternal, God does not act "before" human action, as there is no "before" or "after" for God.[18] Second, because God is infinite in every respect, human acts cannot add anything to the being of God. For this reason, contingency cannot be introduced into God because of the contingency of human agency aggregating to God by additional cooperative acts.[19] Further potential objections are headed off by adverting to the already established notions of extrinsic predication and those things that are necessary on the supposition of themselves. Human acts do not change God because agency is extrinsically predicated of agents, and so true propositions about God's causal role in human acts are true of God by reason of the existence of the human acts and not some transformation in God. Finally, the necessity with which free human acts are produced by God's action is the aforementioned necessity upon the supposition of itself, by which it is said that insofar and as long as something exists, it necessarily exists.[20]

All of this is to say in various ways that God stands outside the order of all other causes. God's effects are, in themselves, necessary or contingent at God's choice. If God does "this," it must be. But the necessity of a "this" can be absolute or it can be hypothetical (as when God wills that B should exist because of A). Which "this" in fact is depends on God's chosen action. As chosen, then, these acts are intended, that is, foreknown with the priority of causal priority. Whichever "this" is, contingent or necessary, as from God's action it necessarily is.[21] Thus God's operation in every created operation is *ad modum naturae*. Indeed, it must be, because *deus operatur in omni operante* is a theorem, not a datum. By extension, God operating in the human will does not prevent human minds from causing their own acts formally, nor deprive our wills of the freedom to contingently act or not to act. God causes our causality in its mode of emergence—namely, as contingent freedom. At the same time, God irresistibly produces the effect God intends, but again *in its*

18 Lonergan, 323.
19 Lonergan, 323–24.
20 Lonergan, 325–28.
21 Lonergan, 336–37.

mode of being, including the mode of freedom/liberty.[22] This is simply the specifically human volitional instance of the general relation of temporal and contingent causes predicated of God as the effects of God's irresistible action.

The Nature of Habits

Additionally, there is the relevance of the dynamic pattern of the universe on the question of human freedom. Free causes no less than nonrational agents require premotion in order to be applied to their effects. God's providence intends the cosmic, spatio-temporal order and thereby irresistibly creates the circumstances and dispositions in which free agents can be efficacious in producing contingent or necessary effects contingently or necessarily as the case may be. Still, as God's instrument, the order of the universe produces what God intends irresistibly and efficaciously.[23] But this cosmic ordering— application by premotion—has an analogue in the human being as free cause: the habit.

Lonergan notes that perfection in the dynamic order of operation— that is, action—is radically one with perfection in the order of being, and perfection in the order of being is measured by the proportion of potency and act. God alone is *actus purus*, "with potentiality at zero and act at infinity," and so only God operates with absolute perfection.[24] This is the impeccability proper to God and God's transcendence. Angels, for their part, are compounds of potency and act, but are beyond time. Consequently, they can fail in their action in some cases, but, as atemporally "created in the full development of their natures," are fixed by a single act toward their goal.[25] Humans, though, are essentially temporal and so the development of our nature emerges in a *series* of acts. At birth, Lonergan says, our "higher powers are the spiritual counterpart of *materia prima*." This indeterminate potentiality is ordered to the good in general, but human beings never happen upon the good in general. What is good is always concrete. This concreteness means that the good is "ever unique" and, by contrast, evil is manifold. In other words, there is the right thing to do and then nearly endless ways to fail to

---

22 Lonergan, 337–38.
23 Lonergan, 338–39.
24 Lonergan, 45.
25 Lonergan, 55–57; *De veritate*, q. 24, aa. 10–11.

do it.[26] Humans begin with the odds stacked against us morally. We are *agens imperfectum*.[27] We *can* act properly in any and every instance, but because our moral potential is realized in time and space, it will in the course of things act properly only, as Lonergan says, "*in minori parte*."[28] It is, to put it in more modern terms, improbable that we will do what is right.

The only remedy to this situation is to set about actualizing our moral potential so that we act rightly with greater regularity. Habits and dispositions meet this need by making the external moral demands of the universe the internal form of our operations. Dispositions do this inconstantly, but habits do so more perfectly. Habits actualize our moral potential, determining some principle or power of our nature, "forming a certain quality in (it)."[29] Because habits are a perfection of an indeterminate potency, their immediate effect is formal.[30] They make this moral form of the universe, as Lonergan put it, our "second nature."[31]

The theorem of the supernatural, to which I had previously appealed in order to account for the disproportion between divine agency and created causes, also allows a distinction in the order of habits. We may distinguish between acquired habits and infused habits. Acquired habits or virtues are those caused by acts. This notion is familiar: practice makes perfect. But Thomas's argument for why it is that acts cause habits may seem a bit strange to those not acquainted with it. In *ST* 1–2, q. 49, a. 2, he says that in agents possessing only the active principle of their acts, a habit cannot be caused by that agent's own acts. However, some agents possess both the active and passive principles of their acts, as when a human will acts if moved by the object presented to it by the intellect. In these agents, acts can cause habits in their agents.

Why does the introduction of passivity make habit formation possible? First, as already stated, effects of action inhere in what is moved—that is, in the patient. The passivity of the will to receive determination from a *bonum apprehensum* is a being-moved. Thus, if one recalls our discussion of premotion above, what is moved is disposed by the action of the agent.

---

26 Lonergan, *Grace and Freedom*, 45.
27 Lonergan, 350.
28 Lonergan, 350; *Super I Sententiarum*, d. 39, q. 2, a. 2, ad 4m.
29 *Summa theologiae*, 1–2, q. 51, a. 2.
30 Lonergan, *Grace and Freedom*, 48; *Summa theologiae*, 1–2, q. 49, a. 4.
31 Lonergan, *Grace and Freedom*, 46.

Second, acts of the will are free precisely because the will can, in principle, act or not act to will the means to the end presented as *bonum apprehensum.* That which acts only out of an active principle cannot have a habit (cannot be "accustomed or unaccustomed," Thomas says), because it cannot fail to act if in the proper external disposition or relation to what it would move. But free agents *can* fail to move themselves to act and so need not only external disposition and relation to what would be moved by its action but also an *internal* disposition toward moving itself. Some of these dispositions are natural and occur spontaneously, others are acquired, and yet others (the theologian knows) may be infused.

Acquired habits are formed in us by our actions. Now, intellectual habits can be formed by a single act, as when one comes to understand something and, coming upon the same intelligibility in the future, continues to understand. But volitional habits, because the apprehensive powers are, Thomas says, "inclined variously," require multiple successive acts to be formed.[32] In so doing, we both actualize our moral potential and determine it, concretizing it. Humans, then, as temporally free agents, have the opportunity (within the constraint of those ends and means cosmic premotion ordered by God's providence has made available in our time and place) to be the artisanal governors of our souls by giving the actualization of our natures a determinate character—forming it and realizing it at the same time. In this way, our action is analogous to God's: we finitely and temporally can create the microcosm of ourselves in much the same way that God infinitely and eternally acts to determine and realize the cosmos in its every moment of emergence.

Of course, what God makes is neither materially nor formally before God makes it. What we make and what we cause by our action is materially before we make it. But it is important not to hypostatize after the fact the abstraction by which we identify its material "existence." What we will is not yet, but what *would be.* The deployment of the subjunctive mood here will prove of central importance when I return to consider free human action in more detail in chapter 10. That is an essential part of what makes the action by which it is caused free. The object of the will is, prior to action, an *intellectual* object. Though it may be part of an extant species (like an automobile) or not (like faster-than-light starships), it is not yet substantial until caused to be in cooperation with God by our action. It is as much a mistake to think of what

32 *Summa theologiae,* 1–2, q. 49, a. 3.

we will in the way that Lonergan warns us not to think of what we know by our intellects: as "already out there now" entities.[33] To think of what we will as "already out there now" covers over the way in which what we efficaciously will and do, we *make*. This point will be of fundamental importance for the modern problem of the supernatural.

All of this brings us back to the problem of human beings as *agens imperfectum*. Good acts need to occur regularly to inculcate virtue in the appetitive powers of our souls. But the structure of our moral nature—as temporal and requiring insight into phantasm—make these acts improbable and so irregular. Unfortunately for us, the only thing that can make them probable is virtue. But we cannot have acquired virtue without those acts occurring regularly, at least for a time. Worse, moral failures also have a formative effect on the soul, imbuing vices where virtues should be and further impeding the actualization of our moral potential. On top of concupiscence, there is moral impotence, and on top of our moral impotence, there is our sinfulness. This is not to say, I should reiterate, that free, right action is impossible. It remains possible for us by nature, but as in the more general treatment of causality above, *possessing proportion to an act is, by itself, to be only possibly acting*. Actual action requires the further ordering of physical premotion for all created causes. Similarly, the proportion to free, right action still requires a proper spiritual or psychological disposition—a kind of moral instance of application—to be efficacious, to be actual for the most part, and to realize itself as an *agens perfectum*.[34]

Happily, the theologian may recognize a second category of habits: infused virtues. The theorem of the supernatural does the heavy lifting on this point. We are, by nature, proportionate to the acquired virtues, but the proper disposition or relations (internal or external, in either case) are likely to be lacking that would allow the proportion of our nature to become actually efficacious in the moral realm. The infused virtues, then, are entitatively disproportionate to our natures. For one, they are received as a gift from God and not by means of our own operation. Second, they transform the disposition of our nature under circumstances in which, though perhaps

---

33 On the "already out there now," see Bernard Lonergan, *Insight: A Study of Human Understanding*, ed. Frederick E. Crowe and Robert M. Doran, CWL 3 (Toronto: University of Toronto Press, 1992), 276–78.

34 Lonergan, *Grace and Freedom*, 46.

proportionate to the operations needed, we lacked the disposition to make them efficacious. Third, they can also (in the case of the theological virtues: faith, hope, and charity) communicate a moral form that is, in itself, beyond the proportion of our nature to operate or develop habitually. In these three ways, the infused virtues address both the specific theorem of the need for grace (the state of our nature as fallen) and the generic theorem of our need for grace (the disproportion of eternal life in God to our created natures).

What is important here, however, is that whether one operates according to his or her created nature in developing acquired habits (of justice, say, or courage) or one receives as grace from God the infused virtues (whether, under our dire moral circumstances those virtues proportionate to our nature, but unavailable to our moral impotence, or those virtues of faith, hope, and charity disproportionate to our natures), *in both cases we see the created human agent cooperating with divine agency.* Not only does God act to create and conserve the human acts that issue from both kinds of habits, but God provides both the external and internal relations and dispositions in which the habits are acquired, received, and/or consist.

Thus, Lonergan has collected and arranged for us an array of philosophical and theological tools that Thomas deployed to get a better handle on the "natural" or philosophical element in the speculative problem of grace and freedom. From these Thomas could derive speculative theological solutions by analogy. My emphasis, however, has been on the developments on the philosophical side that accrued from Thomas's efforts in theology by this speculative method. If Lonergan's read is correct, I have presented a perhaps permanent achievement with regard to the relation of divine and created causality in general, and that of divine and human agency specifically. It is a medieval solution to the medieval problem of the supernatural in its full generality.

Conclusion

Tracing Lonergan's retrieval of Thomas over these preceding chapters has led to this perhaps surprising double conclusion. First, I have shown how the commerce between philosophy and theology produced advances for both fields. A theological problematic spurred Thomas's appropriation and augmentation of Aristotle on to philosophical developments that, whatever dividends they paid in his speculative theological enterprise, stand on their own merits. Developments on the specific form of the specific medieval problem generated developments on the generic and specific forms of the generic medieval problem. These, in turn, scaffold Thomas's eventual solution to the specific form of the specific medieval problem of the supernatural. The integration of these, then, constitutes a medieval solution to the entirety of the medieval problem of the supernatural.

The benefit philosophy accrued from its commerce with speculative theology also saddled it with a new problem. When separated from its cooperative concern with theology, philosophy will discover that these new developments suggest a fundamental ambiguity from which it cannot, by its own powers, loose itself. There is the general ambiguity regarding the explicability of the universe (if any), and alongside it the specific ambiguity of human freedom and its purpose (if any). Of course, the theologian may recognize how the doctrines of creation and redemption provide a resolution to these ambiguities. However, insofar as these doctrines must be affirmed by faith, the theologian cannot absolve us of the philosophically undecidable choice to which we are called by these ambiguities. In this way the theologian cannot, so to speak, snatch the analysis of this choice and its grounding ambiguity out of the hands of the philosopher. It will remain a perennial ambiguity for philosophy and, as perennial, it calls out for a philosophical pluralism that can mediate between those philosophies generated out of the existential postures taken by philosophers. Above I indicated that what in our free agency we do, we also make in cooperation with God. What is made by our action, including the fully human worlds of cultural meaning and value, cannot therefore be bracketed out of our philosophical and theological inquiries. Chapters 9 and 10, then, will indicate how the medieval account of human and divine cooperation might itself cooperate with modern concerns about the constitutive function of cultures to suggest a modern problem of the supernatural. Chapter 11, then, will work to sketch a heuristic for an adequately modern approach to theologies of the supernatural.

PART III

AMBIGUITIES

CHAPTER 6

MEDIEVAL AMBIGUITIES, MODERN MENTALITY

My path through Lonergan's mid-twentieth-century Thomism had an ulterior motive. Thomas's solution to the medieval problem of the supernatural ultimately leads to a pair of ambiguous philosophical conclusions. The first is a general ambiguity that regards the intelligibility of the universe. This is the titular ambiguity of this work: the ambiguity of being. The second is a specific ambiguity that regards the meaningfulness of human agency and action. I might call this "the ambiguity of being (free)." For the purposes of keeping their nested correlation in view, however, here I will call the former the "general medieval ambiguity" and the latter the "specific medieval ambiguity." Now, these ambiguities are not medieval in the sense that they appear on the scene during the middle ages as a historical epoch. I call these ambiguities "medieval" first of all in the loose sense that they pertain to a medieval mentality and specifically to the results of a medieval ideal of science. But I call these ambiguities medieval in a more precise sense, one internal to the argument and technical apparatus of this book. My contention is that these ambiguities are rendered thinkable by the medieval solution to the medieval problem of the supernatural, and so are in this logical respect subsequent to it. In another respect, however, these ambiguities also lurk beneath and behind both the general medieval problem and its solution, undermining the notion that the medieval solution consists entirely in an apodictically demonstrated formal ontology. To appreciate the philosophical force of these ambiguities, it was necessary to know both the synthetic philosophical and theological positions that suggest them. It was necessary as well to know something of the cooperation between ancient and medieval philosophy and theology that produced them in the mind of Thomas Aquinas.

That it became *possible* to take stock of these ontological ambiguities in light of Thomas's synthesis did not mean that, in the near term, anyone actually did. In order that the illumination of the medieval ambiguities becomes not just possible, but *probable*, another factor is required: a modern philosophical mentality. This mentality eventually forced the medieval ambiguities down stage in the performance of ontology. Although I have called these ambiguities "medieval" according to the era of speculative development that made them possible, putting them in the spotlight is a distinctly modern achievement. This chapter, then, is our pivot from the medieval ambiguities to the distinctly modern form of the problem of the supernatural. But first, I will turn to the ambiguities directly.

The Generic Medieval Ambiguity

Lonergan praised the theorem of the supernatural for the release it effected in the thirteenth-century theology of grace, enriching the sense in which grace is at once gratuitous and necessary. It also cracked open the difficult question of God's creative and providential agency. To say that every created cause cooperates with God's action to bring about the universe that God intends can, for those prone to praying with their metaphysics, have profound spiritual significance. But this same theological insistence on universal instrumentality, resting on the theorem of the supernatural, also produces a certain deflationary effect on the role that common sense might attribute to God's agency in the world. To borrow the words of Matthew Lamb, the truth of the statement, "from 'all eternity' … God understood and knew and loved such and such to happen," only requires *that it happen*.[1] God's agency causes *every* cause, without exception or restriction. But then the question arises: if God causes every cause, what difference does God's agency make in the world? This question is at the heart of the first, general medieval ambiguity.

At one level, this question is easy to answer. God's agency makes the biggest, most important, and most fundamental difference there can be: God's agency causes the universe, everything in it, and its order of causal unfolding to be at all. If this difference is not made, between existing and not existing, no other differences matter. But is this fundamental, binary

---

1 Rev. Matthew L. Lamb, "Fr. Bernard J. F. Lonergan, S.J.: The Gregorian Years," in *Lonergan's Anthropology Revisited: The Next Fifty Years of Vatican II*, ed. Gerald Whelan (Rome: G & B Press, 2015), 57–80.

difference between what is and what is not all there is to it? Now, if one affirms universal instrumentality and causal cooperation with God within a speculative theological context controlled by a doctrine of creation, then one has reason to believe that God's agency, even though it is unrestricted in scope, is still determinate. God understands and knows and loves this possible world to be actualized in the temporal unfolding of the universe. God intended to cause *this* world and its various beings, causes, and events.

But if one withdraws from a theological context and enters into a strictly philosophical method that explicitly prescinds from religious doctrine, the answer to this question becomes ambiguous. It becomes ambiguous, in particular, whether God's agency is determinate or not. From the vantage of the creature's experience of creaturely being, untutored by religious doctrine, the data of experience do not so clearly suggest a determinate relationship to the transcendent. After all, if God's causal agency acts in every created cause without limit or exception, what contrast or definition can one trace in the available evidence that would suggest whether or not God causes the universe to be and to be thus ordered with any kind of determining or determinate intentionality? Robert Cummings Neville, for example, comes to the conclusion in *God the Creator* that God is the purely indeterminate act of creation, the *ur* indeterminacy against which every other thing has determination, and so being.[2]

Certainly, one can extrapolate from human conceptions of alternative possible cosmic orders to divine knowledge thereof, but this approach is vulnerable to suspicions of projection: why does the presence of alternate possible (where possible simply means "intelligible") cosmic orders in *our* minds necessitate an intentional mind in God whereby God would know those possible worlds by knowing our conception of them? And why does it necessitate a decision for this determinate order in God? After all, the whole account of free agency provided above rests on the essential affirmation that apprehended goods (like possible world orders) are not enough to necessarily move a free will to act. In the case of God, this point is amplified: for how could a finite good (even if it is the good of the entire universe of created being) compel the infinite and eternal divine will to action? Moreover, only secondarily did the account of liberty above involve the determination of some means—in this case, the whole unfolding of cosmic process—and

---

2 Robert C. Neville, *God the Creator: On the Transcendence and Presence of God* (Albany: SUNY Press, 1992).

perhaps this is only a condition of temporal freedom. In other words, perhaps God causes what is, but trivially and not at all lovingly.

One can bring this ambiguity into higher contrast by applying this Thomistic theory of divine agency to the modern natural scientific method. One discovers more-or-less immediately that God's agency applies to every side of every explanatory functional equation. Every term in every scientific theory, insofar as it is intelligible, and moreover every concrete correlate of such terms and theories, insofar as they exist, depend on God for reality. God's agency can, therefore, be cancelled off every side of every equation without remainder and without making any difference for the correlations, laws, frequencies, and so forth, with which the natural sciences are concerned. Appeal to God's agency answers two questions that, while relevant to the prosecution of the scientific method, are not strictly speaking scientific questions. God's agency answers whether anything exists at all and whether the universe is fundamentally intelligible—that is, whether it has a sufficient reason for existing. However, the procedures of natural scientific inquiry operate quite happily when these two elements are merely assumed rather than demonstrated.

Let us suppose (as there is ample evidence to do) that the natural sciences emerged from a Christian horizon of speculative theology, passed through a broadly Christian period of natural philosophy, only to now emerge in the modern era as a separated, secularized project.[3] The efficacy of their methods has been well proven, both in the annals of natural knowledge and in the arena of applied engineering and technological advance. It has carried through all of this a grounding insight into a distinct line of reference called "nature," and a fundamental assumption that skeptical suspicions about the existence of the universe or its basic intelligibility get one exactly nowhere. It has, however, quite practically excised the remote principle of these grounding assumptions: an account of the transcendent creating God. After all, in this limited respect, Laplace was right: the scientist really does have no need of that hypothesis to explain the relations among intra-mundane realities (even if he was wrong about their mechanically determinist character).[4]

---

3 For a fascinating and detailed (if now a little out of date) look at one much discussed, but commonly misunderstood, transition point in the development of the modern natural sciences, see Willam A. Wallace, *Galileo and His Sources: Heritage of the Collegio Romano in Galileo's Science* (Princeton, NJ: Princeton University Press, 1984).

4 On Laplace's mistake, see Patrick H. Byrne, "God and the Statistical Universe," *Zygon: Journal of Religion & Science* 16, no. 4 (1981): 345–63.

The modern natural scientific method, because it assumes the fundamental intelligibility of the universe, may come around to ask after its own fundamental assumption. But the intended term of this question—the reason there is anything at all and that all of it is the way it is—would have to be transcendent at the very least with regard to time and space. Consequently, there will be, by definition, no direct sensory data on the term intended by this question. There remains what Lonergan calls the data of consciousness on the intention of complete intelligibility itself and this could be taken as data on the term of this fundamental question. One can, it is true, trust the intellectual thrust of this intention of complete intelligibility and so extrapolate from it a heuristic for the transcendent term that explains the existence of the universe and its order. This is what Lonergan himself does in chapter 19 of *Insight*.[5]

One can also suspect that to take this questioning intention of being's complete intelligibility as evidence that there is in fact an answer to one's fundamental question is an act of androcentric projection. One can affirm the intention itself (after all, there are data on it among the data of consciousness) and still demand further evidence on its term. But such data, in principle, cannot be forthcoming. Thus, one might come to the inverse insight that the universe is only intelligible proximate to our evolved intellectual powers. When it comes to the fundamental question regarding the explanation of existence and the existing cosmic order, there is no intelligibility where one expects it to be. At bottom, the existence of the universe is a bare matter of fact and so an absurdity. And while this would be radically unreasonable to the horizon of one who practices trust in the thrust of intellectually intentional consciousness, the decision to practice trust or suspicion with regard to this thrust is, as I will discuss at some length in the next chapter, constitutive of what counts as "reasonable" in the first place. The possibility of this radical intellectual suspicion reveals that there is a generic medieval ambiguity and that this is its negative pole. Moreover, it shows how one begs the question if one applies the standard of one fundamental horizon of reasonableness to the other.

With regard to the generic medieval ambiguity, the answer at which one arrives depends upon the basic existential comportment one has

5 Bernard Lonergan, *Insight: A Study of Human Understanding*, 5th ed., ed. Frederick E. Crowe and Robert M. Doran, CWL 3 (Toronto: University of Toronto Press, 2000), 657–708.

toward the question that reveals it. If one chooses to trust the thrust of the questioning intention of complete intelligibility, one can come to an ontologically affirmative, if formally heuristic answer with regard to God and the explicability of the universe. If, however, one chooses to be suspicious and distrusting of this same thrust, one enacts warrant for coming to the opposite conclusion. In either case, there are no sensory data on the term of inquiry to adjudicate between these fundamental options and the data of consciousness regard its intention, not its fulfillment. Moreover, in each case, one can look back at the courses of inquiry by which one was led to either basic posture, whether trusting or suspicious, and reinterpret what one knows of the universe accordingly. For the first course, one finds a world known, chosen, loved by a God transcendently operating in every effective mundane operation. From the second existential posture, one can read the universe as a determinate, but accidental, being that seems to permit us to understand it up to a certain point (where understanding mostly means pragmatic success), but if the demands of understanding are pushed too far, it rebuffs our human-sized minds and turns a cold shoulder to any naïve, anthropomorphic projections of intelligence or intention. The ambiguity resides in the givenness of finite, contingent existence as apprehended from the abstractive viewpoint of what below I will call a "separated philosophy." Which basic posture one comes to follows from a pre-philosophical and philosophically undecidable decision because it is a decision about how much and how far to trust the very wonder-expressing questions in which philosophy begins enacted immediately in the very performance of philosophy per se.

More importantly, one can look back from the conclusion of one line of inquiry initiated by such a basic posture and see the possibility of the other. This, after all, is what I have just done. Following Lonergan, with the aid of the Christian dogmatic context and Thomas's speculative innovations and syntheses, the above spelled out a philosophy that takes the complete intelligibility of the universe as its proper heuristic expectation and so baptizes the thrust of the human mind toward total explanation. Consequently, a theory of transcendent divine agency can emerge to fill in precisely how the existence and intelligibility of the universe is grounded. Nonetheless, the very same theory can reveal, as it has above, the possibility of an alternative interpretation from within the abstractive viewpoint of a separated philosophy. Conversely, because the suspicious cosmological nihilist cannot find data to confirm his or her inverse insight into the explicability of the universe within the universe itself, he or she is also invited to construct an alternative interpretation that cannot be conclusively ruled out. Even pain of performative inconsistency cannot derail them, for it is the meaning of cognitional performance itself that they suspect. A theory of universal divine *concursus,* grounded in the theorem of the supernatural, invites philosophy to discover that what conclusions it can generate on its own about the fundamental explicability of being are unavoidably ambiguous.

The Specific Medieval Ambiguity

Human action, *qua* cause, has cooperation with God in common with all created causes. In this way, human action participates in the general medieval ambiguity. This was already implied above, insofar as the basic posture and interpretation an inquirer chooses with regard to the fundamental explicability of the universe has implications for his or her read of what is already known, but also for how he or she will conduct him or herself as an inquirer (and person) in the future. But this only hints at the further, specific medieval ambiguity to which the above theory of divine agency leads us. Human action cooperates with God *freely,* and so as the underlying question of the general medieval ambiguity was, "What difference does God's action make for created causes?" the underlying question of the specific medieval ambiguity is, "What difference does God's action make for free human agency?"

As before, the question is easy to answer at first. God acts in every free human action. God's action first of all causes free human agents to exist and by the providential ordering of the cosmos applies us to our effects. But this is not all. Lonergan summarizes the volitional specifications of this general cooperation as follows:

> In the exercise of a formally free act, a person is the cause per se, inasmuch as having willed the end and deliberated on the basis of this willing of the end, one now moves oneself to willing the means to the end. Yet God too is a cause per se of this same exercise of the will. For a cause of a cause is a cause of the effect; and God causes the act of willing the end, causes the intellectual light by which one reflects and deliberates, and causes all the external circumstances as well as one's interior habits and dispositions. In the specification of this same formally free act, a person is the cause per se inasmuch as by willing the end one wills this particular practical judgment to

be the final one in accordance with which one moves to will the good presented by that judgment. Yet God too is a cause per se of this same specification of the will, since the specification is itself intelligibly contained in the antecedents of that free act. But there is a triple intelligible nexus between this free act and its antecedents; therefore, since God causes the antecedents, he also causes the specification of the free act.[6]

God therefore also causes the act of the will by which human actions are essentially free in several ways: first, by kindling in the will desire for some *bonum apprehensum*; second, by making the means to this end spatiotemporally available to us; third, by illuminating intellectually the process of deliberation by which means are selected; fourth, by having this same causal efficacy upon all our previous actions such that we have the dispositions and habits by which we are not just exteriorly related properly to our chosen end and means, but also interiorly.

These specifications are important for properly understanding how the general account of cooperation between divine and created causality works in the case of free human agency, but they do not eliminate the above, general ambiguity. God causes the will and the mind to be according to their dynamic nature and causes the order of the cosmos by which both external and internal premotions apply possible free human agents to their effects. This causality is as universal in rational, free agents as it is in mindless, physical causes. The same fundamental ambiguity applies, therefore. Is human action fundamentally intelligible as a part of the universe or is it only accidentally susceptible to the manipulations of our evolved conscious powers to navigate and manipulate our habitats and so only proximately and pragmatically intelligible in the final analysis? From a strictly philosophical vantage, the same pre-philosophical decision and attitude haunts the interpretation of the specific case of free human agency as it did the case of created causality in general.

There is a further issue in the case of free human causality. In addition to the radical answer that is God's irresistible creative action, there is also a proximate answer to the question, "Why does this action exist?" This action,

---

6 Bernard Lonergan, "God's Knowledge and Will," in *Early Latin Theology*, ed. Robert M. Doran and H. Daniel Monsour, trans. Michael G. Shields, CWL 19 (Toronto: University of Toronto Press, 2011), 329–30.

as mine and free, exists or not because of my choice to effect it or not. This is not to deny that only God is proportionate to causing existence as an effect but rather to acknowledge that free human agents have a special kind of cooperation with God. Causes that lack freedom, if they are proportionate to an effect and they are brought into the proper relation or disposition to the proper material conditions or circumstances, act of necessity. But God may kindle the desire for an end in our will, may illuminate our deliberations about some means, may put us in both the proper external and internal disposition to some action, and yet we may decide otherwise. These fundamental aspects of our liberty mean that, whatever the antecedents, free human actions have as their proximate explanation the choices of free human persons. Liberty with regard to our actions is not something in excess of God's action in our action. It is precisely that which God effects in irresistibly acting to cause the reality of our freedom, both in its essential generality and its effective concreteness. Your freedom and mine—*as free*—is God's instrument in the universe.

What in a speculative theological horizon is perhaps unproblematic, when tackled from within the horizon of a separated philosophy becomes an inescapable ambiguity. If one's inquiry is controlled (as a speculative theology must be) by doctrines of creation, of divine justice, and of redemption, then this freedom must be considered correlative to the already-affirmed teleology of the moral grain of the universe and the eschatology of humanity's (and all of creation's) ultimate union with God. However, if one withdraws these doctrinal correlates from the inquiry and instead takes a separated philosophical approach, one is again faced with a prephilosophical choice that makes all the difference for how one interprets the data of free human action. As in the general ambiguity, which interpretation one takes follows from a prephilosophical choice. This prephilosophical act of freedom is part of what shapes the ambiguity itself. One might be led by the general ambiguity to suppose that, parallel with its option to affirm or deny the fundamental intelligibility of the universe, the specific ambiguity presents the option to affirm or deny freedom in one's own being. Although such a choice would be likewise *pre*philosophical, and thus not necessarily ruled out concretely on account of performative contradiction, it is at the same time pre*philosophical*, and so would be recognized as a "false start" to any genuinely philosophical account of human being and freedom. If one's philosophical inquiry into the intelligibility of the universe of being leads one to the inverse insight that there is no basic explanation for existence, one might be troubled by the circularity in suspecting the intelligence that anticipated there should be, but there is no contradiction. However, if one comes to the philosophical conclusion that human freedom is not a reality, but then one retrospectively acknowledges that this process began in a choice to be suspicious about the being of freedom, the circularity is overshadowed by the obvious and, more importantly, self-defeating contradiction. Where above suspicions of the cognitive character of cognitive performance were not ultimately an obstacle to skepticism and/or nihilism, here the attempt to perform a denial and negation of performance cannot proceed.

The specific ambiguity, however, is not about whether or not there is any freedom at all, but the significance of the freedom that is. The parallel with the general ambiguity regards the question of ground. In the general ambiguity, one chooses how to primordially relate to the intelligible ground of the universe of causes (if any). In the specific ambiguity one chooses how to primordially relate to the intelligible ground of freedom (if any). If I take the prephilosophical posture toward my freedom that I have it for some reason, even if that reason is unknown, I can appropriate that agency with an aim to discern what that reason is and to exercise my freedom with devotion to its purpose, even if that purpose is unseen. On the other hand, I can take a posture of suspicion toward my freedom, deciding that in the absence of evidence of some ground, I am not justified to suppose it has any ground at all. This suspicion will undoubtedly be confirmed in the long run, since there can be no direct data on a transcendent ground. From the vantage of this posture, my freedom cannot but be exercised arbitrarily, because it exists arbitrarily. My only recourse against the imposition of freedom, then, is to appropriate my freedom for what Camus called "rebellion." Note that, in either interpretation, there is no falling for the myth that my freedom is self-grounding, nor any dodging the fact that, because I am the cause of my acting or not acting, my actions are my responsibility. Either way, I am free and I must freely choose how to comport myself to that fact.

Realizing the Medieval Ambiguities

To review then, the generic medieval ambiguity concerned the possibility of comporting one's self to the question of a transcendent cause of the universe in one of two basic ways: either as a matter of indifference or of fundamental importance on account, in either case, of the very universality of its efficacy.

The generic medieval ambiguity takes an epistemic form insofar as it marks our knowledge of the world of causes. It takes an existential form insofar as it marks our inquiry into the same in order to attain that knowledge. The specific medieval ambiguity of being concerned free human agency among the universe of causes and in relation to a transcendent cause. The specific medieval ambiguity takes an epistemic form insofar as it marks our understanding of free human actions. It takes an existential form insofar as it marks the discernment of our own free human actions. Thus, the specific medieval ambiguity poses an alternative to the free agent, to comport him or herself to the meaningfulness and purposiveness of his or her agency in one of two ways: to suppose it has some meaning and purpose (though transcendent, and so unknown) or as an unavoidable, but nonetheless absurd project.

The Medieval Ambiguities of Being

1) Generic Medieval Ambiguity: "Does the transcendent cause ... *the universe of causes?*"
   a. Epistemic Form: "... make no difference or a fundamental difference in my *knowledge of* ..."
   b. Existential Form: "... make no difference or a fundamental difference in my *inquiring into* ..."
2) Specific Medieval Ambiguity: "Does the transcendent cause ... *free human actions?*"
   a. Epistemic Form: "... make no difference or a fundamental difference in my *understanding of* ..."
   b. Existential Form: "... make no difference or a fundamental difference in the *discernment of my own* ..."

We have also seen how Thomas Aquinas's solution to the medieval problems of the supernatural made cognizance of these medieval ambiguities possible. The transcendence of God's *ad extra* action leaves any account of its immanent effects—which is to say, any ontology—open to one of these two basic, pre-philosophical postures: on the one hand, faith in the basic explicability of the universe and of human action within it; on the other, suspicion that the universe and so human action within it are both mere matters of fact that admit of no fundamental explanation.

Again, that it became possible to take stock of these ambiguities in light of Thomas's synthesis did not mean that anyone actually did. In order that the illumination of the medieval ambiguities becomes not just possible, but *probable*, another factor is required: a modern philosophical mentality. Putting these ambiguities in the philosophical spotlight is a distinctly modern achievement. In what follows, I describe relevant aspects of the modern philosophical mentality and how, at the turn of the twentieth century, Maurice Blondel approached the medieval problem of the supernatural in an explicitly modern fashion. Blondel's treatment of the problem shows how a modern mentality led him to the medieval ambiguities. I will also briefly consider Jean Paul Sartre's *Being and Nothingness* as an example of an alternative ontology made possible by the medieval ambiguities considered from within the modern philosophical mentality. Where Blondel can find no immanent explanation for human action but takes this as evidence that there must be a transcendent and supernatural explanation, Sartre reads the absence of immanent explanation for being as an inexplicability proper to being in-itself. From the abstractive viewpoint of theology and what below I will call a "subordinated" (as opposed to a "separated") philosophy, both interpretations are supported by the evidence on the universe of human action precisely because God's *ad extra* agency is universally effective.

The Modern Philosophical Mentality

What is the "modern philosophical mentality?" What about it makes cognizance of the medieval ambiguities probable? This modern philosophical mentality has, in my view, two salient features. First, it is a "separated" philosophy. Its inquiry does not begin from, nor is it ordered toward illuminating any revealed doctrine. Second, it elevates the *via inventionis*—the path of discovery—to a criterion for the validity of knowledge, where the quality of one's investigation serves as the measure of the investigation's results. Perhaps some will feel I have selected idiosyncratic markers of "the modern" in philosophy, but these seem to function behind and beneath a number of more "traditionally" identified features of modern philosophy. A modern aversion to authority or tradition may be read as a byproduct of a more fundamental transformation in philosophy's understanding of its own project. In the modern frame, theology's handmaid is now self-employed. The privileging of the *via inventionis* can be correlated with the turn to the subject for which modernity is so well known, but that phrase ("turn to the subject") carries with it a host of problematically dualistic assumptions about consciousness and knowledge that tend to muddy the waters. I will briefly address some of those assumptions below, but for now suffice it to say that characterizing this focus on the operation of the investigator does not have to be a move "inside" our heads, nor a move "away" from *das Ding an sich*. Rather, it amounts foremost to a demotion of the logical criterion for validating knowledge that drove the construction of late-scholastic treatises and early-modern rationalist philosophical systems.

Subordinated Philosophy

In the medieval situation, Thomas Aquinas identified two kinds of argument in theology. He writes,

> One kind of argument is directed to removing doubts as to whether something is so. In such arguments in theology, one relies especially on the authorities that are recognized by the persons with whom one is disputing. . . .
>
> But another kind of argument is that of the teacher in the schools. It seeks not to remove error but to instruct the students so that they understand the truth that the teacher hopes to convey. In such cases it is important to base one's argument on reasons that go to the root of the truth in question, that make hearers understand how what is said is true. Otherwise, if the teacher settles a question simply by an appeal to authorities, the students will have their certitude that the facts are indeed as stated; but they will acquire no knowledge or understanding, and they will go away empty.[7]

Speculative theology begins from difficulties understanding the coherence of doctrines that are already affirmed, individually and in aggregate, as true by faith and on the authority of the Church. "A person who is seeking an understanding of the mysteries is not asking," Lonergan writes in *The Triune God: Systematics*, "whether there are mysteries or whether they are true."[8] Instead, speculative theology deploys a subordinated philosophy to better understand how these already-affirmed doctrinal elements cohere.

---

7 Thomas Aquinas, *Quaestiones quodlibetales*, 4, q. 9, a. 3.

8 Bernard Lonergan, *The Triune God: Systematics*, ed. Robert M. Doran and H. Daniel Monsour, trans. Michael G. Shields, CWL 12 (Toronto: University of Toronto Press, 2007), 15.

Subordinated philosophy, therefore, has its program set for it by the speculative theological endeavor. This does not mean that subordinated philosophy simply provides logical forms for hashing through the propositional content of the dogmas. Rather, subordinated philosophy operates with a relative autonomy to clarify everything in a theological problem that is not itself the mystery believed by faith. When the work of subordinated philosophy is done, "It leaves to faith not human problems, nor the human element in religious problems, but the pure formulation of the point that cannot be encompassed by the human understanding."[9] It leaves, in other words, that element in the problem that is properly hidden in the mystery of God. As I showed in the previous chapter, philosophy was not necessarily hampered by this arrangement. No small philosophical advances were made from within its unfolding. Beyond this direct treatment of the creaturely element in speculative problems, theology "also finds in the natural order, as philosophically analyzed, the analogies necessary for the scientific conception of purely theological data."[10] In the case of the Trinitarian dogma this is especially important, for there is, strictly speaking, no intrinsic human element in need of clarification.

Speculative theology becomes a *systematic* theology when the questions and answers pursued in cooperation with a subordinated philosophy are sapientially ordered according to their relative priority. This order of priority can take different forms, but its underlying purpose is to provide understanding not of this or that element in a theological problem but of the whole. Lonergan identifies two basic forms of this ordering: the *"via inventionis"* and the *"via doctrinae."* Following the *via inventionis* (as I did in the first part of the chapter detailing the development of St. Thomas's philosophy of agency), the material is organized by the process of inquiry and insight to show how the required speculative elements came to view such that the final position is now possible. Following the *via doctrinae* (as I did when stating Thomas's synthetic position on *ad extra* divine agency), one can arrange these elements for the purpose of communicating directly the whole position, so that the answer to any particular question does not presuppose some answer not already provided. For Lonergan, the *via doctrinae* "begins with concepts

---

9 Bernard Lonergan, *Grace and Freedom: Operative Grace in the Thought of St. Thomas Aquinas*, ed. Frederick E. Crowe and Robert M. Doran, CWL 1 (Toronto: University of Toronto Press, 2000), 171.

10 Lonergan, 175.

that are fundamental and especially simple, so that by adding a step at a time it may proceed in an orderly way to the understanding of an entire science."[11] For speculative theology the *via doctrinae* is given pride of place, because its doctrinal elements are affirmed with certainty on the authority of the Church and the aim is to understand their coherence to the extent our finite minds are able. The *via doctrinae* is the properly systematic presentation of a systematic theology, communicating an imperfect, analogical, persistently obscure but nonetheless fruitful understanding in its present state of always-ongoing development.[12]

Separated Philosophy

A separated philosophy, by contrast, does not receive its marching orders from a theology. It is perhaps obvious that the dogmatic context is that from which a separated philosophy is separated. Too often, though, this is taken in the flatfooted sense that a separated philosophy is liberated from the obligation to come to points of doctrine as the ready-made conclusion to its arguments.[13] But for speculative theology on Lonergan's model, philosophy is never working directly toward the doctrines themselves as conclusions. Rather, separated philosophy is separated from its obligations to answer first those questions that concern the created element in a theology's problem(s) of dogmatic understanding. Separation from a dogmatic context, moreover, does not mean that a philosophy has no doctrines whatsoever but rather that its doctrines are not accepted on the authority of the Church, of scripture, and so forth. A separated philosophy's doctrines are accepted in the provisional fashion of the dialectician, which is to say they are accepted until they can be established on independent grounds or overturned. In this way, for a separated philosophy, credulity and suspicion are placed on equal footing (and so one may notice already the correlation between a separated philosophy and the basic alternatives posed by the medieval ambiguities).

11 Lonergan, *The Triune God: Systematics*, 61.

12 Lonergan, 15–19.

13 This seems to explain the short shrift given Thomas Aquinas by Bertrand Russell in his *History of Western Philosophy*. For Russell, Thomas's subordination of philosophy to a theological program, insofar as it seems to reason to predetermined doctrinal conclusions, cannot be considered philosophical at all. See Bertrand Russell, *A History of Western Philosophy* (New York: Simon and Schuster, 1945), 452–62.

How, then, are the doctrines of a separated philosophy established or overturned? As I suggested above, the modern philosophical mentality makes of the philosophical *via inventionis* both a measure for and a form of argumentation about philosophical doctrines, considered individually or as a unified system. The ideal of coherence proper to the theological *via doctrinae* is no longer an appropriate measure of a separated philosophy's provisionally accepted doctrines. Separated philosophy installs in its place the relative rigor and authenticity of the intellectual labors by which various philosophical doctrines have been derived. How one came to this or that bit of philosophical insight, for the modern philosophical mentality, becomes a way of adjudicating the reliability and validity of the insight itself. Moreover, arguing in support of one's philosophical doctrine becomes, in no small part, a matter of rehearsing the path travelled to it. Let us consider below an example of these two elements at work in a pivotal work of modern thought.

Descartes's *The Discourse on the Method*

René Descartes, in *The Discourse on the Method*, provides a famous early example of the modern philosophical mentality for which I have been setting the scene. Close reading reveals that ontology remains a core, even central, concern for Descartes, even though ontology *as a method* has been deprioritized in favor of epistemology. Still, as I suggested above, this "turn to the subject" is a secondary effect of this more basic transition that Descartes will help us illustrate below. In the *Discourse*, Descartes expresses his dissatisfaction that, though "it had been cultivated by the best minds for many centuries," philosophical doctrines were widely disputed, with many learned figures defending "different opinions on the same subject."[14] More than this, he expresses his further dissatisfaction that the fashion in which these various doctrines were defended amounted to no more than a defense of their "plausibility." Their coherence was asserted by something like what above I called a *via doctrinae*. This coherence only served to show that these positions *could* be true, not that they in fact were. Indeed, this seems to him the chief "virtue" (read: vice) of the philosophy of his contemporaries: it "provides

---

14 René Descartes, *A Discourse on the Method of Correctly Conducting One's Reason and Seeking Truth in the Sciences*, trans. Ian Maclean (Oxford: Oxford University Press, 2006), 10.

us with the means of speaking *plausibly* about anything."[15] Even logic seems to him a device for rigorously and carefully communicating to others what one thinks one already knows, or (worse) speaking rigorously and carefully to others about that of which one is ignorant.[16] It does not, in any case, seem to hold much value for Descartes in generating knowledge *de novo*. While he in many places affirms his devotion to the teachings and authority of the Church, he assiduously denies that he has possession of the elevations of grace necessary for direct insight into matters theological.[17] Because he feels inadequate to evaluate those doctrines independently, those teachings cannot themselves serve as the kind of philosophical ground for the philosophical doctrines of which Descartes found himself bereft. Consequently, Descartes's philosophy is going to be a *separated philosophy*.

As famous as Descartes has become for his methodical doubt, he begins the *Discourse* with an affirmation of reason that one might easily overlook. "Good sense is the most evenly distributed thing in the world." Moreover, "the power of judging correctly and of distinguishing the true from the false ... is naturally equal in all men." Facility in applying reason well, however, is distributed unevenly.[18] In other words, reason as a native power in human beings is unproblematic; the problem comes when reason has to be concretized by application to reality. Consequently, Descartes's procedure of persuasion consists in sharing with his reader the path he takes on the ways to his philosophical doctrines, thereby detailing the application of his powers of reasoning to the problem of knowledge. He even gives a kind of short intellectual biography to frame his investigation.[19] The method by which he derived and (in his own estimation) grounded his doctrines features centrally in this rehearsal. Surveying the path to his philosophical doctrine and its attendant method will, Descartes tells us, provide what is required that "everyone may come to a judgment about it."[20] Notice what Descartes has done: he has proposed from the beginning that his *via inventionis*—his path of discovery—should serve as the criterion by which his philosophical doctrines should be measured and evaluated. Moreover, he has explicitly appealed to

---

15 Descartes, 8.
16 Descartes, 16.
17 Descartes, 8, 21, 50.
18 Descartes, 5.
19 Descartes, 7–17, 25–27.
20 Descartes, 6; for Descartes's summary of his method, see 17–20.

the transcendence and so cognitional disproportion of revealed doctrines to human minds to justify pursuing a separated, rather than subordinated philosophical project. Descartes, then, embodies an instance of the modern philosophical mentality where its two salient features serve an integral function.

Descartes's philosophical method comes with a host of problematic assumptions. He assumes that philosophical principles must function like geometric axioms. He assumes that this geometric approximation means a philosophical method can be followed automatically insofar as one knows the rules of operation.[21] He assumes that there is a hard binary in knowledge between what is certain and what is dubitable and that it justifies universal methodical doubt.[22] Indeed, he assumes that universal methodical doubt is possible at all. He assumes that individual control of thought is obviously to be preferred to the communal aggregation of understanding.[23] Several of these assumptions—about methodical doubt and about the individual control of thought especially—lend credence to the impression that the modern philosophical mentality is foremost a skeptical turn inward to the subject and away from the world of really real things. But Descartes does not come to a philosophical viewpoint "trapped" inside the mind of the subject. His basic position is not merely epistemological, but also explicitly metaphysical. *Cogito ergo sum* implies that thinking is indubitable to itself, but also, do not forget, explicitly asserts that thinking *is*. Thought turned to itself is at once a fact, an activity, and an apprehension of being. Thinking recognizes itself in act, and this act exists. It exists in that which I cannot but call "I," and so exists substantially. But substantially existing things have essences, and so Descartes determines that the thing that I call "I" is a "thinking thing."[24]

It is important, therefore, not to be led too swiftly down a "subjectivist" or "immanentist" road by what Descartes is arguing because he is discussing thought. Having just established that thinking can know itself *as being*, he wonders whether those thoughts a thinking thing thinks, because they are about entities other than its own thinking, have an extra-mental reality— whether they have what he will later call *res extensa,* distinct from *res cogitans.*

---

21 Descartes, 31.

22 Descartes, 17, 25–28.

23 "Things made up of different elements and produced by the hands of several master craftsmen are often less perfect than those on which only one person has worked" (Descartes, 12).

24 Descartes, 28–29.

That Descartes imports a dualistic, "in-here" and "out-there" distinction conflicts with his own insistence that what keeps people from apprehending the force of his arguments is a failure to "rise above" the sensible in their thinking, so that "everything which seems unimaginable seems to them unintelligible."[25] Descartes's dualism evinces his own failure to follow all the way through on his methodical doubt of the sensible. Although he insists himself that it is the insensible intellect that knows being, and not the senses, he makes of the extended and sensible a distinct "nature."[26] Nonetheless, though one might wish Descartes had taken up a more intellectualist realism in general, the above muddle turns out to be beside my main point. Descartes's foundational position only serves his philosophical aims if it is a *metaphysical position*. To defend his metaphysical doctrine, Descartes appeals to his process of inquiry as the criterion for the validity of his knowledge. He explicitly deploys his *via inventionis* as the argument for the verity of his position. In this way, Descartes's project is modern because it operates in separation from the dictates of a dogmatic theological project and it gives intellectual operation pride of place as its internal criterion of validity.

Conclusion

This chapter has effected a perhaps disorienting transition, from the tight logical controls of medieval ontology to the habits and objects of thought commonly termed "existentialist" and back to an account of the modern philosophical mentality. It is important, however, not to lose sight of the medieval solution to the medieval problem of the supernatural that anchored this dual transition. For it was the affirmation of a transcendent cause's universal efficacy, grounded in the theorem of the supernatural, that set the stage for both. If what God causes to be God causes to be *ex nihilo*, then the effects of God's creative action are different from nothing. It becomes both possible and reasonable to ask whether this affirmation makes any difference at all. While there seem to be two basic answers (answers that constitute the above ambiguities), there are neither data on God, nor on the nothing from which God creates that might provide warrant for one answer or the other. This ambiguity opens up the practical possibility of bracketing the question of ultimate explicability, of assuming without saying so that the universe is

25 Descartes, 32.
26 Descartes, 31.

completely intelligible, and *successfully* exploring the universe of being on its own terms without reference to God. In this way there emerges a separated philosophy, but also the modern natural sciences of the Enlightenment and, eventually, the modern human sciences of the Second Enlightenment. Afterall, if one brackets the causal efficacy of the transcendent, certainly one also brackets any self-revelation of the same. And finally, in this newly opened field of separated inquiry, the veracity of doctrines can no longer rely in the first instance on the authority with which they are taught. And so, into the consequent crisis of authority that has marked so much of these early stages of modernity, there has appeared the modern tendency to treat an inquiry's *via inventionis* as its criterion of validity. This tendency, keep in mind through subsequent chapters, spontaneously gives autonomy (intellectual and otherwise) an exalted place in the modern mentality. It remains to be seen whether this exaltation is justified or not.

CHAPTER 7

BLONDEL OR SARTRE?

et us turn now from the brief illustration of the modern philosophical mentality in chapter 6 to its substantive influence on the problem of the supernatural and the medieval ambiguities of being. If the medieval solution to the problem of the supernatural made cognizance of the medieval ambiguities possible and the modern philosophical mentality made it probable, Maurice Blondel's philosophy of action made it *actual*. On the eve of the twentieth century, Blondel made bold to raise the problem of the supernatural in a thoroughly modern way for a modern audience.[1] By articulating the medieval solution to the medieval problem of the supernatural in a thoroughly modern fashion, Blondel can make the attendant medieval ambiguities apparent to the modern mind, preparing the ground for the genuinely modern form of the problem of the supernatural to arise. The following, then, will ask and answer a series of questions about Blondel's philosophy of action and the supernatural. How is Blondel's approach modern? How does it raise the medieval problem of the supernatural in this modern fashion? How does it answer that problem in a modern way? How does it articulate the medieval ambiguities in light of this answer? Finally, in what ways does Blondel's modern philosophical approach to the problem of the supernatural fail to be yet-fully-modern?

In an effort to highlight the respect in which these ambiguities are genuinely and thoroughly *ambiguous*, I will consider a contrasting exploration of the same questions in the work of Jean-Paul Sartre. A generation after Blondel, Sartre became an international celebrity arguing for a thoroughly atheistic account of

---

1 I should note from the outset, however, that Blondel's philosophy, although its procedure is modern in the ways described, still does not yet set out to face a modern form of the problem of the supernatural, nor, therefore, does he alight upon a corresponding modern solution.

human freedom and, in turn, of being itself. Indeed, part of what is remarkable about Sartre's philosophy of being and of human freedom is how clearly it faces up to the ontological problems occasioned by thorough-going atheism. Although Blondel makes note of the general and specific ambiguities of being, he does so from one pole of the ambiguity itself. Sartre, for his part, tackles the question of human action and of being from the opposed pole. It was unavoidable that they should take one angle or another on the problematic, and I too will fail to escape this basic alternative in my exposition.

Blondel's Modern Philosophical Method

Blondel called his philosophical method a "method of immanence."[2] It consists in "trying to equate, in our own consciousness, what we appear to think and to will and to do with what we do and will and think in actual fact."[3] It recognizes that any and every idea of the transcendent is just that: an idea, and not the transcendent itself. Therefore, short of the transcendent revealing itself to us, we must critically investigate it by surveying and evaluating our immanent notions and motives.[4] Blondel specified his notion of a method of immanence in distinction from a philosophically unfounded, but what he found quite common, "doctrine of immanence." The doctrine of immanence tries to "make a transcendent truth of the negation of the transcendent or of the supernatural ... content (with) explaining the manifold interdependent and heterogeneous aspects of thought by one another and to reintegrate all forms

---

2 Blondel's most famous excursus on philosophical method can be found in an essay written shortly after the publication of *L'Action (1893)*, in 1896, "*Lettre sur les exigences de la pensée contemporaine en matiere d'apologétique et sur la méthode de la philosophie dans l'étude du probleme religieux*," since translated and published in English under the somewhat misleading, but rather more pithy, title "The Letter on Apologetics" (Maurice Blondel, *The Letter on Apologetics and History and Dogma*, trans. Alexander Dru and Illtyd Trethowan [Grand Rapids, MI: Eerdmans, 1994]). Blondel would later become embroiled in the Francophone debates about the possibility of Christian philosophy. For an excellent overview and a handful of freshly translated primary texts, see Gregory B. Sadler, *Reason Fulfilled by Revelation: The 1930s Christian Philosophy Debates in France* (Washington, DC: The Catholic University of America Press, 2011). Henri de Lubac's synthesizing intervention is also well worth reading ("On Christian Philosophy," *Communio* 19 [Fall 1992]: 478–506).

3 Blondel, *Letter on Apologetics*, 157.

4 Blondel, 158–59.

of life into the unity of a single determinism."[5] Blondel was convinced that a philosophical doctrine of immanence, a priori foreclosing the transcendent and supernatural from philosophical discourse, was incompatible with thought that proceeds according to modern philosophy's highest principles and aspirations. Moreover, he thought that "the only possible religious philosophy, which is truly religious and truly a philosophy, results from these principles."[6] Though he was quite explicit that the secularizing *doctrine* of immanence was modern philosophy's great error, Blondel thought of the *method* of immanence as one of modern philosophy's great achievements.[7]

Blondel was fond of such conceptual pairings, often giving them mnemonically impossible appellations: the willed will and the willing will; afference and efference,[8] integrism and integralism,[9] mobiles and motives,[10] and so forth. This pair in particular—the method of immanence and the doctrine of immanence—crystallizes Blondel's philosophical approach. Blondel did not tend to oppose an idea or philosophical outlook by brute force. He instead showed how an ostensibly self-standing idea betrays its incompleteness by its internal structure. He writes of this technique,

> We must, taking within ourselves all consciousnesses, become the intimate accomplice of all, in order to see if they bear within themselves their own justification or condemnation. They have to become arbiters of themselves; they have to see where their most frank and their most interior will would lead them; they have to learn what they do without knowing it, and what they already know without willing it and without doing it.[11]

---

5 Blondel, 178–79.

6 Blondel, 158.

7 See James Le Grys, "The Christianization of Modern Philosophy according to Maurice Blondel," *Theological Studies* 54, no. 3 (September 1993): 455–84.

8 See Michael A. Conway, *The Science of Life: Maurice Blondel's Philosophy of Action and the Scientific Method* (Frankfurt am Main: Peter Lang, 2000), 368–73.

9 See Maurice Blondel, *Une alliance contre nature: Catholicisme et intégrisme, La Semaine sociale de Bourdeaux 1910* (reprint; Brussels: Éditions Lessius, 2000). For helpful context, see also Peter Bernardi, *Maurice Blondel, Social Catholicism, and Action Française: The Clash over the Church's Role in Society during the Modernist Era* (Washington, DC: The Catholic University of America Press, 2009).

10 Maurice Blondel, *Action (1893): Essay on a Critique of Life and a Science of Practice*, trans. Oliva Blanchette (Notre Dame, IN: University of Notre Dame Press, 1984), 111–20.

11 Blondel, 12.

When Blondel accused modern, secular philosophies of adhering to a doctrine of immanence, he did not just accuse them of being unfairly hostile to religion in general or theology in particular. Nor did he merely point out the scotoma of prejudice in their worldview and its effect on their philosophies. By pointing out the doctrine of immanence at work in modern, secular philosophies, Blondel accused philosophers of being *insufficiently modern* in their approach. Instead of attacking the anti-religious self-understanding of modern philosophy headlong, Blondel subverted it, insisting modern philosophy follow its own core methodological commitments to their limit. There is no rectilinear genealogy of decline or wish-dream of repristination at work in Blondel's criticism of modern philosophy. Blondel encouraged modern philosophy to be both more philosophical and more modern, not less so. Only in this way could modern philosophy show to the modern mind the necessity of making the supernatural a philosophic term (albeit in a methodically controlled and, as we will see, strictly heuristic sense). Blondel's philosophy of action, then, is self-consciously *modern* philosophy.

In what way is his philosophy modern? It shares the two basic commitments outlined above as "the modern philosophical mentality." First, it is separated philosophy, unsubordinated to a dogmatic context. Second, it treats the philosopher's *via inventionis*—that is, his or her path of philosophical investigation and discovery—as the basic criterion of validity, even truth. Theologians and Christian philosophers sometimes see these elements of modern philosophy as inimical to the prospect of integrating philosophy with Christian faith. Separated philosophy seems to a priori rule inadmissible a core Christian commitment: that there are revealed and authoritative doctrines and that these doctrines are true. The elevation of the *via inventionis* to a criterion of validity and truth seems a fortiori to foreclose the very category of revealed doctrine. After all, if conclusions can only be verified to the extent the philosopher can exposit the validity of their derivation, then doctrines of supernatural provenance cannot be verified or, in the strongest form of the claim, be true at all. The startling genius of Blondel's *Action* appears when these basic commitments are shown as the very source of philosophy's necessary affirmation of the supernatural in general and supernatural religion in particular.

Blondel contends that a critical attitude toward the authority of religiously revealed doctrines can be the very thing that makes modern, separated philosophy practicable for Christians. True, the dogmas of faith cannot be entered into philosophic discourse as is, nor can they anymore control its procedure or direct its outcomes. But Blondel's radicalized method of immanence *also* excludes the philosophical doctrine that only purely immanent accounts of reality are admissible as philosophic explanation. This position would arbitrarily privilege certain prospective doctrines over others.[12] Modern philosophy must be willing to admit doctrines containing transcendent terms so long as they have been derived according to the method of immanence. Thus, Blondel's argument in *Action* shows how the modern commitment to philosophy's autonomy should prevent modern philosophers from excluding the supernatural from their philosophies. "It would be strange, therefore," he writes, "if it were scientific to exclude what it is not scientific to admit."[13] Taking the separatedness of philosophy to mean that the supernatural, a priori, cannot be a term in modern philosophy makes this exclusion itself into an inviolable doctrine, subordinating philosophy to a secularizing program. This ironically violates the principle behind an appropriately modern "method of immanence" and only gives these philosophies the *appearance* of separated autonomy. For Blondel, modern philosophy gives pride of place to autonomy and autochthony. Indeed, his notion of what counts as philosophical immanence is controlled by these twin characteristics.[14]

Blondel's is a "method of immanence" for an even more basic reason. His refusal to privilege any doctrine presupposes a commitment to only considering doctrines insofar as they are the product of human reasoning

12 "Thus, for the problem of action to be raised scientifically, we should not have any moral postulate or intellectual given to accept.... Thus everything is called into question, even where there is a question. The spring for the entire investigation must come from the investigation itself; and the movement of thought will sustain itself without any external artifice" (Blondel, 11).

13 Blondel, 359.

14 "In a phrase which must be explained but which indicates at once the seriousness of the conflict [between philosophy and Christianity], modern thought, with a jealous susceptibility, considers the notion of immanence as the very condition of philosophizing; that is to say, if among current ideas there is one which it regards as marking a definite advance, it is the idea, which is at bottom perfectly true, that nothing can enter man's mind which does not come out of him and correspond in some way to a need for development and that there is nothing in the nature of historical or traditional teaching or obligation imposed from without which counts for him, no truth and no precept which is acceptable, unless it is in some sort autonomous and autochthonous" (Blondel, *Letter on Apologetics*, 151–52).

and willing. True, prospective philosophical doctrines can enter into Blondel's philosophical dialectic from any quarter (including, it turns out, that of supernatural religion). However, only those doctrines that can be evaluated and verified according to the native resources of the philosopher can survive this dialectic to be affirmed and not merely entertained. From a certain angle, this is what it means to call his notion of modern philosophy "critical": it can give an account of itself both as a body of doctrine but also as giving rise to and even verifying those doctrines. "The difficulty," Blondel writes, "is to introduce nothing external or artificial into this profound drama of life; it is, if need be, to correct reason and the will through reason and the will themselves."[15] But recourse to the *via inventionis* in this way means that all affirmed philosophical doctrines presuppose their own proportionality to human powers of reasoning. Hence Blondel's appellation: a method of immanence.

Blondel's Modern Philosophy of the Supernatural

Blondel's "critique of life and science of practice" in *Action* is modern because it proceeds under these twin conditions of the modern philosophical mentality. How then does Blondel's philosophy of action raise the medieval problem of the supernatural in a modern way? First of all, contrast it with Aquinas's way of raising the problem. Blondel does not a priori privilege or refuse to consider any plausible philosophical doctrine. Even more than this, if his *via inventionis* will demonstrate the truth of his conclusion and not just its plausibility, then Blondel must rigorously survey and dialectically disqualify other explanations of human action. He writes,

> As I approach the science of action, then, I can take nothing for granted, no facts, no principles, no duties. It is to strip myself of every precarious support that I have been working.... We must enter into all prejudices, as if they were legitimate, into all errors, as if they were sincere, into all passions, as if they had the generosity they boast of, into all philosophical systems, as if each one held in its grip the infinite truth it thinks it has cornered.[16]

Thus, where Thomas considers alternative opinions in the ancillary space provided for objections, Blondel centers the internal logic of a succession

---

15 Blondel, *Action*, 13.
16 Blondel, 12.

of philosophical doctrines purporting to provide an adequate explanation of human action on their own. Where Thomas incisively reveals the mistaken assumptions behind mistaken objections, Blondel goes to great pains showing how these candidates for the complete explanation of action fail to meet even their own internal criteria for validity. The aesthete, for example, makes a single-minded purpose of distractedly flitting from project to project.[17] The nihilist cannot detach his or her denial of meaning from the "something" it denies.[18] The positive scientist cannot provide sense data on the intelligibilities he or she finds in the observed.[19] The secular humanist cannot avoid being superstitious in his or her repudiation of superstition.[20] Because the rigor of Blondel's demonstration relies on showing his phenomenological procedure, he cannot rely on an analytic argument that would exclude these perspectives a priori. According to his method of immanence, Blondel must take up an a posteriori procedure, and so he moves methodically from arena to arena of human action, from doctrine to prospective doctrine, excluding every purely immanent candidate.

It is common to hear expositors of Blondel emphasize how his philosophy demonstrates the necessity of the supernatural by following the *élan* of the human will from its interior movement, through its various efforts to satisfy itself, and then out beyond the limits of the whole universe, showing that nothing in creation is adequate to the native desire of the human will. In the contemporary, anglophone controversy over the *surnaturel*, this is often equated with the theologian's notion of a natural desire to see God.[21] Blondel, of course,

---

17 Blondel, 16–35.

18 Blondel, 36–50.

19 Blondel, 56–93.

20 "Nothing is more true, nothing is more necessary than to look, almost to the point of pride and naïveté, upon the metaphysician fascinated with his constructions, upon the artist in love with his work, the devotee of the moral ideal, or the apostle of action for the sake of action, as savage fetishists: in each instance, it is the same pretention and the same presumption. All are equally persuaded they can make their god without God. To lay bare the nothingness of such human effort is to do a work of pious impiety. For if he stays only with his negative conclusions, if he takes satisfaction in them, with the hope of having confiscated and as it were dissolved the divine, if he is triumphant for having dug within himself an abyss deep enough to bury, once and for all, his action and all things, the impious critic is not yet impious enough. He still retains the superstition of not having any; he remains an idolater" (Blondel, 285–99).

21 See David Braine, "The Debate between Henri de Lubac and His Critics," *Nova et Vetera (English Edition)* 6, no. 3 (Summer 2008): 543–89; Sean Larsen, "The Politics

does in part argue according to this trajectory and did affirm something like the natural desire to see God (he called it the "trans-natural" character of the human will in his defense of Social Catholicism).[22] But if one attends only to Blondel's analysis of the will's infinite dynamism and desire, one can overlook the way in which Blondel installs the medieval problem of the supernatural in the very heart of *Action*. Blondel shows how even the most sincere and sophisticated effort to explain human action does not just fail in its highest aspiration to explain human destiny per se. A fortiori, he shows that it fails *at any and every level of analysis*.[23] Whether at the first stirring of our interior life or our orientation toward creation as a whole or anywhere in between, whether one appeals to the positive sciences, the structure of rational agency itself, or to the universal moral law or any other doctrine, there always remains missing some explanatory element, some required something that cannot be disclosed philosophically. The causal circle cannot be rounded off with only immanently derived terms. The progressive expansion of Blondel's inquiry reveals not just the *élan* of the human will but also the exhaustive, "deterministic" nature of his philosophical survey of human action. It is not just that each level of analysis fails to answer the ultimate question of human action, but it even fails to give an adequate account *of itself at that level*. If one will admit only immanently derived

---

of Desire: Two Readings of Henri de Lubac on Nature and Grace," *Modern Theology* 29, no. 3 (July 2013): 279–310; Guy Mansini, "Henri de Lubac, the Natural Desire to See God, and Pure Nature," *Gregorianum* 83, no. 1 (2002): 89–109; Mansini, "The Abiding Theological Significance of Henri de Lubac's *Surnaturel*," *The Thomist* 73, no. 4 (2009): 593–619; Raymond Moloney, "De Lubac and Lonergan on the Supernatural," *Theological Studies* 69, no. 3 (2008): 509–27; Aidan Nichols, "Thomism and the *Nouvelle Théologie*," *The Thomist* 64, no. 1 (2000): 1–19; Thomas Joseph White, "Imperfect Happiness and the Final End of Man: Thomas Aquinas and the Paradigm of Nature-Grace Orthodoxy," *The Thomist* 78, no. 2 (2014): 247–89.

22 On Blondel and Social Catholicism, again see Bernardi, *Maurice Blondel, Social Catholicism, and Action Francaise*.

23 In *Theology and Social Theory*, John Milbank alights on this point and makes a great deal of it to characterize Blondel as presaging both Rorty-esque pragmatism and post-structural postmodernism. The levels of equilibrium in Blondel's analysis hang together a bit too tightly for this characterization to ring true for those who have spent much time with *Action* or Blondel's other works. However, it goes a long way to explain Milbank's possibly puzzling claim in the introduction that, though Milbank rejects Alasdair MacIntyre's philosophic realism, his thought will assume "a realist cast within [his] final *theological* perspective" (Milbank, *Theology and Social Theory: Beyond Secular Reason*, 2nd ed. [Malden, MA: Blackwell, 2006], 5, 212–13).

philosophical terms, one runs inevitably into the reality that none of these can provide a complete explanation of human action. Thus, Blondel raises the specific medieval problem of the supernatural in a distinctly modern fashion. He suggests that the way in which modern philosophy championed immanence did not excise the transcendent once and for all, but only provisionally bracketed it. Eventually, if what one wants is complete explanation, the borrowed explicability of the immanent was always going to have to be returned to its transcendent source. Of course, as I will discuss below in the section on Sartre's *Being and Nothingness*, if one is willing to give up ontological explanation per se, to allow philosophy to declare ontological bankruptcy, then the theoretical debt to the transcendent is effectively cancelled.

How does Blondel answer the medieval problem posed in his modern idiom? In a sense, he responds to the medieval problem with a version of the medieval solution but transformed by the strictures of his modern philosophical method. The aggregation of explanatory failures in which his phenomenology of human action results provides the warrant for a negative, but heuristic, conclusion: there remains "one thing necessary" to explain human action and it cannot be produced by human thinking or willing. It is something that must be supposed on account of the fact of human action, but that philosophy cannot produce according to its *via inventionis*. This is, for Blondel, the philosophical meaning of the term "supernatural": a heuristic term indicating this "one thing necessary." The term "supernatural" indicates an answer to a question, the very question with which *Action* begins: "does human life make sense and does man have a destiny?"[24] Action appears to be free and purposive, and yet we cannot avoid action and find ourselves in the middle of it without knowing what its purpose is. For Blondel, the supernatural is that which we must will in order to act freely and for our action to find its purpose.

The theologian, however, must not jump too quickly to some ready-made sense of the supernatural and its place in the drama of human being. Because Blondel's philosophy is separated from the Christian doctrinal context, his "supernatural" cannot be read as synonymous with, for example, Lonergan's *ens supernaturale* or de Lubac's *surnaturel*.[25] First of all, within the frame set by

---

24 Blondel, *Action*, 3.

25 Bernard Lonergan, "The Supernatural Order" in *Early Latin Theology*, ed. Robert M. Doran and H. Daniel Monsour, trans. Michael G. Shields, CWL 19 (Toronto: University of Toronto Press, 2011), 53–256.

Blondel's method of immanence, the supernatural is an answer anticipated, but not yet known. Blondel's investigation reaches the very limit of the universe of human action and does not comprehend its term. It seems to be an answer that, by a method of immanence, cannot be known. But *that* there is some answer seems a necessary presupposition. Blondel has to his own satisfaction already ruled out doctrines of aesthetic indifference and nihilism as prospective answers to his question, though we will see below that perhaps this exclusion was not yet sufficiently worked out and will return in a more radical and so more serious form. Nonetheless, Blondel argues that the answer to the question of action cannot be that there is no answer. Though philosophy must anticipate an answer, no philosophical answer can be forthcoming. As we will see, there is a certain moral squeamishness to Blondel's conclusion on this point; it may well be that both the question and the anticipation that it must have an answer are a kind of illusion that modern philosophy's suspicious or skeptical aspect ought to expose and repudiate, even if it means all philosophy is ultimately self-immolating. But Blondel believes too much in philosophy as a practice for this kamikaze line of reasoning. For him, the supernatural serves as a heuristic term standing in place of the answer that cannot but be anticipated by philosophy. The supernatural, thus, is what modern philosophy would know if it could answer Blondel's question of action.

This negative implication is not totally fruitless. It has philosophic value in its heuristic function: the supernatural is, even as unknown, that "one thing necessary."[26] This one thing necessary is produced in every action. There is no arena of human action in which it is not operative. By extension, it is willed in willing any realized action (what Blondel calls the "willing will"). Although the human agent cannot fail to will that the supernatural be operative in his or her action, the supernatural is not in any action because a human agent wills it to be. The will, for Blondel as for Thomas, is an intellectual faculty. Thus, when the human agent wills an idea of some determinate action (Blondel's "willed will"), reason presents a manifold of appetites ("mobiles") to the will as a multiplicity of ideas ("motives") and one of these ideas is promoted by the will for execution.[27] Consequently, what cannot be willed also cannot be thought, because that which is willed is always already presented by reason

26 Blondel, *Action,* 314–29.
27 Blondel, 109–44.

for consideration. The thought of an action never provides the one thing necessary to reason, let alone to action itself. Neither does reflection on an effected action comprehend the one thing necessary, though reflection must affirm that it is operative. Therefore, modern philosophy cannot completely explain human action in general or (per Blondel's underappreciated and more radical claim) any human action in particular. It cannot provide in its concepts the one thing necessary to all, any, and every action. But modern philosophy also cannot a priori rule out the supernatural as a heuristic term without violating its own root principles that a) all doctrines can be considered, b) no prospective doctrine gets special status, c) the rigor and expanse of inquiry is its measure, and d) the soundness of a philosophy is the soundness of its method. Thus, Blondel's notion of the supernatural stands as that which would explain human action to thought, in the concrete realizes every human action, and yet cannot be produced in and by human volition or thought.

Though Blondel does not rely on Thomas for the scaffolding beneath his philosophy of action, it turns out his modern form of the answer to the medieval problem of the supernatural comports nicely with the solution offered in part 2. Every human action relies upon a transcendent term to be rendered explicable. This term must be operative in every action for that action to itself be actual. Thus, the reliance of every human action upon the operativity of the transcendent term amounts to cooperation between the immanent and the transcendent. Blondel does not consider the broader case of cooperation between the transcendent agent and finite causes in general. He begins with the unique case of human causality and the intensifications that come along with its free mode of agency. Thus, the reliance of human agency upon transcendent agency and the problem of free, rational cooperation with transcendent agency are carried forward together in his investigation. Though the generic medieval ambiguity can only be found in Blondel's *Action* by implication, it both begins with and culminates quite explicitly in the specific medieval ambiguity. Blondel asked generally about the explicability of human freedom, but he comes to specify his question with regard to the significance of human freedom before its transcendent cooperator: the supernatural. In the next section, we see how Blondel poses the specific medieval ambiguity as an existential dilemma brought about by his philosophic recognition of the supernatural.

Once the supernatural becomes an explicit term in philosophy, it at the same time becomes also an active idea in the life of the philosopher. In the mode of this idea, the supernatural poses a dilemma to the philosopher as a person: there is necessarily something I cannot know or determine at the heart of my action. It is necessary to my actions and may even have been mobilizing my action in some invisible way. But now appearing under this heuristic term, the supernatural functions as more than an invisible and unknown appetite. It can be a motive for my action, something willed purposively. Blondel thinks that every human agent faces this choice in the course of living a life, but the philosopher knows this dilemma not by mere implication or with the simple sincerity of the morally circumspect. No, the philosopher faces this dilemma with critical rigor. Because this choice is present to me as an idea—however slight, however heuristic—it can itself be an object of my willing. Because the one thing necessary is necessary in and for all human action, I may explicitly and affirmatively will it in, with, and by my determinate actions. Blondel speaks of willing the supernatural in this way as "ratifying" the supernatural and its place in one's living. Now, plainly the supernatural cannot be willed in and of itself by human agents. It can, at this stage, only be thought and willed as a known unknown. But even this formal ratification occurs under a terribly difficult constraint: if I choose to explicitly will the supernatural in and with my various finite human actions, I must relinquish a certain power to determine what I will. For in ratifying the supernatural in my agency, I knowingly will an unknown. Blondel speaks of this as the "mortification" of action.[28] In order to will what is necessary for my action (and so, in fact, to be fully autonomous in the literal sense), I have to include in my willing an acknowledgement and acceptance of the fact that my action is not completely my own. In order to grasp fully human autonomy, I have to embrace the fundamental heteronomy of my action and to submit the significance of my action to something I cannot fully determine.

This already-uncanny alternative, between refusing to ratify the supernatural in my action (presumably by somehow acting against its transcendent source) or ratifying the supernatural by willing in my human way that the supernatural operate integrally with my action (as it necessarily must) comes with a further wrinkle. To this point we have considered the supernatural insofar as it is a heuristic term, and so the prospect of willing the supernatural has been restricted to this notional sense. But if willing the supernatural in our finite actions would amount

---

28 Blondel, 187–91, 350–54.

to anything more than an empty formality, changing nothing about how we live, we require some mediation of the supernatural. If we would will the supernatural in any determinate way, it must be rendered susceptible to the proportion of our volitional and rational powers. Consequently, Blondel argues that the development of human freedom calls out for not just a notional acknowledgement that our action comes from a transcendent source but what Blondel calls a "literal" supernatural practice by which our ratification of the one thing necessary can be concretized. In a word, the development of human freedom calls out for religion. In religion, the supernatural operates in our agency with the same necessity as always, except now we can explicitly or "literally" cooperate with it in the fullness of free, purposive agency. We are invited to enact by our willed will more fully that which our willing will silently intends.[29]

Because this mediation accommodates our finitude so that our lives can carry out the ratification invited by the critical acknowledgment of the supernatural, modern philosophy can in principle work out a number of further heuristic determinations for its character. Blondel, by his own admission, allowed his deeply formed Catholic imagination to overdetermine his derivation of these characteristics in *Action*.[30] But he corrects this tendency in a later, revised version of the work, excising these passages and substantially reworking them in *La philosophie et l'esprit chretien*. Even if the particular content of Blondel's treatment of this mediating "supernatural religion" violates the principles of modern philosophical method in *Action* (and this point is debatable; Blondel's dissatisfaction may have owed more to others's persistent misinterpretation of these passages than their inherent failure), the task itself fits squarely within his vision of the modern philosophic method of immanence pushed to such a radical extent that it reveals the impossibility of a doctrine of immanence. In Blondel's hands, modern philosophy has to admit that considering religious phenomena *as supernatural* is admissible, even though philosophy cannot penetrate into the supernatural content thereof. Such content would only be available materially in the religious practice as concretely lived, formally recognizable only to the eyes of faith. Adequate reflection upon it would remain the province of the theologians who, in a secondary fashion, reflect on that practice and its constitutive faith.

Blondel does consider what might follow from the alternate choice to resist the influence of the supernatural in one's action. Action is ineluctable, of

---

29 Blondel, 373–88.
30 Blondel, xxiii–xxiv.

course, and so one has to take some action to oppose the necessary operation of the supernatural in one's action. But this amounts to implicitly accepting the gift of realized action in order to explicitly reject it. This state of contradiction constitutes what Blondel calls "the death of action." One cannot make nothing of the actions realized in cooperation with the supernatural, but one wills that—if they cannot be entirely my own—they would not be. Blondel considers this a kind of perdition for human agency. These actions, once effected, cannot not have been and so have an indelibly eternal valence to them, such that Blondel describes our relationship to them as like that of a man tied to his own corpse forever.[31] It is, as Augustine had it, a kind of living death.

Blondel's Contribution

One can see how Blondel's conclusions comport with the medieval solution to the medieval problem of the supernatural, albeit as transformed by the strictures of a separated modern philosophy. The explicability of human action (and the world in which it operates) relies upon the efficacy of a transcendent term. What does Blondel add? He contributes the explicit "modern" mentality in which the medieval solution appears with its attendant ambiguities. His inquiry begins not from the effort to understand a supernaturally revealed doctrine but the native situation of human action considered according to the method of immanence. The results of his inquiry derive their validity from their ability to make sense not of supernaturally revealed doctrines in light of available philosophical opinions but of philosophical doctrines that would purport to completely explain human action to the satisfaction of human intelligence. His philosophical investigation culminates in the anticipation of (indeed, need for) a transcendent term explaining what, on Blondel's analysis, is only proximately, but not completely, intelligible to human intelligence: the concrete universe of human action. This anticipation cannot be unambiguously satisfied, because if there is a transcendent term, there can be no human actions that, as human, produce it.

Therefore, Blondel provides a robust articulation of modern philosophy's basic alternative, at least up to that point. Separated, modern philosophy can either a) extrapolate from its own proximate successes in action and understanding to affirm that, though it cannot be produced within a method of immanence, there must be a transcendent term if there is to be complete explanation, and so

---

31 Blondel, 344.

generate a heuristic anticipating it or b) alternatively conclude from the absence (and, indeed, impossibility) of immanent data on the transcendent term that this anticipation is misleading, and thus reject the actuality of a transcendent term and the demand for complete explanation with it. Strictly speaking, however, one cannot find refuge in agnosticism on this question. One either desires complete explanation or one does not. There is no third, neutral position to occupy on the question. However, one can simply decide not to ask the question, but this is explicitly anti-philosophical and obscurantist/quietist and so amounts to a tacit decision to not pursue complete explanation.

Either option is selected on the basis of the same available data, the same methodical outlook, and in response to the same absence of data where one would expect to discover some intelligible term. The reason for selecting one option over the other resides, therefore, in the free choice of the subject facing this irreducibly ambiguous situation. Subsequent to this choice, either option can be intelligently pursued, though the status of either option as rational is complicated by the "knock-on" effect of this prephilosophical choice on a philosopher's operative notion of rationality. This will be of the utmost importance in assessing the conflicts between the philosophical positions that follow from each prephilosophical alternative posed by the medieval ambiguities of being. These ambiguities regarding human action and its universe can become the object of both modern separated philosophical inquiry (as in Blondel's *Action*) and modern subordinated philosophical inquiry (as here). Both forms of philosophy can thematize the ur-choice from which these two basic postures originate and be clear about philosophical differences that emerge from them. In the main, a modern separated philosophy cannot decide on the issue in the absence of data and data cannot be forthcoming. Modern philosophy can at best come to find these medieval ambiguities already waiting for it in the very structure of the medieval solution to the problem of the supernatural.

Sartre's Modern Philosophical Alternative

Blondel's analysis of the life and death of action, however, fails to consider another framing of the basic option faced by human agency, one that he thought he had foreclosed in his discussion of nihilism.[32] Blondel's account

---

32 For Blondel's discussion on why "nothing" cannot be the answer to the problem of action, see *Action*, 36–53. I am echoing here Milbank's criticism of Blondel

of action's perdition operates on the belief that the operativity of the supernatural in human action has been so thoroughly demonstrated by his investigation that it cannot be notionally accepted or rejected as a conclusion, but only practically accepted through the process of cooperative mortification or rejected by an attempt to refuse cooperation with God. Now, Blondel's alternative is one way to frame what I have been calling the specific medieval ambiguity: a philosophically undecidable alternative between acting as though human freedom has a fundamental, but transcendent meaning or purpose, or, acting as though the liberty to determine our actions is, in its autonomy, basically arbitrary and inexplicable, lacking any fundamental meaning or purpose. But Blondel frames the dilemma (as every philosopher must) from the vantage of one who has already, in a pre-philosophical way, decided with regard to the transcendent meaningfulness of his own freedom—and so, by extension, made a decision to operate out of a presumption of complete explicability for the being of human action and the being of the universe in which it unfolds.[33]

One is free, however, to interpret the broad strokes of Blondel's argument and its conclusions another way. Perhaps the gap in explanation that Blondel finds, not just at the extremity of action's orientation to destiny, but in every nook and cranny of its universe, does not evince a deficiency in the phenomenality of the immanent. Perhaps it reveals a deficiency— indeed, a negativity—in philosophy itself. Perhaps Blondel's philosophical procedure evinces a philosophically unjustified "practical prejudice" in favor of ontological explicability. The evidence that supports Blondel's supernatural realism might also support an atheistic, existentialist nihilism. This would not

---

that he does not take seriously enough the challenge posed by a thoroughgoing nihilism to any ontology that radically rests its realism on a transcendent term. See Milbank, *Theology and Social Theory*, 218.

33 It should be noted from the outset that this decision is prephilosophical not in the sense of being some explicit and controlling premise from which a philosophy derives conclusions. That would be to confuse the very important difference between judgments and decisions. Rather, it is a prephilosophical decision in the sense that, because the derivation of philosophical conclusions is an activity undertaken by an agent, the basic orientation of that agent in its active reasoning sets out, in broad strokes, the character of the reasoning itself and so of the conclusions that result from it. What I am calling a decision (because it pertains to the order of agency) may in many cases not be thematized by philosophers in their writing, nor to themselves, and may only be inferred on the basis of the activity and the products that evince it.

be the simple, straightforward nihilism Blondel considered at the beginning of *Action* that wants to wave away the problem of action by cheap appeal to nothingness. No, it would be a wisened nihilism aware of its own penchant for illusion and "bad faith," full of the knowledge that it cannot but pose a problem for which there is no answer—or better, for which the answer is nothing. Blondel wrote of a process of mortification for the sake of liberation, of losing one's life in order to more fully receive it as a gift. But under the weight of his own Christian imagination, he did not (and perhaps could not) consider a philosophy that takes death as the limit and measure of its authenticity. One can call to mind a philosophy that would transcend every boundary, not in order to approximate the boundlessness of God but to approximate the indeterminacy of human being per se. Blondel does not seem to notice that his demonstration suggests this ambiguity running deeper than the alternative he envisions. Nonetheless, it is an ambiguity made available to modern thought by the medieval solutions to the problem of the supernatural. It has stowed away in the very logic of a transcendent cause of every created cause on which Blondel's philosophy of action relies. His radicalization of the method of immanence transported this medieval implication into a modern philosophical milieu and, by centering the problem of action, lifted it up just below the surface of modern Catholic thought. Below, I will consider one version of this alternative, embodied by Sartre's *Being and Nothingness*.

The Generic Medieval Ambiguity and Sartre's Being and Nothingness

Blondel's philosophical approach rests on a prephilosophical commitment to explaining completely what is. The various determinations of determinate being need to be explained and his philosophy discovers that what philosophy cannot do is explain any of them completely. The supernatural is imposed on modern philosophy because it is precisely the *being* of determinate being that needs explanation and no immanent term proves adequate to the task. The supernatural is Blondel's heuristic indication of that in which an explanation of determinate being insofar as it *is* would consist. I might note as well that, for Blondel, although the various *determinations* of determinate being are at least partially intelligible (supposing one sets aside the infinite remainder that is the supernatural), determinateness itself needs no explanation. Determinateness (being-determinate, one might say) is a kind of negative quality born by finite beings, a shadow cast by being at all. When thought in terms of a fundamental relation to an infinite "supernatural," determinate being is (to borrow a turn of phrase from Paul Ricoeur), "struck with nothingness." To be finite, temporal, immanent, and so forth is to be (again in Ricoeur's words) "surrounded by nothingness." This nothingness is not and cannot be an explanation for determinate being, because, for this philosophical posture, nothing is explained by nothing. It is simply the fact of a "radical ontological difference that separates the creature from the creator."[34] In sum, then, Blondel's basic ideal of philosophical rationality—resting on his prephilosophic commitment to completely explaining what is—includes the entailments that being needs to be explained and determinateness itself need not be explained because it cannot be explained.

As noted above, this normative ideal or horizon of philosophical rationality, embedded in a particular posture one brings to the philosophical task *as an activity*, has an alternative and it rests no less on a prephilosophic decision, commitment, and posture. Jean Paul Sartre's *Being and Nothingness* is instructive here because it embodies this alternative and so helps us to indicate in a more concrete fashion what I have been calling the medieval ambiguities of being. For Sartre, it is not the being of determinate being which calls out for explanation but its *determinateness*. "Being," he writes, "is empty of all other determination than identity with itself."[35] Being, because it is "absolute plenitude and entire positivity," seems to need no explanation.[36] Determinateness, however, needs some explanation. For Sartre, "Being can not [*sic*] be the support of any differentiated quality."

---

34 Ricoeur uses these formulations when discussing the relationship between time and eternity in Augustine's *Confessions*, but the same relationship of disproportion holds. See Paul Ricoeur, *Time and Narrative*, vol. 1, trans. Kathleen McLaughlin and David Pellauer (Chicago: University of Chicago Press, 1984), 25–27.

35 Jean-Paul Sartre, *Being and Nothingness: A Phenomenological Essay on Ontology*, trans. Hazel E. Barnes (New York: Pocket Books, 1966), 48.

36 It is telling that Sartre characterizes knowledge as an ekstatic adventure in the *affirmation* of being in-itself by being for-itself, an affirmation that can have no determinate content (indeed, no content at all) because it must be an unmediated presence of the world to the self—in other words, a presence that lacks the distance of a presence-to. What would be apprehended as a content is not the being of a being, but a meaning which has a being of its own, immediately present to consciousness. See Sartre, *Being and Nothingness*, 25–26, 295–96.

Something needs to "release" the "undifferentiated mass of being" that it might be a world of particularized and relativized beings.[37] What effects this release and so explains determinateness for Sartre? Nothingness. "Thus reversing the statement of Spinoza," Sartre writes, "we could say that every negation is determination."

At first blush, the difference between Blondel and Sartre on this point may seem minor, perhaps a matter of emphasis. After all, one might point out that they agree "nothing" explains determinateness. This agreement, however, is merely verbal. Sartre and Blondel take opposed philosophical postures, and it is my contention that this opposition owes a) to differing prephilosophical attitudes toward the meaning of what is and b) a basic ontological ambiguity that poses this choice to any philosopher prior to any philosophical act. To reiterate then, for Blondel, being is in need of explanation, both in general and in its concrete determinations, but the determinateness of these determinations does not need to be and cannot be explained. For Sartre, by contrast, being in-itself calls for no explanation, but determinateness by contrast needs to be accounted for. One can diagnose Blondel's basic philosophical posture because it is the necessary practical presupposition behind his entire argument in *Action*. What is it about Sartre's philosophical procedure, then, that leads me to think he holds a posture opposed, even inverse to Blondel's?

For Sartre, what can be said of being in-itself is that being *is*. He writes,

> Being is what is. In the in-itself there is not a particle of being which is not wholly within itself without distance. When being is thus conceived there is not the slightest suspicion of duality in it; this is what we mean when we say that the density of being of the in-itself is infinite.... The in-itself is full of itself, and no more total plenitude can be imagined, no more perfect equivalence of content to container. There is not the slightest emptiness in being, not the tiniest crack through which nothingness might slip in.[38]

Being cannot be absolutely and at the same time be relative to something, qualified by something, or somehow determined. Being cannot, in itself, even be "present to" itself. Sartre explains,

---

37 Sartre, 48.
38 Sartre, 120–21.

> This presence to itself has often been taken for a plenitude of existence, and a strong prejudice prevalent among philosophers causes them to attribute to consciousness the highest rank in being.... Actually, *presence to* always implies duality, at least a virtual separation. The presence of being to itself implies a detachment on the part of being in relation to itself. The coincidence of identity is the veritable plenitude of being exactly because in this coincidence there is left no place for any negativity.... Presence to self, on the contrary, supposes that an impalpable fissure has slipped into being. If being is present to itself, it is because it is not wholly itself.[39]

For this reason, being-in-itself is absolutely and can be relative to nothing. This means that making being present to itself, being-for-itself (that is, the being that characterizes conscious human reality for Sartre) brings nothingness to being through the very transcendence of its reflexive distance.[40] Thus, Sartre characterizes conscious human reality as self-nihilating—as a nothingness with borrowed being that being can be present-to. It is, by extension, through conscious human reality that the various determinations (explained by the nothingness of world-transcending consciousness) come to things: possibility, necessity, impossibility, and so on. But this nothingness of the determinateness of the various determinations is founded upon the fact of a self-nihilating being-for-itself.

Conscious human reality is separated from being only by this nothing given in its transcendence of the world as consciousness. It is the cause of the nothingness of determination (i.e., determinateness), and so it can be a term of explanation for determinateness "within the limits of the real."[41] Throughout the phenomenological and dialectical machinations between the in-itself and the for-itself of *Being and Nothingness,* it is being-dependent "nothingness" which explains the determinateness of determinate being. This nothingness, in other words, is present-to-as-related and so constitutes being-explicable. No transcendent term can serve this explicability function since all transcendence is a relativity, a dependent realm of nothing. Explanation can only come from within the world present-to being-for-itself

---

39 Sartre, 124.
40 Sartre, 17, 50–57.
41 Sartre, 56.

because explicability is constituted along with it. Determinateness *needs* to be explained because determinateness is what *can* be explained.[42]

Sartre's philosophical posture toward being seems on its face to be quite ontologically positive. Sartre heaps metaphysical superlatives on being-in-itself. However, it turns out that nothingness carries the day philosophically, since it is the borrowed existence of nothingness that admits attestation of any (pardon the pun) substantive kind. The being of being-in-itself resists even the assertion of identity ("A is A"), since the unity at the heart of identity is nonetheless a determination introduced by being-for-itself.[43] Put another way, Sartre's philosophy lives concretely as a nihilism, for that of which it can speak is only the nothingness that it brings to being. It is a nihilism despite its avowal to itself that it is an existentialism. It devotes itself to the explanation of nothingness and denies that what is can be explained. Moreover, insofar as the basic posture of his philosophical inquiry consists in a pre-philosophical attitude that does not endeavor to understand being, Sartre's philosophy in fact has *decided* to be a nihilism—or, more accurately, Sartre has decided his philosophy will be a nihilism. In a bit of irony, *Being and Nothingness* turns out to be a work of "bad faith," a great body of philosophical argumentation insisting to itself that it is not what it is: the product of a basic, prephilosophical decision to act as though being is inexplicable.[44]

On the other hand, if I am right that *all* philosophical ontology must begin from such a basic, prephilosophical decision and posture about how the philosopher shall comport him or herself to being, that *Being and Nothingness* is in bad faith does not compromise the internal validity of Sartre's argument, at least according to the ideal of rationality corresponding to such a commitment. I can say descriptively and by way of weighing the evidence for the medieval ambiguity of being that contingency and determinateness give a certain nothingness together with the positivity of what exists in the world

---

42 This approach is almost precisely inverse to Blondel's. For Blondel, existence itself is that which calls out for explanation because existence is what can be explained (even if philosophy, as a practical matter, can do nothing more than affirm this obligation founded on this possibility). The negativity that marks determinate being in its determinateness needs no explanation because it cannot be explained. What is given but cannot be explained at all is a mere matter of fact.

43 Sartre, *Being and Nothingness,* 120.

44 On Sartre's famous notion of "bad faith," see *Being and Nothingness,* 86–116.

of human reality. A philosophy that reads being as a mere matter of fact and the determinateness of what is as a question thus takes a basic interpretative posture vis-à-vis the data on offer. This basic posture, however, has to be taken prior to any investigation of determinate being, because it constitutes the overall character of the investigation itself. It is, in fact, not so much a decision about the object of philosophical inquiry as it is about its operative subjectivity. Through its anticipatory ideals, the posture of the operative philosophical subject invests philosophical inquiry with its immanent norms and it implies an ideal of rationality against which the results of any inquiry must be measured. To critique Sartre's argument for failing to meet its own ideals is one matter, but to demand it meet another ideal notion of rationality is to ask the philosopher to make a different existential decision on the basis of ambiguous data—namely, the data on being a conscious, inquiring agent. Such a request amounts not to an exercise in philosophical dialectic but rather an invitation to convert to another way of life. The notion of such a request also tips us toward the place held by the specific medieval ambiguity in *Being and Nothingness*.

The Specific Medieval Ambiguity
in Being and Nothingness

By focusing on Sartre's ontology, I have tried to suggest that *Being and Nothingness* embodies an opposed alternative to Blondel. But what of the specific ambiguity that regards human freedom and agency? How can holding Sartre's account of freedom and agency up beside Blondel's help us to better appreciate the ambiguity of human freedom after a Thomistic solution to the medieval problem of the supernatural? In both cases, the basic posture of their ontology is carried through, framing their theory of freedom. Moreover, both ontological postures can be thematized in terms of the theory of freedom by which it is framed, so that the circle of reflexion can be closed according to the ideal of rationality immanent to either posture or, if you prefer, the horizon it sets out.

Recall how, for Blondel, the being of determinate being calls out for explanation, but determinateness itself does not need to be explained. Between being and determinateness, philosophy can offer some partial account of the various determinations of determinate being in their various equilibria but cannot ultimately provide complete explanation for any determinate being at any level. Recall as well how Blondel frames the inquiry that arrives at this heuristic ontological conclusion by a question about the meaningfulness of human action. In Blondel's case, the ontological conclusion is derived by generalizing from the specific case of human agency. Because human action has its being and so explanation, and so meaningfulness beyond itself, but moreover beyond even the universe in which it acts, Blondel is able to argue that though the being of our action calls out for explanation like every other determinate being, a philosophy of action has to affirm that there is some transcendent, supernatural ground to the meaningfulness of our action. However, a philosophy of action cannot produce this ground, much as our willing does not of itself produce the being of our action. Human freedom, then, provides some explanation for the determinations of being in which human actions consist insofar as it places before itself the determinate purposes for which it acts. But as to why the whole complex of motives, decisions, and actions *is*, philosophy cannot say. The agent instead faces Blondel's version of the alternative: to act either in a manner that supposes there is some unknown meaning for action and aims to cooperate in some mediated and finite way with its supernatural purpose or to reject the heteronomy implied by this heuristic conclusion and aim to act in such a way that rejects cooperation with any supernatural meaning or purpose.

For Sartre, by contrast, freedom is the being of the for-itself and, though any exercise of freedom in action contains causes, motives, and ends, "freedom has no essence."[45] Much like being-in-itself, the freedom that being-for-itself is has no explanation. All of the ontological superlatives that could be heaped onto being-in-itself can, in freedom, be transferred to being-for-itself insofar as it expresses itself in action. As being is what *is*, so freedom is what is free, what "cannot cease being free," and so is, famously, "condemned to be free." Bad faith can, thus, be understood as the effort of freedom to "hide its freedom from itself."[46] The act, like knowledge, can only be a matter of affirmation for philosophy: it simply is and is free. Once this "nihilating rupture with the world [of the in-itself]" is effected and the act is, then we may speak of the experience of the act and the philosophical discernment of its causes, motives, and ends. But we may speak of them for the same reason we may speak of any determination of being—because its

45 Sartre, 565.
46 Sartre, 567.

very determinateness is what is explicable. But all of these determinations of action are nonbeing. They are projections in the transcendence of conscious human reality of what is not, of nonbeing. Thus, Sartre gives the example of the laborer who only finds a sufficient reason for revolution in the projection beyond his daily circumstances of a different set of circumstances which do not exist and yet, in their nothingness, render his life suddenly intolerable.[47] But note that the cause of the worker's will to revolt resides not in the being of his circumstances but only inside himself. He has made himself miserable and so he is the true cause of his own will to revolt. Therefore, even when one turns to elucidate the determinations of human action, one finds that, although they formally admit of explanation, what explains them is "nothing." For our actions, Sartre says in *Existentialism Is a Humanism*, "we are left alone and without excuse." Once cast into the world, we are responsible for everything we do.[48]

Above I accused Sartre's philosophy of being in bad faith. This accusation rests on an internal ambiguity that haunts these modern realizations of the specific medieval ambiguity. It is the same internal ambiguity Blondel exploits to reveal the insufficiency of every effort to explain action in purely immanent terms. This ambiguity resides between a philosophy considered as an intention, a thinking, *an activity,* and a philosophy considered as an intended, as a body of thought, as *a product.* I have already said that both Blondel and Sartre adopt a prephilosophical posture toward the practice of philosophical investigation and its object (as I hold every philosopher of being or action must). Adopting this posture amounts to a decision, a commitment to follow in one's philosophy a certain course of action. It devotes the philosopher to a way of philosophizing. This way of philosophizing, in turn, constrains the sort of philosophy that he or she will likely produce. However, because this prephilosophical decision does not *determine* the philosophical product (for the exercise of intelligence has immanent norms of its own that can be corrupted, even subverted, but never entirely suppressed without ceasing thought altogether), the philosophy that is intended, thought, produced is all too rarely an impeccably apt thematization of the basic comportment to being and/or freedom that gave it rise. Indeed, Blondel and Sartre, both in different

---

47 Sartre, 560–63.

48 Jean-Paul Sartre, *Existentialism Is a Humanism*, trans. Carol Macomber (New Haven, CT: Yale University Press, 2007), 29.

ways, imply that this internal ambiguity is as philosophically undecidable as the ontological ambiguities themselves. For Blondel, the impracticable character of the "one thing necessary" means that any philosophy that includes an element claiming to meet his anticipation of complete explanation must be a philosophy inadequate to the reality of even the action of thought that produced it. For Sartre, because freedom is prior to thought and freedom is always other than what can be said about it, any philosophy of freedom (even, he does not seem to notice, his own) has to be alienated from the being of freedom in the nothingness of conscious human reality.

Nonetheless, it turns out that neither Blondel nor Sartre manages to give an account of the pre-philosophical condition that constrains his own thought: an exercise of freedom with regard to how to determinately realize the task of philosophizing. A more fully articulated and genuinely modern philosophy of the medieval ambiguities would make explicit the *de facto* choice faced prior to philosophizing. However, because any philosophy must proceed *from* such a choice, that explicitation would have to be expressed via a doubling, in which the alternative is narrated from within one horizon of commitment and then renarrated from within the other. The anticipation at the heart of the modern philosophical mentality that the philosopher's *via inventionis* will serve as a criterion of validity calls out for this rigorous double explicitation. Unavoidably, one of these narrations would consist in an act of ventriloquizing that could never quite throw its own voice entirely away. In the case of this study, I cannot disavow my own basic comportment to being and to freedom as fundamentally, but transcendently, explicable, and I cannot deny that my characterization of Sartre's alternative is, in ways both evident to me and probably subterranean too, marked by my practical prejudice for Blondel's philosophical posture. But there is no need to effect such a disavowal, since the ideal norm of rationality governing my philosophical task comes to bear on it from within the horizon opened up by my practical prejudice for explicability. Modern philosophy's separation from a dogmatic context precludes an appeal to the doctrines of a higher, putatively more certain science like theology that could settle the matter in the extrinsic fashion appropriate to a subordinated philosophy (even if I find Lonergan's retrieval of Thomas on the transcendence of God's creative and redemptive agency convincing).

Thus, even when a philosopher gives voice to his or her basic prephilosophical posture toward philosophizing and, subsequent to this avowal, pursues it with single-minded devotion, still the ambiguity is not extinguished. From Blondel's perspective, such a basic decision does have a reason, but it is precisely this reason that philosophy cannot produce by its philosophizing. Rather, a philosophy can only show its faith in the reality of some transcendent meaning and purpose by its intellectual works. Philosophy's very resoluteness with regard to the supernatural foundation of its practice and its products is a source of instability for an authentically modern philosophy: the most important part of its *via inventionis* cannot be produced to validate itself. Sartre, by contrast, would deny that, even if the causes, motives, and ends of its determination can be experienced and described, the act of freedom in which philosophy begins has any essence. It needs no explanation because it can have no explanation. It is simply a matter of fact for which the philosopher is responsible, left alone and without excuse.

Conclusion

Readers may notice how I have hewed away from the more usual controversies about grace in which Blondel's name is sometimes invoked. I have not, however, taken this tack in order to dodge the problematic of grace. Rather, in both this chapter and its predecessors, I have considered the relation between divine and created agency that would provide the categories and analogies for a speculative theology of either creation *or* grace. In part 2, I considered that relation according to the subordinated philosophical approach characteristic of the medieval theological mentality. At the beginning of the previous chapter, I gave some indication of the ambiguity that could result from the solution to the medieval problem of the supernatural, but subsequent to a change in philosophical and/or scientific method. Then I considered the same relation in light of just such a change in method. I have called this the modern philosophical mentality and characterized it as a general method in separated philosophy that takes its *via inventionis* for its criterion of validity.

This has been a transitional chapter, pivoting between a detailed account of medieval achievements and the fully modern problem of the supernatural in part 4. I showed how two modern philosophical minds appropriate the generic and specific ambiguities made available to thematization by theorematic achievements of the high Middle Ages. I discussed the knock-on effects of the medieval solution manifest in these modern philosophical ontologies as an irreducible ambiguity. It is an ambiguity manifest in the radically different philosophical postures taken by Blondel and Sartre. It is an ambiguity manifest in Blondel's basic alternative in the face of the "one thing necessary." It is an ambiguity manifest in the temptation to "bad faith" diagnosed by Sartre. It is an ambiguity manifest in both Sartre's and Blondel's failure to fully take stock of the philosophically undecidable, prephilosophical act of freedom behind their philosophies of being and freedom. It is an ambiguity manifest in the fact that, while narrating these ambiguities, I too had to confess to my own practical prejudice in favor of one pole over the other and its effects on my study here.

This ambiguity has various elements, but its root grows up from a pair of ontological ambiguities faced by the inquiring agent, one generic and the other specific. The inquiring agent encounters a world of beings that are not completely explicable on their own and must decide to pursue complete explanation or not. The inquiring agent must decide, in general, to act from the anticipation that being is completely explicable (even if complete explanation perpetually eludes every determinate inquiry) or if being simply is a matter of fact, the pursuit of any explanation for which would amount to a flight into nonbeing, to a philosophical problem that arises when language has "gone on holiday."[49] The inquiring agent must decide, specifically, if his or her action, originating in his or her freedom but realizing itself among every other determinate being, has a basic meaningfulness, a fundamental purpose. But every act of freedom has its proximate meaning and purpose in the freedom of the agent him or herself, a determinate being the fundamental explanation of which always eludes philosophy. The free agent must decide whether to act as though his or her freedom has some meaning and purpose (even if that meaning/purpose is transcendent and so unknown) or if he or she will act as though freedom has no essence and so, like every other being, is a mere matter of fact admitting no explanation, and so no meaning and no purpose. This specific ambiguity in turn rebounds upon the generic ambiguity, since the free agent's posture toward his or her own freedom includes the prospect of pursuing philosophical inquiry as one of its possible exercises of freedom. In this way, the circle of ambiguity closes upon its own philosophical undecidability for those who inhabit the modern philosophical mentality.

---

49 Ludwig Wittgenstein, *Philosophical Investigations*, trans. G. E. M. Anscombe, P. M. S. Hacker, and Joachim Schulte, 4th ed. (Malden, MA: Wiley Blackwell, 2009), 23.

It remains to ask: how can it be that philosophers have left behind a medieval mentality of speculative theology and subordinated philosophy to inhabit this modern philosophical mentality instead? Why, if the modern mentality results in such confounding ambiguity, do they not just beat a hasty retreat back into the state of mind that served St. Thomas so well? The answer to this quandary will occupy us in chapter 8. The question has to do with the mediation, but especially the constitution of the fully human world by human and divine meanings. This further element will usher onto the scene what I believe is the genuinely modern problem.

TOWARD THE MODERN PROBLEM

To move from the medieval problem of the supernatural to what I am calling the modern problem of the supernatural requires a significant transition. In chapter 6, I explored how the modern philosophical mentality rendered probable a philosophical cognizance of the medieval ambiguities of being. This realization occurred in an intellectual context at some remove from the medieval theological mentality that made the medieval ambiguities merely possible for subordinated philosophy. This realization also occurred at the nexus of a set of questions about atheism, secularism, individualism, politics, and history. In chapter 2, I noted some of these questions insofar as they appear in but are also sidelined by the contemporary controversy over the supernatural. In what follows, I will begin to argue that the problem underlying these questions is distinct from and irreducible to the set of medieval questions that made up the horizon of the medieval problem and so the horizon of Thomas's medieval solution thereto. In order to articulate how the modern problem is distinct and irreducible, to elucidate its character, and to communicate its force requires that one make this transition. It requires I show how the modern problem is insoluble by means of the medieval solution or any metaphysical theory at all. Indeed, neither possession of a solution to the medieval problem of the supernatural nor a grasp of the medieval ambiguities of being, nor a crucial, but ultimately prephilosophical commitment to the explicability of being and of free human actions can *of themselves* resolve the modern problem. Rather, possessing these at most makes it possible for us to recognize how the twenty-first-century questions about the supernatural contain a distinct and irreducible modern problem of the supernatural. I have expressed this problem by the somewhat informal question, "What is God doing in free human action?" What difference is God making in human freedom and its products? What is God up to in the world generated by these? How do we discern the substance of God's action in a world constituted by freely constructed human meanings?

The Natural Desire to Know God

First, and belatedly, I might consider an objection to my procedure so far. In this work ostensibly on the controversy over the supernatural, I have yet to discuss at any length the central point of disagreement both in the francophone debate of the 1940s and its contemporary anglophone cousin: the natural desire to know God. Much of the contemporary debate over the supernatural has been sparked by Lawrence Feingold's tome on the topic, *The Natural Desire to See God according to St. Thomas Aquinas and His Interpreters.*[1] Was it not this very question that de Lubac raised in his effort to find the roots of modern secularism, atheism, materialism, in so forth, in decadent scholastic theology?[2] If I am now turning to the *modern* problem of the supernatural, then must I not engage with this question of the natural desire for God directly and at length? Yes and no. In what follows, I engage the question directly, but only briefly. My brevity will owe, ultimately, to my reasoned conviction that a) this question is a microcosm of the undifferentiation endemic to the contemporary controversy (insofar as it intends to pose a medieval metaphysical solution to a modern problem irreducible thereto), but also b) even an adequate metaphysical answer to this precise question can only restate the ambiguity to which Thomas's medieval solution to the problem of the supernatural led us by way of the modern philosophical mentality described in chapter 6.

Henri de Lubac and others appeal to the Thomist credentials of the doctrine that there is a natural desire to know God by his essence (*videre Deum per essentium*). Both Feingold and Steven A. Long make *Summa theologiae* 1–2, q.

---

1 Lawrence Feingold, *The Natural Desire to See God according to St. Thomas Aquinas and His Interpreters*, 2nd ed. (Naples, FL: Sapientia Press, 2010).

2 See Henri de Lubac, "Remarques sur l'histoire du mot 'surnaturel,'" *Nouvelle Revue Théologique* 61 (1934): 225–49, 350–70; *Surnaturel: Études historiques* (Paris: Aubier, 1946); *The Mystery of the Supernatural*, trans. Rosemary Sheed (New York: Herder and Herder, 1998); *A Brief Catechesis on Nature and Grace*, trans. Richard Anandez (San Francisco: Ignatius Press, 1984); *The Drama of Atheist Humanism*, trans. Mark Sebanc (San Francisco: Ignatius Press, 1995).

3, a. 8 central for their framing of the topic.[3] The *respondeo* is worth quoting in its entirety:

> Final and perfect happiness can consist in nothing else than the vision of the Divine Essence. To make this clear, two points must be observed. First, that man is not perfectly happy, so long as something remains for him to desire and seek: secondly that the perfection of any power is determined by the nature of its object. Now the object of the intellect is "what a thing is," i.e. the essence of a thing, according to *De anima* III, 6. Wherefore the intellect attains perfection, in so far as it knows the essence of a thing. If therefore an intellect knows the essence of some effect, whereby it is not possible to know the essence of the cause, i.e. to know of the cause "what it is;" that intellect cannot be said to reach that cause simply, although it may be able to gather from the effect the knowledge *that* the cause is. Consequently, when man knows an effect, and knows that it has a cause, there naturally remains in the man the desire to know about the cause, "what it is." And this desire is one of wonder, and causes inquiry, as is stated in the beginning of the *Metaphysics* (I, 2). For instance, if a man, knowing the eclipse of the sun, considers that it must be due to some cause, and knows not what the cause is, he wonders about it, and from wondering proceeds to inquire. Nor does this inquiry cease until he arrives at knowledge of the essence of the cause. If therefore the human intellect, knowing the essence of some created effect, knows no more of God than, "that He is," the perfection of that intellect does not yet reach simply the First Cause, but there remains in it the natural desire to seek the cause. Wherefore it is not yet perfectly happy. Consequently, for perfect happiness, the intellect needs to reach the very essence of the First Cause. And thus it will have its perfection through union with God as with that object, in which alone Man's happiness consists, as stated in a. 1, 7 and q. 2, a. 8.

The very desire that we have by nature to know the quiddity of things is also, in the limit, a desire for God. Moreover, because the God we desire to know as cause is disproportionate to our unaided ability to know, our natural desire

---

3 Steven A. Long, *Natura Pura: On the Recovery of Nature in the Doctrine of Grace* (New York: Fordham University Press, 2010), 15; Feingold, *Natural Desire*, 3–6.

for God is also a natural desire for the supernatural, for a communication of the divine nature. Moreover, because the will is a rational faculty, the desire of the will for the *bonum in genere* is also a natural desire for the supernatural, for some participation in the divine life. The theologian knows that this desire is not in vain, because he or she affirms with the certainty of faith that the beatific vision and so spiritual union with God is promised to the elect. When we consider the human being concretely, the neo–de Lubacian contends, there is in us by nature an innate desire for the communication of God that is supernatural grace.

Certain neo-neo-scholastics object to such *prima facie* reading of this passage and others like it.[4] Feingold and Long, for example, observe that the desire described is "elicited."[5] This is to say that the desire to know "what" God is has as its condition some prior knowledge, that is, "that" God is cause of creation. Thus, it cannot be a natural—which is to say, innate—desire to know God by God's essence.[6] A corollary governing objections of this kind is that the natural desire, if it is natural and innate, is a priori (even unconscious, on Feingold's read), but if it is "elicited," then it is a posteriori, and so manifestly not natural. Long, in fact, goes further to make the remarkable claim that to desire to know God "under the *ratio* of 'cause of the world,'" is "strictly speaking not truly to desire God, Who is infinitely more than cause of the world."[7] The desire to know God as the cause of

4 Reinhard Hütter trains his sights at length on *Summa contra Gentiles* III, c. 25, in a 2009 article ("Aquinas on the Natural Desire for the Vision of God: a Relecture of *Summa contra Gentiles* III, c. 25, *après* Henri de Lubac," *The Thomist* 73 [2009]: 523–91), though he couples this analysis to a wider historical frame in chapter 6 of *Dust Bound for Heaven* ("'Thomist Ressourcement'—A Rereading of Thomas on the Natural Desire for the Vision of God," in *Dust Bound for Heaven: Explorations in the Theology of Thomas Aquinas* [Grand Rapids, MI: Eerdmans, 2012], 183–248).

5 Feingold acknowledges that this term and its opposite ("innate") are contemporary not to Thomas but to Suarez (Feingold, *Natural Desire*, 15).

6 Feingold, *Natural Desire*, 13–16, 397–406; Long, *Natura Pura*, 17, 19n15.

7 Long, *Natura Pura*, 20. The concept "cause of the world," according to Long, is predicated accidentally of God, for it "signifies something in the world, whereas God infinitely transcends the world." First, it is strange for a Thomist to claim that a true statement predicated of God is predicated "accidentally." It seems to me a deeply held Thomist doctrine that the divine being admits of no accidents. But what could a true statement predicated of God accidentally impute to God but an accident? It is true, as I have said above, that God's creative agency is predicated of God by extrinsic or "contingent" predication, but this is hardly the same thing as accidental predication.

contingent, finite being may have God as its material object, but does not have God's essence as its formal object.[8] How can a desire and its proper fulfillment not have the same formal object? By metaphysical analysis, are not operations specified by their objects?

One should alert to a fundamental problem here, however. The desire to know *as desire* must always will an end or object, to use Long's terms, under a *ratio* that is "accidentally denominated" of that which would fulfill the desire. For what is desired is the quiddity, but if the intellect could present to the will a concept derived from the desired quiddity, the intellect would already be in possession of that which it desires to know. Long's example gives this away. He claims that desiring to know God under the concept "cause of the world" is like desiring to know Einstein under the concept "man wearing a raincoat."[9] It is true, of course, that desiring to know the man in the raincoat (who happens to be Einstein) is only materially and not formally specified as a desire to know Einstein. However, desiring to know "the man called Einstein" is also only materially and not formally a desire to know the person who is identical with the famous physicist. The proper noun "Einstein" is predicated of the person identical with the famous physicist no less accidentally than "man wearing a raincoat." And, more to the point, if I already know the famous physicist, I can hardly be said to *desire* to know him according to the formal understanding on which that knowledge rests. Lonergan makes this same point with considerable brevity in his essay, "The Natural Desire to Know God": "The desire [to know] and its fulfillment must have the same material object. But a desire to understand cannot have

---

However, perhaps that is substantially identical with what Long intended, only by an infelicitous term. After all, he is right that to be "cause of the world" is predicated of God on the basis not of something intrinsic to God but of the contingent fact of something extrinsic to God existing. However, to truly be the cause of the world— which is to say, the cause of every finite and contingent thing without exception—is necessarily to be infinite, and so it is not the world's finitude that is implicitly predicated of God by the *ratio* "cause of the world," but precisely God's own unrestrictedness. How God's *ad extra* unrestrictedness can be ostensibly "transcended infinitely" by God's *in se* infinitude such that some meaningful distinction between the God who causes finite and contingent being and the God who necessarily is (whether He creates or not) can be drawn eludes me.

8 "Materially the object is the same, but the formal specification of the desire is quite different" (Long, *Natura Pura*, 19n15).

9 Long, *Natura Pura*, 20.

the same formal object as the fulfilling act of understanding. A desire to understand is specified by what we already know. The fulfilling act is specified by what as yet we do not know."[10] One can see, then, how Long and those who level this objection to the natural desire to know God elide the formal object (God as known to exist) specifying the desire to know God's essence and that formal object (beatific vision) specifying the act which would fulfill that desire.

The foregoing analysis considers the desire to know any particular quiddity and specifically considers it as *desire*. But I might also consider the natural desire to know in general. The essential and adequate object of intellect is the transcendental *ens*. Whatever can be known is, and besides what is, there is nothing. One may express the human intellect's desire for this object by two basic kinds of questions, "*quid sit?*" and "*an sit?*"[11] Not even the doctrinaire Kantian, Lonergan notes, will deny that human beings may ask, "*an sit?*" about anything at all, including God. But a rational and affirmative answer to a question is a fulfillment of the desire expressed by the question. However, one may philosophically affirm that God exists by extrinsic denomination, saying that it is true of God that He is the necessarily existing cause of every contingently existing being on the supposition that contingent things in fact exist. Concomitantly, one may ask "*quid sit?*" about anything at all as well, including God. Asking *quid sit Deus* expresses a desire to know God's essence specified by the knowledge of God's existence. It is indeed an elicited desire. However, desiring to know the essence of any being is a natural operation of the human intellect: it requires no acquired habit, nor the aid of supernatural grace.[12] Moreover, desiring to know the essence of God as specified by knowledge of His existence is not excluded from the field of the intellect's essential object, for besides *ens* there is nothing. Thus, the desire to know in general is natural in origin and transcendental in its object. The specific desire to know God is no exception when considered *as desire*.

---

10 Bernard Lonergan, "The Natural Desire to Know God," in *Collection*, 2nd ed., ed. Frederick E. Crowe and Robert M. Doran, CWL 4 (Toronto: University of Toronto Press, 2005), 87.

11 Lonergan, "Natural Desire," 81. See also Lonergan, *Verbum: Word and Idea in Aquinas*, ed. Frederick E. Crowe and Robert M. Doran, CWL 2 (Toronto: University of Toronto Press, 1997), 10, 70, 100, 105, and *passim*; Thomas Aquinas, *In Aristotelis libros Posteriorum analyticorum*, 2, lect. i.

12 Lonergan, "Natural Desire," 81.

The elicited character of the desire to know God by His essence impinges on its naturalness not at all.

If it is objected that this sense of "natural" is not commonly what is meant by a natural desire to know God by His essence, but rather de Lubac and others have in mind an a priori tending toward God as end, we can note that the *desiring desire* to know has *ens* as its object and God is. Indeed, God is infinitely and so "infinitely more" than any creature we might inquire about according to some particular *desired desire*.[13] Thus it is that we can say the mobilizing wonder diagnosed in human nature by Aristotle in the *Metaphysics* is, as to the formal object specifying its fulfillment, a desire for God.[14] Lonergan again:

> We are not content to ask *quid sit* solely with regard to material things, and we are not content with merely analogical knowledge of immaterial things. We keep on asking why, and we desist ultimately not because we do not desire but because we recognize our impotence to satisfy our desire. Even the Kantian, who denies to speculative intellect any knowledge of God, nonetheless appeals to some transcendental illusion to account for our desire. The fact seems to be that, just as the natural desire expressed by the question, *an sit*, has its range fixed by the adequate object of intellect, so also the natural desire expressed by the question, *quid sit*, has an equal range. Since, then, acts are specified by their objects, and the object of natural desire is the transcendental, *ens*, we may say that the desire of our intellects is natural in origin and transcendental in its object ... [and] the question, *quid sit Deus*, expresses a desire that arises naturally as soon as one knows the existence of God. This is but a corollary of the twofold affirmation that the desire to understand is natural and transcendental. Moreover, analogical knowledge of God does not satisfy this desire completely: not only is this clear *a posteriori* from the

---

13 This notion of an operative desiring desire distinguishable from an operated desired desire is borrowed and adapted from Blondel's notion of the willing will and the willed will. The human being's willed will is always finite, but the willing will to which any willed will aims to be adequate and a fulfillment always transcends it. See Maurice Blondel, *Action (1893): Essay on a Critique of Life and a Science of Practice*, trans. Oliva Blanchette (Notre Dame, IN: University of Notre Dame Press, 1984), 134, 153, 309, and *passim*.

14 Aristotle, *Metaphysics*, book I, 1, 980a, 21.

fact that natural theology and Trinitarian theory are not completely satisfying but only what we have to take because we cannot do better; it also is evident *a priori* since analogical knowledge is knowledge not only of similarity but of difference as well, and so of the limitations inevitably resulting from the difference. Hence, it is only proper knowledge of God that fully can meet the question, *quid sit Deus*.[15]

Note (as Lonergan does subsequently) that this desire considered as desire "neither includes nor excludes the Blessed Trinity," even if the theologian may affirm by an act of supernatural faith that this desire is only properly fulfilled by an act of understanding specified by the substance of the beatific vision as its formal object. That conclusion, of course, is theological and not properly philosophical. "It can be thought," Lonergan writes, "only because one has the faith, knows the fact of the beatific vision, and so must accept its possibility."[16] Affirmation of potency, as ever, is derived from act.[17]

The philosopher, however, is in a rather different position. Human beings do not possess intellect *simpliciter*. Rather, our intellect comes to be in potency brought to act by illuminated phantasm. As Aristotle had it, "Intellect grasps forms in images," which is to say by inquiry into the sensible.[18] While the field of the sensible is restricted, the transcendental *ens* is unrestricted, for besides being there is nothing. Thus, the philosopher faces a paradox: it would seem that, because the naturally attainable fulfillment of our desire to know is restricted, so too should the desire be. But, Lonergan observes, "The facts are otherwise."[19] There is nothing about which we cannot ask, "*quid sit?*" or "*an sit?*" because nothing is excluded from the range of our natural desire to know. Thus, the essential object of our intellects *qua* intellect infinitely outstrips the totality of proportionate objects (*quidditas rei materialis*) of our intellects considered concretely. The wonder mobilizing the philosopher

15 Lonergan, "Natural Desire," 83.

16 Lonergan, 83.

17 If this treatment of Lonergan's views on the natural desire to see God proves unsatisfactorily summary, please see his detailed treatment of the topic in general, "The Supernatural Order," in *Early Latin Theology*, ed. Robert M. Doran and H. Daniel Monsour, trans. Michael G. Shields, CWL 19 (Toronto: University of Toronto Press, 2011), 53–255. The entire treatise is to be considered, but those in a hurry might turn specifically to Excursus 1 of Thesis 4 of the same (139–60).

18 Aristotle, *De anima*, III, 7, 43ib, 2.

19 Lonergan, "Natural Desire," 83.

to discovery and reasoning and the episodic triumph of rational judgment may, it turns out, itself prove an absurdity. The task of finite spirit appears Sisyphean. Such is the negative pole of the general medieval ambiguity.

But if the human intellect has a field of proportionate objects, could we not call complete and adequate knowledge of that field a proper end of the human intellect, one in which some natural if imperfect felicity could be found? Could we not have as our completely intelligible but purely natural end knowledge of creatures and of God insofar as God is their creator? Could we not worship God as source of creaturely being and divine the natural law from the theonomic order among creatures?[20] Yes and no. Certainly, any knowledge of creatures, of any *quidditas rei materialis*, brings with it a eudaimonic satisfaction. Also, aggregate knowledge of the whole of proportionate being is in principle possible for the unaided human intellect. Further, the existence of God may be affirmed on the basis of a valid inference that the totality of contingent finite beings must have a necessary and infinite cause. Still, knowledge of *what* the cause of contingent finite being is would necessarily elude us. We can know that there is sufficient reason for creaturely being, but not (without divine aid) what that reason is in itself. And this is no merely extrinsic matter to the intelligibility of that which depends upon the sufficiency of reason. For if I do not know the sufficient reason of creaturely being, whatever else I may know about creatures, I still as yet do not know *why* they exist, but only that they exist and that their existence is in principle intelligible. But if I do not know *why* something exists, I hardly know that thing completely. And so in the end the aggregate knowledge of creaturely being, no less than the universal existence of creaturely being depends entirely upon God. This dependence is absolute, for the difference between existence and nonexistence is absolute. As a consequence, if separated (rather than merely distinguished) from its founding relation to the God who is, the proportionate end of the human intellect proves to be nothing at all. This, then, signals the important role played by natural knowledge of God's existence: it heuristically indicates where the causal order of being continues infinitely beyond the ken of unaided human minds, situating the restricted field proportionate to human knowledge within the unrestricted intelligibility that provides its proximate integrity.

---

20 A line of reasoning approximating one Long attributes to "some authors," in a footnote (Long, *Natura Pura*, 20n20).

If my treatment of this widely controverted point seems terse[21] and, furthermore, somewhat tart, it is because I am convinced that the thesis on the natural desire to know God, especially when considered according to separated philosophy, amounts in the end only to a restatement of the medieval ambiguity articulated in chapter 6 in terms of a medieval metaphysical psychology. To desire to know God under the *ratio* of the cause of finite, contingent being is simply to have affirmed that there is a sufficient reason for finite, contingent being and to ask what it is. If, however, one denies that there is some sufficient reason for the existence of finite, contingent being (perhaps on the basis of the paradox into which affirmation seems to lead philosophical reasoning), it would be absurd to thus ask what that sufficient reason is. Conversely, if there is no sufficient reason for finite, contingent being, then being is not at bottom completely intelligible and the partial intelligibility one finds is not part of any whole, thus in fact no part at all. Being is mere matter of fact. Thus, the activity of inquiry itself must be judged worth pursuing on the basis of an intelligibility desired, but in principle beyond the attainment of the human intellect and so of any separated philosophy. Concretely, what is posed to the philosopher conceptually as a paradox is posed existentially as a prephilosophical decision for or against the complete intelligibility of being (and so, the theologian knows, materially for or against God).

What has been posed in the last century as the problem of the supernatural is, I contend, not the modern problem of the supernatural properly so-called, but a residue of efforts to think up to the mind of Thomas Aquinas on the medieval problem, using his medieval terms but only occasionally achieving his medieval solution. The medieval solution consists necessarily (though in the case of grace, not sufficiently) in the application of the theorem of the supernatural. We may say without contradiction or competition that God

---

21 I have chosen, for example, not to engage with the neo–de Lubacian positions on the question at all in this chapter, nor with Jacob Wood's *via media* (which closely resembles Lonergan's position on the topic), nor David Hart's avowedly neoplatonist foray into the topic, in part to avoid needless repetition of material in early chapters, but also because (a) they all broadly agree on the question, (b) I find Lonergan's account goes most incisively and efficiently to the heart of the neo-neo-scholastic objection without also collapsing important elements into indistinction, and (c) whatever differences of detail—inarguably important on the natural desire question itself—there may be are ultimately rendered moot by the more fundamental point I make above that any of these reduce to the medieval solution and its attendant ambiguities.

acts in all of my actions, making them actual and intelligible. Even when my willing outstrips the proportion of my efficacy, it is God that makes my desiring make sense at all and so lets it be *as desiring*. But this conclusion cannot be drawn unambiguously in a separated philosophy. This ambiguity, however, fails to invalidate the conclusion. Rather, taking cognizance of the ambiguity allows us to recognize what Blondel insisted on at the end of the nineteenth century: that there is infinitely more in action than in thought.[22]

If a tidy solution to the quandaries of the natural desire to know God like the one sketched above only manages to restate the medieval ambiguity of being, then I have still not yet posed the modern problem of the supernatural. Perhaps I can pose the question according to Aristotle's two basic questions. In part 2, we answered a kind of *"an sit"* question. I followed Lonergan's reconstruction of Thomas's metaphysical argument for divine *concursus*. I elucidated the theoretical conditions for the possibility that God is at work in all our actions. I showed that these conditions can be affirmed. In turn, I affirmed that God acts in every free human action. But as I may desire to know the essence of the God that is the cause of every creature (and who thus operates in every created cause), I can more specifically ask after the nature of God's operation in free human action. If I commit myself to the prephilosophical decision that such a question is worth asking, if I commit myself to the hypothesis that free human action is fundamentally intelligible, then as a theologian I may naturally wonder after what as a philosopher I could not hope to know: "What is God doing in human action?" This question cannot be answered by more metaphysics. This question does not ask for the synchronic and causal conditions of possibility for God's involvement in free human action. Instead, it asks after the diachronic manifestation of God's providential and redemptive intent

---

22 "For, once reflexion, through the initiative of spontaneous life itself, rises to the conception of an ideal order, once we have understood that there is more in human action than all of nature can offer, once the will takes over what is autonomous and transcendent within it, it is no longer in the real facts, nor even in the ideas that regulate the understanding, that man seeks support and finds the end for his conduct. It is in practice alone that he aspires to equal the amplitude of his acting will. And henceforth, action (far from seeming a phenomenon conditioned by an infinity of other antecedents, whether objective or subjective matters little) appears as conditioning all the rest. Considered in all its purity apart from facts and ideas, action commands and produces the ideas and the facts; it organizes itself freely; it creates the organs of its necessary functions" (Blondel, *Action*, 280).

in and through human actions. It is, in other words, a *hermeneutical* question as much as it is an ontological one. Still, if the contemporary controversy over the supernatural has been any indication, the abstract universality, the logical control, and the disclosure of formal necessity offered by a medieval ideal of science will continue to prove too tempting to set down, however provisionally. Therefore, in what follows I spell out why the modern problem of the supernatural cannot be answered according to that ideal of science because it arises in a different horizon set out according to a different ideal. My effort to elucidate why the modern problem of the supernatural cannot be solved exclusively in terms of metaphysical analysis proceeds in two parts. In the first part, I argue that a metaphysical answer to the question, "What is God doing in human action?" only restates the problem. In the second part, I will argue that the problem thus restated is manifestly and unavoidably diachronic and, moreoever, hermeneutical in the radical sense that appeared with the "Second Enlightenment." This latter claim requires no small amount of explanation, but if the circumference of the medieval solution is to be fit within the horizon of the modern problem, I must survey at once both the area it covers and those places where its efficacy drops off.

A Metaphysical Attempt
to Answer the Modern Problem

What is God doing in free human action, metaphysically speaking? St. Thomas says God is "governing" it.[23] Bernard Lonergan spells out four ways in which God governs free human actions. God governs the will's willing of the end, the specification of the free act as to its means, the exercise of the free act once means have been decided upon, and the whole series of an individual's free acts. God governs the will willing the end of free human action by what Lonergan calls "the direct exercise of power" (*immediatio virtutis*).[24] God is the immediate cause of an act of willing insofar as God creates and conserves the will. God not only causes the will to be itself according to its essence but beyond essence in the actuality of its operation that wills the end.[25] God also

---

23 Thomas Aquinas, *Summa theologiae*, 1, q. 103, a. 5, ad 3m.

24 Bernard Lonergan, "God's Knowledge and Will," *Early Latin Theology*, ed. Robert M. Doran and H. Daniel Monsour, CWL 19 (Toronto: University of Toronto Press, 2011), 325. See also "The Supernatural Order," 183.

25 On the manner in which operation is "beyond essence," see Lonergan, *Verbum*,

governs the intellect in its operation by which the end is presented to the will and in this same direct or immediate manner, that is, through creation and conservation. God governs too the will's willing of the end as mediate cause (*mediatio suppositi*), applying causes to their effects and adapting causes to be instruments of His will.[26] This is to say that God applies the agent objects of sensation to the senses, applies the senses in act to the intellect, and applies the agent intellect to the passive intellect, thereby illuminating the phantasms impressed there.[27] Thus, God governs the operation of the will with regard to the end by causing the will and its operations to be at all (*immediatio virtutis*) but also by arranging the spatiotemporal conjunction and disposition of the intellect and will with regard to the agent objects that bring them to act in space and time through the order of the universe (*mediatio suppositi*).

Of course, one may object that if God moves our will to the end, both by the immediate and mediate exercise of divine power, how may such a willing be said to be free? In one respect, this objection loses hold of the medieval solution to the problem of the supernatural. "Now what," Lonergan asks, giving voice to this objection, "does the ... will moved by God, when it is moved by God, while it is moved by God, confer or contribute?" His response presupposes the transitive relation of causality that is divine *concursus*: "(The will) operates. It wills.... The will operates inasmuch as it is the will that is actuated. The will contributes inasmuch as an act received in the will has to be a 'willing.'"[28] In other words, what I receive from God in my action is the activity itself. But that is simply to say that my action is contingent rather than necessary. In another respect, however, having simply willed the end is not yet a formally free act, according to Lonergan, but only a virtually free act. This is to say, it is free to the extent that it produces a formally free act.[29]

God also governs the specification of our free acts whereby we select the means through which to reach our intended end.[30] God effects this governance by ordering through application all the intelligible factors that contribute to

---

115: "But there also are elements of reality that are over and above essence; sight is an essence, but seeing is more than that essence; still, seeing is not a further essence, for seeing and sight have the same definition, which they share as act and potency."

26 Lonergan, "God's Knowledge and Will," 325.

27 On the role of "agent objects" in bringing operations to act, see Lonergan, *Verbum*, 106–51, but especially 149–50.

28 Lonergan, 147.

29 Lonergan, "God's Knowledge and Will," 327.

30 Lonergan, 329.

it. God orders the matter of the act, which is to say the circumstances that bound feasibility and so the range of means actually available. God orders the subject of the act through his governance by application of our habits and dispositions of the body, the senses, the intellect, and the will. He also governs the subject of free acts through his governance by creation and conservation of the intellectual light of deliberation and the love for the end motivating our deliberations. In the explicitly theological register, God governs so many of our free acts by the grace that makes them possible, by *mediatio suppositi* in supernatural habits and through *immediatio virtutis* in the gift of enlightenment of our intellect and inspiration of our wills.[31] As I argued at length in part 2, God also governs the exercise of our free actions through the transitive relation of causality that is divine *concursus*. As agents, we are not proportionate to have existence as an effect, but the effects of the exercise of our free actions exist. God, thus, causes both this existential efficacy in our action as well as the operation by which we commit ourselves to realizing it. God causes our causing, and so is cause of our effects. This is no less true when we are moved than when we move ourselves.

Finally, Lonergan argues that God is solely the cause of the entire series of an individual's free actions. Lonergan offers both conceptual and concrete support for this claim. Causes, he reminds us, are one in themselves, but an individual's acts are multiple. Therefore, even if one intends and chooses the series as a whole, that act itself would be part of the series, for "no one act of a person is simultaneous with all that person's acts."[32] Concretely, Lonergan points out, we experience our freedom as effective here and now, such that "it is not today's freedom but tomorrow's that is going to carry out the resolution made today."[33] Indeed, this inescapable temporality rules out the prospect that we might have causal mastery of the whole series of our actions. No, God wills the order of every ordered series in God's infinite wisdom and so is the cause per se of each person's free acts.

The above elucidation of God's governance of human action, however compendious, only restates the modern problem. Each point in Lonergan's catalogue of God's governance of free human action serves to specify the formal content of a decision to affirm the positive pole of the specific medieval ambiguity, of a decision to operate on the heuristic anticipation

31 Lonergan, 331.
32 Lonergan, 333.
33 Lonergan, 333.

that free human action is ultimately intelligible. Each point fills out a respect in which one may affirm, yes, there is an explanation for the being of free human action. That explanation is what the theologian means by God. Moreover, by providing free human action with its efficacy (and so being), God does not deprive it of its liberty. The metaphysical answer tells us *that* free human actions are intelligible because of their dependence upon God and so also that God is acting in them. No doubt one can, by learning what human actions are, learn what God is doing in making them to be. This is of the utmost importance in answer to *an sit* questions about the work of God in human actions. Nonetheless, it produces a trivial answer to *quid sit* questions about the same: *whatever* God knows, wills, or does necessarily is, but only with the minimal necessity resulting from the supposition of itself.[34] That triviality with regard to the quiddity of God's *ad extra* agency grounded the medieval ambiguities of being we saw in chapter 6. If by asking, "What is God doing in human action?" one wants to know the intelligible nexus between free human action as the freely produced effects of God's action and the end for and toward which they are governed and effected by God, this sheds no light at all. One has as yet no purchase on *what* God is doing in free human action.

Conclusion

So far, my argument for the impossibility of answering the modern problem of the supernatural metaphysically is primarily metaphysical. This might seem odd on its face. Although the metaphysical attempt to answer the modern problem only restates the problem, one need not consider that approach entirely fruitless. In principle, careful exposition of this metaphysical restatement should serve to both articulate the elements of the problem and also to communicate its force. One might, through analysis, reveal not just the fact that a metaphysical approach cannot answer the modern problem, but also reveal some of the reasons *why* it cannot do so and thereby uncover some determinations of the problem itself. For example, I have expressed the modern problem of the supernatural by the somewhat informal question, "What is God doing in free human action?" Diffusely and at length in part 2, but more directly and tersely in this chapter, I have considered "what God is doing." I have, in other words, kept the focus on God's *ad extra* agency in

34 Lonergan, 279–81.

human action. Free human action in itself has gone little defined, except when considered as the object of God's action. In the next two chapters, a close look at Lonergan's account of Thomas's metaphysical psychology provides both the needed articulation of the modern problem and communication of its force. This close look consists in a metaphysical analysis reducing free human action to its principle in free acts of the will, and so involves a reconstruction of Lonergan's Thomist theory of the human will. This reconstruction, in turn, includes an account of rationality in general for the sake of clarifying precisely how the will is a *rational* faculty. For my purposes, underlining the role of *meaning* in human rationality and so in human volition proves most important. The constitutive function of meaning in human action, fundamental for human action *as free*, reveals why the modern problem of the supernatural is a) diachronic, b) radically, ontologically hermeneutical, and c) irreducible to metaphysical solutions.

PART IV

MEANING

CHAPTER 9

RATIONALITY AND MEANING

How are free human actions discerned as both free and human? There is a temptation, because agents are predicated as such extrinsically, to think one must distinguish free human action on the basis of the "action-as-effect" itself.[1] For example, one might suppose that those actions that go unimpeded are thereby free. Of course, that which is impeded does not come to be at all and without an extant effect/product, there is no action to speak of, much less a free and human one. If it is objected that there is an effect, but it is simply not the effect intended, this also tips us away from the effect/product as the determinant of an action as free. For effects do not have intentions, but rational agents do, and so implicitly one must distinguish free human actions on the basis of the agent.

If one cannot distinguish the free and human character of an action-as-movement on the basis of its effect/product, then one may turn to its other term: the agent. How is agency distinguished as free and human from the agent? I will proceed by metaphysical analysis, which is to say by reduction

---

1 In chapter 4 I reviewed Thomas's augmentation of Aristotle's theory of action. Within a unitary action, a single "movement," the patient or effect or product is distinguished on the basis of its dependence upon another—the agent—for its act. Agency, then, is predicated extrinsically, from the existence of an effect really dependent upon the agent for its act. It is from within this general metaphysical framework, then, that I am asking how free human actions are distinguished. First, we need to acknowledge a looming ambiguity. Action can be taken to mean the movement as a unitary whole within which agent and patient/effect/product are distinguished. We might approximately associate Aristotle's use of *poiesis* with this sense of "action." However, action can also refer to the effect or product itself, and here we might associate, with matching approximation, Aristotle's sense of *praxis*. I will do my best to be clear about which sense I am employing along the way, referring to the former sense with "action-as-movement" and the latter as "action-as-effect."

to principles. Thus one moves from the object(s) of an act to the nature of the act and then from the nature of the power to act thusly to the nature of the being that possesses that power. One might begin by positing vaguely and heuristically that the object of free human action is "some good." Now, this does not carry one very far, because every being that becomes in time and space tends toward "some good." These goods-as-ends remain in need of specification. Here metaphysical analysis takes on a dialectical nature, pivoting between terms to gain traction. Thus, one may specify goods by their proportion to the nature of the acts, powers, and natures that tend toward them.

Humans, plainly, tend toward nutritive ends. While this distinguishes human actions from the actions of the inanimate, we have this specific tending in common with all living things. Humans also tend toward sensible goods (the "pleasurable"). Moreover, we tend toward nutritive goods under the aspect of their sensible goodness perceived. In other words, our desire for nutritive goods depends upon, in the concrete, our tending toward sensible goods. However, we have this tending in common with all sentient living things and so it gets us only so much closer to specifying actions as free and human. Finally, then, humans also tend toward intelligible goods, as evinced by the desire to know for its own sake and the love we have for knowledge possessed. This, at least according to present knowledge of the cosmos, seems a uniquely human tending. Moreover, we tend toward nutritive and sensible goods under the aspect of their intelligible goodness as known. In other words, our desire for nutritive goods depends, in the concrete, on our tending toward intelligible goods based in our understanding of their relative nutritional value for our physical health or the relative sustainability of the economies in which agriculture consists. Our desire for sensible goods also, in the concrete, depends on our tending toward intelligible goods, as evinced by the intellectual character of our delight in the beautiful.[2]

Thus, the objects of human actions are desired or loved under two aspects: primarily as good, but secondarily and integrally as intelligible. Of course, intelligibility and goodness pertain to everything toward which any being tends, since *bonum* is among the transcendentals of being. This does not help us specify actions as free and human, however. Every end toward which a being tends in its becoming is, insofar as it is, intelligible and good. Noting that they are desired *as* good and intelligible does aid such specification, however. One may say that, although free human actions produce effects that

---

2 Thomas Aquinas, *Summa theologiae*, 1, q. 5, a. 5.

are intelligible and good (like all effective actions), specifically free and human actions follow from prior acts of knowing and desiring as their ontological principle. Consequently, the potency for these acts is called a "rational appetite."[3] But prattle of the Thomist definition for the will only occasionally raises the essential questions: what is rationality? How does rationality modify the tending in which appetite consists? These questions will occupy me for the remainder of this chapter.

What Is Rationality?

Fundamentally, rationality is an intellectual process. But when one thinks of intellectual process, one may think only of the forms of inference "found in an abbreviated and very formal textbook on deductive logic."[4] One might, in other words, think of rationality as a fairly mechanical process whereby concepts and their contents are assembled into arguments according to rules or laws. These rules or laws, then, are what one learns in logic courses and rationality would consist in their rigorous application. But such a process would be merely intelligible and not as such intellectual. It would be what Lonergan calls a "natural process." He notes three differences between a natural process and an intellectual process. He writes,

> [First] the intelligibility of natural process is passive and potential: it is what can be understood; it is not an understanding; it is a potential object of intellect, but it is not the very stuff of intellect. [Second,] the intelligibility of natural process is the intelligibility of some specific natural law, say, the law of inverse squares, but never the intelligibility of the very idea of intelligible law. Thirdly, the intelligibility of natural process is imposed from without: natures act intelligibly, not because they are intelligent, for they are not, but because they are concretions of divine ideas and a divine plan.[5]

---

3 David Gallagher notes how Thomas seldom contents himself with anything so straightforward as the simple notion of an appetite that follows cognition (David M. Gallagher, "Thomas Aquinas on the Will as Rational Appetite," *Journal of the History of Philosophy* 29, no. 4 [October 1991]: 559–84), so here as throughout, I will be presenting a synthesis of "Lonergan's Thomas" on the will.

4 Bernard Lonergan, *Verbum: Word and Idea in Aquinas*, ed. Frederick E. Crowe and Robert M. Doran (Toronto: University of Toronto Press, 1997), 51.

5 Lonergan, 46–47.

Intellectual process, then, will be not just intelligible, but also intelligent. Intellectual process is not just governed by laws or rules but is generative of laws/rules.[6] Thus these governing principles are not heteronomous to intellectual process. Intellectual process is not just governed by intelligible law, but creates, constitutes, and so grounds "the intelligibility-in-act of law."[7] In this sense, intellectual process is *autonomous*, rather than automatic.

Even more significantly, intellectual process is not merely the autonomous assemblage of ready-made concepts generated through "metaphysical mechanics."[8] "Conceptualization comes as the term and product," Lonergan writes, "of a process of reasoning."[9] If intellectual process produces concepts themselves, the autonomous process of deductive, syllogistic reasoning is not therefore basic but a derived form of rationality. The rationality of deductive inference rests on this still-more-basic rationality. As I have previously argued, any positive philosophy that would come to ultimately unambiguous conclusions in ontology operates on the presupposition that "all causation is intelligible," and so "any effect has sufficient ground in its cause."[10] Concepts are the result of a process and so are, in that sense, effects dependent on their cause as sufficient ground. Moreover, concepts are the result and product of a specifically intellectual process, and so their sufficient ground is not just intelligible, but intelligent. This ground cannot be intelligence merely in potency, and therefore the ground cannot be the intellectual power as such. No, the ground of concepts must be *intelligence in act*, understanding or, in humans, what Lonergan famously called "insight," because effects receive their act from their cause. But the intellect in act, that is *intelligence* in act, is intellectual operation. It is *intelligere*, understanding, insight. The sufficient ground of the concept-as-effect is "a knowing," and it is "operative precisely as a knowing, knowing itself to be sufficient."[11]

The intelligent intelligibility of intelligence in act, according to Lonergan, is the "basic and essential rationality of rational consciousness" to be

6 This latter point is perhaps obvious in the divine (and so paradigmatic) instance of intellectual process, but I shall argue below that it is also true in human intellectual process. The law-generative character of human intellectual process constitutes rationality's autonomy and, furthermore, human freedom's character as autonomous.

7 Lonergan, *Verbum*, 47.

8 Lonergan, 22n45.

9 Lonergan, 51.

10 Lonergan, 47.

11 Lonergan, 47.

observed "in all concepts."[12] But here one runs up against the limits of metaphysical analysis alone. Lonergan argues that Thomas seems to have noticed such a limitation in his effort to follow Aristotle's lead on questions of conceptualization and its ground, for Thomas abandoned *to ti ên einai* and its Latin equivalent.[13] Aristotle, on Lonergan's account, distinguished essence (*to ti estin*) from form (*to ti ên einai*). *To ti ên einai* functions in the logical order for Aristotle. It is that which undergirds what Lonergan calls "the core of identical meaning" between a defined term and its definition or concept. But *to ti ên einai* can also directly name the formal cause of a particular thing. Thus, form is not strictly identical with essence for Aristotle. It plays an integral role in the kind of scientific, essential definition in which concepts consist. By this procedure, however, it remains opaque how understanding why this concrete thing is the thing it is should produce a concept of that kind of thing.

Lonergan notes that Thomas only rarely invokes the Latin equivalent of *to ti ên einai* outside of the commentaries on Aristotle. When Thomas makes reference to it there, he often identifies it with essential definition itself, though sometimes more specifically with the ground of essential definition.[14] Lonergan thinks that Aristotle's by-the-way efforts to isolate the concrete apprehension of form from the abstract articulation of essential definition in concepts proved unsatisfactory to Thomas and that Thomas consequently chose a different strategy. Lonergan explains the difficulty:

> The Aristotelian term [*to ti ên einai*] was a logical effort to isolate understanding and form, and one has only to consider the difficulties of such isolation to grasp why Aquinas dropped this Aristotelian effort as abortive and proceeded on lines of his own. Because the act of understanding—the *intelligere proprie*—is prior to, and cause of, conceptualization, because expression is only through conceptualization, any attempt to fix the act of understanding, except by way of introspective description, involves its own partial failure; for any such attempt is an expression, and expression is no longer understanding and already concept.[15]

12 Lonergan, 47.

13 Lonergan, 30–38.

14 Lonergan, 36. In one instance, it is identified with formal cause (Thomas Aquinas, *Sententia libri Metaphysicae*, lib. 6, lect. 2, §764 [paragraph numbers from the Marietti edition]).

15 Lonergan, *Verbum*, 38.

In other words, Lonergan thinks that Thomas discovered a conceptualist liability to any purely logical ideal and procedure on questions of knowledge. Aristotle, though the progenitor of that logical ideal in many ways (through the wide-ranging influence of the *Posterior Analytics*), does not exhibit the rarified logicism of so much scholasticism. And so Thomas, Lonergan thinks, was able to turn instead to Aristotle's emphasis on the role of diagrams in mathematical discovery, and thereby augment the logical technique of metaphysical analysis with introspective, psychological description. "We can all experience in ourselves that, when we try to understand something," Thomas writes, "we form for ourselves images, by way of examples, in which as it were we inspect what we desire to understand."[16] The need for diagrams in mathematics (whereby necessary and immobile forms are represented and re-represented) provided Thomas his heuristic for what would be more generally the case: abstract definitions of things are derived from their multiple representation in concrete things.[17] In what follows, I will follow Thomas and Lonergan in pairing these techniques, metaphysical analysis and psychological description, toward three complementary ends. First, the pairing will help concretize the causal relation between *intelligere* and the *emanatio intelligibilis* of the concept. Second, it will clarify the function of the concept in rationality considered more widely, from its origin in sense to its termination in true judgments of fact to the development of a classical *scientia*. Finally, it will prepare me to speak articulately in the next chapter and with detailed control about the rational element in willing, and by extension in free human action. Again, for my purposes, the most important insight will be to see how *the rationality of human volition places meaning in a constitutive role vis-à-vis human action.*

I have already noted that concepts depend on intellectual operation to bring them to act. Human intellect, however, is not perpetually in act like God's. "Angelic, and still more, divine knowledge is exclusively that sort of thing, a continuous blaze of the light of understanding." We human beings

16 *Summa theologiae*, 1, q. 84, a. 7 c.

17 "When the geometer argues about two triangles similar in all respects, he deals with two triangles, and not with some one triangle; but if they are similar in all respects, then they do not differ in idea, in essence, in nature, or in any accidental characteristic; there is mere material multiplication. In Aristotelian and in Thomist psychology, the second 'one' or the second 'triangle' is accounted for, not by a second concept, but by the reflection of intellect back to phantasm where the many instances of the one idea are represented" (Lonergan, *Verbum*, 40). See also Thomas Aquinas, *Sententia libri De anima*, III, lect. 8, §713, and *Summa theologiae*, 1, q. 86, a. 1; q. 84, a. 7.

"shout our rare 'Eurekas' with Archimedes," Lonergan writes, "but for the most part we have to reason."[18] What brings human intellect into act, to operation? For Lonergan, following Thomas, it is *quidditas rei materialis*. How does this come about? In and through phantasm illuminated by agent intellect. But, again, it is easy enough to trot out these terms, to exposit their logical relations and metaphysical determinations, but remain obtuse to their meaning. So, I will break down cognitional process along two lines: according to a metaphysical analysis and a parallel psychological description.

As I noted in the discussion of application in chapter 2, it is not sufficient for a cause that it be in act to produce its effect. It must also be in proper disposition and relation to the material of this effect, as a lit match cannot ignite a candle's wick if each would remain in its opposed corner of a room. So it is too with the agent object of understanding. The intelligibility in act of a material being cannot bring the intellect to act unless it is in the right relation to the intellect. *Quidditas rei materialis*, by virtue of its substantial materiality, comes into relation with or disposition to other beings in space and time. The intellect, of course, is immaterial, and so does not come into relation with or disposition to its objects spatiotemporally. But besides intellect, there is sense. Sense is intentional, but also materially dependent on its bodily organ. Integral to the process by which intellect comes to act is the application of sensible objects to the sense powers of a human being, whereby the sensible in act (i.e., *as sensed*) serves as agent object to sight or hearing, and so forth, bringing them to act, to operation. Thus sensibility in its intentional rather than material mode—that is, the sensible-as-sensed—can bring *quidditas rei materialis* into the proper relation with the intellect so that its role as agent object might be realized.

But the spatiotemporal disposition of material being to sense organs is not the only instance of application needful to bring intellect to act. Nor is the immaterial relation of sensibility in act to the intellectual power sufficient. So also there is needed a further immaterial, indeed properly spiritual, relation and disposition. This, in my view, is the metaphysical function of the agent intellect as a specifically efficient potency in the intellectual faculty.[19] The

---

18 Lonergan, *Verbum*, 45. See also Thomas Aquinas, *Super Ioannem*, c. 1, lect. 1; *Super III Sententiarum*, d. 23, q. 1, a. 2.

19 "The distinction between agent intellect and possible intellect is a distinction between an efficient potency that produces and a natural potency that receives" (Lonergan, *Verbum*, 149).

agent intellect is that which brings the intellect itself into right disposition to and relation with the quiddity, the intelligibility-in-potency now present intentionally in and through sensation. The effect of this disposing function falls not only upon the intellect in an illuminating and preparatory fashion, as when we feel the desirous tension expressed by our genuine questions, but also upon the sensations themselves, organizing and selecting among sensations that which is potentially relevant for understanding. It is the effect of this organizing and selecting function that distinguishes phantasms properly so called from mere sensations. Once the proper material, intentional, and spiritual applications have been effected, the intelligible in act immanent in the sensible in act and illuminated by the light of agent intellect may bring the intellect to act.[20] Then what is sensed is also understood.

Alongside this metaphysical analysis of powers, operations, objects, and application, so too it is helpful to consider a description of the same process under its psychological—which is to say, conscious—aspect. One has perhaps had the experience of "spacing out" or being "lost in thought." In such experiences, we do not cease to be conscious, nor do we cease to have consciousness of the flow of sensation. We see, hear, smell, taste, and feel during such episodes. But it is so little organized, so little selected, deemed of so little relevance to our waxing or waning curiosity that it goes un-attended-to and largely unremembered. If, rather than fading into twilight consciousness, one puzzles and if one puzzles not over the imagined, but over the presently perceived, then one finds the pattern of experience highly organized, highly selective according to the heuristic force of some incipient question. This question is operative, one may recall in retrospect, as a criterion of relevance that tunes out the hum of the HVAC system, but sees the lines of some diagram or hears the words of the lecture in sharp relief. Such are phantasms, not as a function or object of metaphysical analysis, but as experienced. One may tinker with the relevant sensible matter for as long as the tension of inquisitive consciousness can be maintained. One may reread one's notes or ask the professor to repeat herself. One may pivot from example to example to example, endeavoring to understand that of which they are, in fact, examples. Alternatively, one may lose heart and go in search of some anesthetizing distraction from the discomfort of inquisitive consciousness, whether in the television, the bottle, or the chatter

---

20 As to any controversy over whether *sentire*, *intelligere*, and even *velle* can be a *pati*, see Lonergan, 139–43.

of social media. But also one may also be relieved of this tension by the sudden—indeed, instantaneous—shift from perplexity to apprehension, from not-understanding to understanding. This transition is from understanding as a live and desired possibility to understanding as a reality of one's conscious experience. It can result from a change in disposition among the sensed (perhaps one reorganizes the diagrams or fixes upon a new example), but it can also result from a change in disposition internal to one's consciousness (a renewed attentiveness, a rephrasing of the operative question, or a newfound willingness to realize the significance of what one has seen or heard all along). In any case, the effect is the same: the synchronic "flash" of insight, of understanding, of *intelligere*.

Having considered both metaphysically and psychologically the process by which intellect comes to act, I am nearly ready now to turn back to the basic rationality that consists in the process by which intellect in act produces a concept or *verbum mentis*. The production and procession of the *verbum mentis* in rational process, keep in mind, will ground the constitutive function of meaning in free human action that is central to the modern problem of the supernatural. But first I must make a few notes. Recall that *intelligere* is, as far as it goes, a knowing. It is the immediate apprehension of its object as immanent in phantasms. This immediacy, of course, is an integral element in the realism proper to any genuinely Thomist theory of knowledge. However, this immediacy has certain limitations that can be enumerated both metaphysically and by psychological description. Metaphysically considered, that which is immediately related can admit of no further application, for any change in relation would deprive the intellect of its agent object, and so that on which it depends for its act. In this way, the human act of understanding considered in itself and in isolation cannot be called 'rational,' for once it is in act, it does not admit of process. The act of understanding, even if considered as the actuality of a movement from potency to act, is a synchronic moment or element in knowledge that cannot serve as part of a diachronic process. To borrow Augustine's language from the *Confessions,* the act of understanding is a pure and complete intending that does not admit of the distention required for consciousness of temporal duration.[21] Without temporal duration, of course, there can be no diachronic process. Finally, intelligibility is distinguished from the sensible, and so is insensible

---

21 Augustine, *Confessions* 11, §§26–27.

per se. Consequently, it cannot of itself be the agent object for the human intellect and so cannot produce the effects in the human intellect in which an intellectual process would consist.

In addition to these metaphysical limitations, the immediate grasp of quiddity by an act of understanding has limits that can be described psychologically. What is immediately experienced is experienced indistinctly.[22] The experience of understanding, the "flash" of insight, is of the understanding itself and also of the understood. One does in fact experience, is conscious of a knowing in the experience of understanding. Still, the act and its object are not distinguished in the experiencing, as seeing is at once experienced as a seeing and also always as a seeing-this. The immediacy of the apprehension and the apprehended makes the apprehension itself, as conscious and intentional, necessarily indistinct. For, if it were distinct, it would not be immediate but rather mediated by the difference by which it is distinguished.[23]

Moreover, the change from potentially understanding to actually understanding is a synchronic, punctual transformation from one state to an opposed state without gradation or overlap. The experience of this transition can be attended to, but as attended to it is no longer immediate, but mediated by the selective (and, as Eugene Gendlin would remind, symbol-facilitated) function of attention. The experience of this transition can be remembered, but as remembered it is likewise no longer immediate, but mediated both by the selective function of attention as well as the dynamics of representing what is past *as past*. As immediate and punctual, the act of understanding is not itself available to serve as the object of inquiry's tension, and so not available to the on-going experience of intellectual process. But intellectual process does not terminate with insight into phantasm, with the immediate grasp of the intelligible in the sensible. As Lonergan writes, "For human understanding, though it has its object in the phantasm and knows it in the phantasm, yet is

22 On the indistinctness of what is immediately experienced see Eugene Gendlin, *Experiencing and the Creation of Meaning* (Evanston, IL: Northwestern University Press, 1997). See also Charles Sanders Peirce, "Questions concerning Certain Faculties Claimed for Man," and "Some Consequences of Four Incapacities," in *The Essential Peirce: Selected Philosophical Writings–*, ed. Nathan Houser and Christian Kloesel, vol. 1, *1867–1893* (Bloomington: Indiana University Press, 1992), 11–55.

23 Robert Sokolowski's centering of distinction-making in philosophical method is in this way also a centering of the mediating function of meaning in philosophy. See "The Method of Philosophy: Making Distinctions," *Review of Metaphysics* 51, no. 3 (March 1998): 515–32.

not content with an object in this state. It pivots on itself to produce for itself another object that is the inner word as *ratio, intentio, definitio, quod quid est*. And this pivoting and production … is an operation of rational consciousness."[24]

With that, I am now prepared to consider this production of the concept, this procession of the *verbum mentis* in some detail according both to a metaphysical analysis and to a psychological description. Metaphysically speaking, there are two kinds of process. There is the emergence of a perfection in and from what is perfected, such as the emergence of an act of understanding in and from the intellect considered above. This is a *processio operationis*.[25] But there is also the procession of the *verbum mentis*, of a concept from intelligence in act, from an act of understanding. This is a *processio operati*. It is the emergence of one thing from another. But lest one think of concepts as extrinsically related to the understanding that produces them, I need to also distinguish two kinds of acts. There are those acts that consist in movement whereby, once the movement is complete, the act ceases. "One cannot at once be walking a given distance and have walked it, be being cured and have been cured, be learning something and have learned it."[26] Such an act is called an *actus imperfecti*. What is moved is in potency, what is in potency is imperfect, and so that movement is the act of the imperfect.[27] Thus, the reasoning that gave rise to the act of understanding, the tinkering with the phantasm under the guidance of inquiry's tension and agent intellect's illumination, all of this is a movement in the sense of *actus imperfecti*. The act of understanding itself, however, is "the act of something that exists in act, inasmuch as it exists in act," and "the act of something brought to completion inasmuch as it is complete."[28] Such is an *actus perfecti*. Such acts are not intrinsically temporal, though we shall see that this transcendence of temporality allows them to have a governing function in ongoing intellectual process as rational.

Concepts proceed by a *processio operati*. They emerge from something else in act rather than as an act in and from something in potency. The *verbum mentis* proceeds from an act of understanding and is produced by that understanding

---

24 Lonergan, *Verbum*, 48.

25 Lonergan, 107.

26 Lonergan, 114.

27 See *Super I Sententiarum*, d. 3, q. 1, a. 1, ad 1m; *In III De anima*, lect. 12, §766.

28 Lonergan, *Verbum*, 114. See also *Super IV Sententiarum*, d. 49, q. 3, a. 1 sol. 1, ob. 2; *Summa theologiae*, 1, q. 18, a. 3, ad 1m; 1-2, q. 31, a. 2, ad 1m; 3, q. 21, a. 1, ad 3m; *Super III Sententiarum*, d. 31, q. 2, a. 1 sol. 2.

as an effect.[29] This act-from-act procession, by the way, is why Thomas can deploy *emanation intelligibilis* as his analogue for the procession of the Word in the *Prima Pars*, for it implies no potentiality in the procession of the divine person. However, this procession is, as I said, not only intelligible but also intelligent. It is the basic rationality that belongs to concepts. Consequently, the procession of the concept must be simultaneous with the act of understanding.[30] If the concept itself is to have the character of rationality in its intelligent and intelligible dependence on an act of understanding, then the concept must also express the *content* of the act of understanding.[31] Again, this is part of its fittingness as an analogy for the consubstantiality of Father and Son in God. As the inner word has entirely the same intellectual substance as the act of insight that produces it, so too the eternal Word is entirely the same substance as the Father that begets Him.

But in the production of the concept, both of the above conditions (simultaneity and consubstantiality) are met because *intelligere* is, in and of itself, an *actus perfecti*. Because in us the act of understanding is the act of a temporal nature, so long as it is in act, it endures through time in act. As enduring in act simultaneously with the procession of the *verbum mentis*, *intelligere* thus governs the production of concepts. This simultaneity of an *actus perfecti* with what is produced from that act by *processio operati* will prove, when I turn to consider the rationality of will as a rational appetite, integral to my account of the relationship between willing of ends and willing of means.[32] This intelligent governance of concepts founds their rationality, as I noted above. They emerge according to a law, but also according to that which is the source of intelligible law. This governance of the concept by understanding also allows the concepts themselves to serve as agent objects

---

29 *De veritate*, q. 4, a. 2 c; q. 3, a. 2; q. 4, a. 2, ad 7m; *Summa theologiae*, 1, q. 34, a. 1, ad 3m.

30 *De potentia*, q. 8, a. 1 c; q. 9, a. 5 c.

31 *De veritate*, q. 4, a. 2 c; *Summa theologiae*, 1, q. 34, a. 1 c.

32 It may also have relevance, when I turn to this governing function's analogue in volitional consciousness, for Lonergan's notion of a "dynamic state," as he develops it later in his career. See Lonergan, *Method in Theology*, 2nd ed., ed. Robert M. Doran and John D. Dadosky, CWL 14 (Toronto: University of Toronto Press, 2017), 102–6, 112–18, and *passim*. For the reintroduction of this notion into the context of psychological analogy and Trinitarian theology, see "Christology Today: Methodological Reflections," in *A Third Collection*, 2nd ed., ed. Robert M. Doran and John D. Dadosky, CWL 16 (Toronto: University of Toronto Press, 2017), 91.

in the intellectual process of deductive reasoning in a manner that is, by extension, likewise rational. Inference is rational not just when it proceeds according to logical rules but when it proceeds according to the autonomy of the intellectual operation from which intelligible law issues.

If the production of the concept, however, is considered only in terms of metaphysical mechanics, a point of central importance will be lost. When considered only in terms of the conditions of possible causal efficacy, it remains unclear why the procession of a *verbum mentis* should be likened unto the speaking (*dicere*) of a word at all. Where my emphasis on rationality as a process ultimately undergirds my claim that the modern problem is irreducibly diachronic, my contention that the procession of the *verbum mentis* is an act of meaning founds my claim that the modern problem of the supernatural is irreducibly, radically hermeneutical. The following provides the psychological description and analysis of concept production on which that claim rests.

As the coming-to-act of understanding is experienced, so too is the procession of the *verbum mentis*.[33] Above I noted that *intelligere* is experienced immediately and synchronically. Still, this act is intentional and so it has an object, which is to say a content, an "about." This content or "about" can be considered in its objective aspect and we can enunciate this consideration by the question, "What did I understand?" Nor is this question unfamiliar to the inquisitive, who having labored with the phantasm and the tension of inquiry, who perhaps basked briefly in the relief of tension provided by insight, and yet who may recall the momentary terror that accompanies putting this question to one's self or having it put to one by a teacher or colleague. This is a dramatic moment in intellectual process, for the flash of insight can, if neglected, fade into obscurity and its content can be "lost." What did you understand? "Ah, damn, I lost it. I can no longer remember." Fortunately, this question has an answer. The "about" of our insights can be formulated, can be expressed both to ourselves and to others.[34]

This question, though it verbally resembles a question for understanding (*quid est?*), is in fact a question for recognition and recollection. It cannot be

---

33 "Meaning is experienced" (Gendlin, *Experiencing*, 44).

34 My analysis here owes much to Gendlin's *Experiencing and the Creation of Meaning,* especially on the role of and function of symbols in making felt-meanings distinct and available for an ongoing process of inquiry. See *Experiencing*, 90–137. See also my "Insight Is a Body-Feeling: Experiencing Our Understanding," *Heythrop Journal* 57, no. 3 (May 2016): 461–72.

a question for understanding, since what it asks after is already understood. Rather, it anticipates and directs attention to something in consciousness that is a) distinct and distinguishable among the various elements in the flow of conscious experience, b) is both intelligible and expressive of conscious intelligence, and c) is available for further reasoning and intellectual procedure. In brief, it is a question ordered to, directed at, consciousness of the *verbum mentis*. The concept, then, is both distinguishable from the act of insight, but it is also distinguishable in experience from the immediacy of that act. The concept distinguishes the understood from the understanding, but nonetheless distinguishes it *as* understood. If I am attentive to *that* I have understood, the concept selects *what* I have understood. In this way, the concept is significant in consciousness. It both carries and refers to the content of intelligence in act, of understanding. It is, in other words, the product of an act of *meaning*. This meaning, because it means what is both intelligible and intelligent (i.e., the substance of intellect in act), does not have the extrinsic significance of the material sign, which signifies, refers to, and carries meaning by convention. Rather, it is the primitive and basic form of meaning. It is important not to miss that *the basic rationality of the concept consists in a mediation of meaning*. In the next chapter, this mediating function in rational process will, in turn, found the constitutive function of meaning in the free human actions that issue from volitional process. That constitutive function is at the heart of the modern problem of the supernatural.

The above only considers the production of the concept as distinct, as generative of distinctness, and as an expression of intelligence. This act of meaning that produces the concept, the procession of the *verbum mentis* is primarily and substantially intellectual. But it is at the same time an integrally imaginal, phantasmatic construction. If it were not, the concept could not play a role in our ongoing intellectual procedure. It could not enter into our processes of logical inference, it could not contribute to the generation and derivation of a *scientia*, because intellectual process comes into act through insight into phantasm, through grasping form in images. We do not stop with the sense that we might "really have it," nor even with the enunciation of what it is we have in answer to our questions. No, the work of intellect continues. We wonder, for example, whether what we have understood in the phantasms is correct, that is, whether it is adequate as an answer to our question(s) and whether that adequacy owes to the truth. Where above I considered inquiry as asking *quid sit?* now recall how it also asks *an sit?*

Understanding that there is sufficient evidence, apprehending the virtually unconditioned in which true judgment consists is itself an operation of the intellect, brought about by the composition of the phantasmatic element of the evidence and the phantasmatic expression of understanding that is the concept under the light of agent intellect in a further insight into the correctness of the understanding expressed in the concept.[35]

This reflective *intelligere* also produces a *verbum mentis*, only it has the much simpler character of an affirmative or negative declaration: it "speaks" yes or no, true or false, correct or incorrect. Moreover, where we judge our understandings correct and so true, we wonder further: what broader significance does this knowledge have? Where does it fit within what else I have come to know and, heuristically, what I hope to discover through further inquiry. Such is the phantasmatic role of concepts in the generation of a science, not through the automatic derivation of implications by the mechanical application of rules but by yet-more-inquiry and yet-more-understanding, by asking more questions about these intelligently intelligible *verba* and the further insights that answer them.

Why can the concept play such a role, mediating meaningfully between some initial act of *intelligere* and subsequent reflective inquiry, reflective understanding, and eventually the derivation of a science? Again, the answer lies in the originary act of all intellectual procedure: advertence to phantasm, the illumination of the agent intellect, and the grasp of intelligibility in images. The *verbum mentis* expresses what understanding apprehends in a mode suitable for its role in the ongoing process of inquiry. Again, this mode is, broadly speaking, phantasmatic. The concept is, in addition to being intelligible and an expression of intelligence, *also* an immanent intellectual image, for our reasoning depends essentially on the sensible or imaginable. It functions on some loose analogy with the diagram, providing a mental object "in which the intelligible species shines forth as an exemplar."[36]

But some images are more suitable to showing forth their intelligibility than others. As any student can attest, many supposedly intellectual images are too ambiguous, able to be interpreted in too many differing respects.

---

35 Lonergan, *Verbum*, 71–78; see also *Insight: a Study of Human Understanding*, ed. Frederick E. Crowe and Robert M. Doran, CWL 3 (Toronto: University of Toronto Press, 1992), 296–340.

36 *Summa contra Gentiles*, 2, c. 73, §38.

And so the concept is a properly intellectual image, specially constructed to convey immanently the substance of the understanding it expresses and *only* the substance of the understanding it expresses. It is precisely in this respect that *intelligere* as *actus perfecti* governs the production of concepts: it accrues only those phantasmatic elements strictly relevant to the intelligible species expressed thereby. Still, where the quiddity apprehended is unitary, the phantasmatic is analogous to the material, and so is multiple. Thus, *the concept is a construction,* both of the intelligible with the phantasmatic but also of available, relevant phantasmatic materials. The concept can make present the intelligible species distinctly and in accord with the fact that what is known no longer needs to be discovered by fresh insight, but only recognized or recalled habitually. The intelligible species so recalled, we may proceed to further inquire about, to verify, to synthesize into a science what we know by insight into phantasms. Without the constructed *verba*, we would understand in the immediate flash of apprehension but could not reason from our understanding, could not verify the correctness of our insights, and so could not develop our knowledge unto a science. What we have understood would not be available to us to recall or to be carried into our reasoning processes.

Even though the *verbum mentis* has an imaginal quality to it, it is not, in Lonergan's language, just some "impoverished replica" of the thing understood. "Abstraction in all its essential moments is enriching."[37] It need not resemble the properties of what is understood, as the word *fire* is neither hot nor bright but only allows us to recall what we have understood about what is hot and bright, and why it is so. Again, one may try, through words that are neither hot nor bright themselves, to evoke the heat and light of a flame, but the definition of combustion will eschew such descriptions. The search for essential definition that gives rise to concepts does not want to know what fire is like, but why combustion is itself. Anything irrelevant to expressing our understanding of the essence of combustion is excluded from the definition. Now, this verbal parsimony is an effect of the prior parsimony of autonomous intellectual process. What the *verbum mentis* carries forward from an act of understanding expresses what was apprehended intellectually and *only* what was apprehended intellectually. If one knows the essential

---

37 Lonergan, *Insight*, 111–12: "So far from being a mere impoverishment of the data of sense, abstraction in all its essential moments is enriching. Its first moment is an enriching anticipation of an intelligibility to be added to sensible presentations: there is something to be known by insight."

definition of a circle (to return again with Thomas and Aristotle to the role of diagrams in mathematics) one can see the uniformity of a plane curve and also apprehend the necessity that its radii be equal. But only the uniformity can be seen. The necessity is known by an act of understanding, not an act of perception. Consequently, the definition of a circle includes equality of radii and neglects to mention the uniformity of the curve produced thereby. In this way, the abstractness of concepts does not impoverish the rich experience of concrete objects, because concepts do not aim to provide a degraded picture of absent things. Instead, concepts inject into the flow of experience the fruits of intellectual apprehension and so enrich the field of consciousness with rationally constructed intellectual images, with its *verba*. Moreover, by expressing intelligence in act with a basic and essential rationality, concepts link together acts of *intelligere* into the derived intellectual processes in which logical inference, empirical verification, and scientific elaboration all consist.

Conclusion

Human rationality consists in an autonomous intellectual process integrally mediated by meaning and productive of intelligently and phantasmatically constructed *verba* or concepts. Human rationality, because it consists in a process, is irreducibly diachronic. Because the process is intelligent and not merely intelligible, it is neither mechanical nor automatic, but rather autonomous. Because the nature of intellectual act consists in the immediate and so indistinct apprehension of form, intellectual process is mediated by some distinct expression of what has been apprehended. The expression of these mediating objects (*verba* or concepts) is consequently an act of meaning. Finally, because subsequent acts of understanding have the same nature as preceding acts—that is, they have *quidditas rei materialis* for their agent object— the mediating objects of human rationality bear, really are borne by some phantasmatic element in addition to their intelligible content. This allows them to be properly disposed as agent object for subsequent intellectual acts in ongoing intellectual process, including the acts of true judgment, the reflective understandings in which knowledge of being consists, and the development of *scientia*. But the intelligent combination of diverse elements into a unity is a construction, a *factum*. In conceptualization, then, we may see how rationality, autonomy, mediation, *poiesis*, and knowledge function integrally.

CHAPTER 10

RATIONALITY, MEANING, AND FREEDOM

Permit me to set down again the main point of the previous chapter: human rationality consists in an intellectual process integrally mediated by meaning and productive of constructed *verba* or concepts. Human rationality, because it consists in a process, is irreducibly diachronic. Because the process is intellectual and not merely intelligible, it is neither mechanical nor automatic, but rather autonomous. Because the nature of intellectual act consists in the immediate and so indistinct apprehension of form, intellectual process is mediated by some distinct expression of what has been apprehended. The expression of these mediating objects (*verba* or *concepts*) is consequently an act of meaning. Finally, because subsequent acts of understanding have the same nature as preceding acts—that is, they have *quidditas rei materialis* for their agent object—the mediating objects of human rationality bear, in addition to their intelligible content, some phantasmatic element. This allows them to be properly disposed as agent object for subsequent intellectual acts, including the acts of true judgment in which knowledge of being consists. But the intelligent combination of diverse elements into a unity is a construction, a *factum*. In conceptualization, then, one can see how rationality, autonomy, mediation, *poiesis*, and knowledge function integrally.

The Rationality of the Will

My central preoccupation remains. In what way is the will a *rational* appetite and how does this rationality ground the liberty of human action? How does rationality as conceived above modify the tending in which the movement of the will consists and the actions follow from it?

Thomas repeatedly affirms that the operation of the will proceeds from a word in the intellect.[1] Thus, in addition to reflective insight into the verity of the understanding expressed by our concepts and the development of a *scientia* from the systematization of our true understandings, we may append "willing" to the list of subsequent operations for which a *verbum mentis* would serve as agent object. It is tempting to skip to the end of our inquiry and affirm that the will is a rational appetite with the borrowed, basic rationality of the concept. Thus, acts of the will would be considered free according to the borrowed autonomy of the intellectual process that gave rise to them. And this is true as far as it goes. What remains opaque is whether a remote and borrowed rationality (and so autonomy) is sufficient to render the tending in which our rational appetite consists both rational and free.

A genuine, albeit preliminary advance is made by recognizing that a certain freedom is bestowed on our rational appetite by the concept from which its operation follows. The concept has been generated by an autonomous intellectual process, and so, as object of the act of willing, it is willed in accord with the autonomous principle on which it depends. This includes both the autonomy of the agent intellect at work in the process of reasoning over the phantasms and the autonomy of construction or *poiesis* at work in the expression of what is understood through the compound of its intelligible species and the phantasmatic element to which it is joined.[2] But the will is essentially ordered to the *bonum in genere*, and so is itself generative of the intelligible "ought" pertaining to willing any particular good. Thus, one anticipates an autonomy proper to the will itself.

Since the concept is the agent object of the will in act, one may ask whether there are conditions for the application of the concept to the will.[3]

---

1 See Bernard Lonergan, *Verbum: Word and Idea in Aquinas*, ed. Frederick E. Crowe and Robert M. Doran (Toronto: University of Toronto Press, 1997), 109n20. See also Thomas Aquinas, *Super I Sententiarum*, d. 11, q. 1, a. 1, ad 4m; d. 27, q. 2, a. 1 sol.; *In III De anima*, lect. 4, §§634–3; *Summa contra Gentiles*, 4, c. 24, §12; 4, c. 19, §8; *De potentia*, q. 9, a. 9, ad 3m; q. 10, a. 2 c, ad 4m, ad 7m; a. 4 c; a. 5 c; *Summa theologiae*, 1, q. 27, a. 3, ad 3m; q. 36, a. 2 c.

2 Be careful here not to conflate the dependence of the agent intellect on God for illumination with a *heteronomy* immanent in willing. Recall that what divine agency provides to agents in the first instance is the act by which they are both existentially and essentially themselves. That the agent intellect receives its immanent norms from God does not at all refute the reality that these norms are its own, and so it is literally autonomous.

3 See Bernard Lonergan, "God's Knowledge and Will," in *Early Latin Theology*, ed.

Because the human being is temporal, there must be some application of the agent object of even spiritual acts to the matter of its potentially operated effect. Thus, as with the *processio operationis* of *intelligere* in the intellect, there is a preparatory disposition of both the power and of the object.[4] The will, then, disposes itself to the good immanent in the concept by its essential tending toward the good in general, but more specifically and concretely by its antecedent habits. Still even more concretely, I would suggest that the will also disposes itself toward particular verified concepts in a manner analogous to reflective inquiry and that can also be expressed in a question: ought this be? Perhaps the concept, constructed with an eye toward verification, is also well disposed toward the evaluative function of the will, but then perhaps not. In either case, one might say that the concept itself must be brought into proper disposition to the will by a felicitous (re)construction, coordinating its phantasmatic and valuative aspects. The concept, in other words, must be rendered meaningful in an evaluative and not just intellectual sense.[5] These prior dispositive conditions having been met, then, the good incipiently apprehended in the verified concept may bring the will to act such that an act of *velle* emerges in the will. Thus, for Lonergan, "as proceeding from the inner word, [the act of love is] *'processio operati.'"*[6]

From another angle, though, *velle* is disanalogous to the act of understanding from which a concept proceeds. Considered not as the term of a process of something like inquiry, and so as the term of an *actus imperfecti*, but instead considered as an operative operation of the will, and so as an *actus perfecti* in itself, an act of willing is more properly analogized to the reflective *intelligere* from which a judgment of fact proceeds. The reflective act of intellect consists in an apprehension that is expressed by a *verbum* as well, that is, by an affirmative "yes" or a negative "no" with regard to the concept whose content it borrows. This affirmative act and expression, then, are the knowing in which cognitional process properly terminates. The

---

Robert M. Doran and H. Daniel Monsour, CWL 19 (Toronto: University of Toronto Press, 2011), 321.

4 "The act of love with respect to an end is, as proceeding from the will, *'processio operationis'"* (Lonergan, *Verbum*, 148).

5 "There can be a twofold apprehension, either of the simple truth or of the truth as it is expanded to take in the good and the fitting—and this latter is perfect apprehension" (*Super I Sententiarum*, d. 27, q. 2, a. 1 sol.).

6 Lonergan, *Verbum*, 148.

reflective act of understanding, as *actus perfecti,* endures through time to govern subsequent intellectual procedure in accord with what is actively known and contemplated. By analogy to the affirmative act of the intellect in a judgment of fact, the act of willing is an *actus perfecti* that a) endures through time and governs subsequent volitional procedures, b) has a borrowed content in what is meant by the concept it "affirms" or "negates," and c) is basically polar in its response, consisting in an unqualified "affirmation," a total "negation," or a spectrally delimited state of intensity tending toward one or the other.

Velle is further analogous to a judgment of fact insofar as the movement, the tending in which appetite and aversion consist are mediated by an uttered "yes" and "no." In other words, willing in act and as expressed in a judgment of value is analogous to reflective *intelligere* in act and expressed in a judgment of fact ("this is so/correct"). Still, it is only analogous, for the affirmative act and expression of the will in act is also a *motive*—a proximate, proper, and rational principle of movement. A judgment of fact may occasion further intellectual procedure, but only extrinsically and *per accidens.* Willing in act and expressed in a judgment of value, by contrast, is the per se cause of some movement. In turn, the good immanent in the concept is in general the agent object of willing in act, but thereby also a *mobile,* a rationally generated "object-for-which" of a movement.[7]

A number of problems present themselves at this point. Is the b*orrowed* autonomy of the concept, or even the proper autonomy of the judgment of value's "ought" adequate to render the movement following from *velle* a free act? If the knowledge expressed in the verified concept is of what *is,* then is the action that follows from an act of the will and a judgment of value superfluous? If the good apprehended in a judgment of value *is,* what could need to be done? What is the movement that manifests the will in act? As knowledge is not a single intellectual act but a compound of acts in an intellectual process, neither is willing a single movement but a compound of

---

7 Lonergan, *The Triune God: Systematics,* ed. Robert M. Doran and H. Daniel Monsour, trans. Michael G. Shields, CWL 12 (Toronto: University of Toronto Press, 2007), 673: "Therefore, the essential notion of will consists in this, that it is an inclination that follows the intellect, so that it not only wills the object presented to it by the intellect but also wills it on account of the motive or end for which the intellect judges that the object ought to be willed." On the function of mobiles and motives in the emergence of action in consciousness, see Maurice Blondel, *Action (1893): Essay on a Critique of Life and a Science of Practice,* trans. Oliva Blanchette (Notre Dame, IN: University of Notre Dame Press, 1984), 112–19.

movements in a volitional process. First, from the *actus perfecti* of the will's operation—that is, from the act of willing—there proceeds the affirmative or negative utterance of the judgment of value. By the mediation of this affirmative or negative word, the *actus imperfecti* of deliberation about means to the willed good proceeds, which is itself unto the *actus perfecti* of willing the selected means themselves, unto the final practical judgment, which is in turn unto the further *actus imperfecti* by which the whole person labors to realize his or her intention.[8]

Let us consider the above process in more detail. The object of *velle*'s motivation is, so to speak, being-conceived apprehended according to its being-valuable, being-good. This apprehension, as I said, is manifest in a mediating word and motivated movement taking responsibility for the being of such a being-conceived and being-valued according to the autonomous "ought" generated by the will in act (understood on analogy with the being-in-act of intelligible law generated by *intelligere*).[9] This movement from the operation of the will mediated by the judgment of value is first to the discernment of means. Such discernment is governed by the *actus perfecti* of willing the good and mediated by a judgment of value. Under the government of this enduring operation and through the judgment of value's mediating *verbum*, a subordinate intellectual process hypothetically constructs means that would be both effective and feasible. Alternative means must be evaluated, but this process of evaluation also proceeds under the enduring governance of the original act of willing. This process applies the good apprehended and affirmed as well as its borrowed intellectual content, to the deliberative process, but also places it under the dual autonomy of intellectual process and of the will's "ought."

This deliberative process, when considered intellectually, can go on indefinitely. There can be no apodictic argument that concludes it with certainty. Any apodictic argument would require affirmation of the fulfilled conditions that would render the hypothetical relation between means and the end virtually unconditioned.[10] However, so long as deliberation continues, one

---

8 See *Summa theologiae*, 1, q. 19, a. 4: "for the inclination to put in act what has been conceived by the intellect pertains to the will."

9 Conversely, the will, its proper disposition in the form of habit, and the act of willing the end are prior conditions for the emergence of an act of willing the means. See Lonergan, "God's Knowledge and Will," 317.

10 For the notion of the virtually unconditioned grasped by a judgment of fact,

of the necessary conditions remains necessarily unfulfilled: a decision to enact the means motivated by the end intended. What fulfills this condition, allowing the practical project to go forward? Initially, it is the will-in-act moving itself to terminate the process of deliberation and utter a final practical judgment as to the selected means. This willing of means is, of course, also a *velle* and so an *actus perfecti*. Accordingly, it manifests its affirmation first in an uttered "yes" that communicates the motivation mobilized by a conceptualized good. In this case, the good conceived consists in those means good for realizing what ought to be. Again, this decision is not just a notional "yes," but also a motivated movement. Once means have been selected to an end intended, there remains only to decide, "yes, I will act," and so to go forth into matter, and to shepherd into being what ought to be. The compound *actus perfecti* of willing the means to the end intended endures through time, governing the *actus imperfecti* by which the entire embodied person moves to bring about the good as an existing effect. But to will this compound of volitional acts in an ordered series is to will not only that order but also the principle of order for its own sake as *value*, the terminal object of willing's "ought."[11]

It is a point of philosophical doctrine that this complete, compound movement of the will is free. But is it only free because it borrows the autonomy of the concept on which it follows? Or is it ultimately free because of the autonomy of the "ought" the will in act generates? The freedom of the complete, compound act of the will is likewise complete only in a compound of elements, and so not reducible to a single element. It is true that the complete compound act of the will is free with the borrowed freedom of rationality's basic autonomy and the proper freedom of *velle*'s "ought." But this is to say that *the will is free insofar as acts of human willing are materially and formally constituted by meaning*. They are materially constituted by meaning insofar as the deliberative process generates its hypothetical means through an intellectual process both autonomously generative of constructed, phantasmatic expressions of intellect in act and governed by the autonomy of *velle*'s "ought." Human acts of willing are formally constituted by meaning insofar as the process of deliberation is governed by and issues from willing brought to act and specified by the good

---

see Bernard Lonergan, *Insight: a Study of Human Understanding*, ed. Frederick E. Crowe and Robert M. Doran (Toronto: University of Toronto Press, 1992), 305–6.

11 "For the will is such that it not only desires good ordered in an intelligible way but also desires it because of the principle of that order, that is, the end—in other words, it desires value" (Lonergan, *The Triune God: Systematics*, 674).

meant in an autonomously constructed expression of intellect in act. In other words, the very substance of the act of willing and so the autonomy of its determinate "ought" is a meaning.[12]

The borrowed and originating autonomy of human acts of willing is matched by a formal freedom pertaining to the will as operated by itself. Complete and compound acts of the will are formally free in two ways. First, there is the freedom of specification. The means selected are not necessary on the supposition of anything else. Thus, the selection of means in light of this indeterminacy reveals an integral liberty of the will to specify for itself the concretization of its own efficacy. Second, there is the freedom of exercise. Because the means selected are not selected as the term of an apodictic argument, in order for the volitional procedure issuing in a free action to be rational, the will must move itself both to the termination of the deliberative process of discerning and evaluating means and also to settling upon a practical judgment and a course of action. In brief, the complete compound act of the will is free insofar as it includes the decision to act or not, and this decision constitutes the outstanding condition on which the action as a contingent effect depends.[13]

The foregoing has been haunted by an *aporia*. Does the gnoseological affirmation of being in the verified concept, from which an originating act of willing the end may follow, render the action manifesting that act superfluous? For what is willed as an end is the good known in a word, immanent in

12 This is an elaboration of what I take Lonergan to mean by the "virtually" free act of the will. Now, Lonergan means that willing the end is virtually free on the supposition that it produces a formally free act of the will. Willing the end, no matter how rationally, cannot be that in which freedom of the will per se consists because it is not an act whereby the will moves itself, but in which the will is moved by its agent object, the good as immanent in a word. For Lonergan's distinction between formally and virtually free acts of the will, see Lonergan, "God's Knowledge and Will," 327. See also Lonergan, *Grace and Freedom: Operative Grace in the Thought of St. Thomas Aquinas*, ed. Frederick E. Crowe and Robert M. Doran, CWL 1 (Toronto: University of Toronto Press, 2000), 96–98, 318–21.

13 "In the exercise of a formally free act, a person is the cause per se, inasmuch as having willed the end and deliberated on the basis of this willing of the end, one now moves oneself to willing the means to the end.... In the specification of this same formally free act, a person is the cause per se inasmuch as by willing the end one wills this particular practical judgment to be the final one in accordance with which one moves to will the good presented by that judgment" (Lonergan, "God's Knowledge and Will," 329).

a concept. But what is good by reason of itself is a whole and a unity. It is intelligible, complete, and existing, for the good is concrete.[14] The good known in a word, immanent in a concept, can be at most whole, unitary, and intelligible. It might even be virtually complete, insofar as the more perfect the act of *intelligere* from which the word proceeds, the more the good known therein will approach perfection. But the good known in a word *merely as known in a word* cannot be existing, nor really complete. If it were, no practical means could prove needful, nor any *actus imperfecti* going forth in matter would be required to realize our volitional intentions. I would say, therefore, that the will "knows" the good in a word "spoken" in the subjunctive mood. Indeed, precisely because it is uttered in the subjunctive mood, it can be willed as the end of a volitional process that contains and, moreover, terminates in the *actus imperfecti* of a practical project.

A distinction is called for, then, between the "ought" of what is and the "ought" of what is not. Admittedly, I have in the foregoing been eliding this needful distinction to underline the distinct autonomy proper to the operation of the will. I have, in other words, been focusing on the productive element in the will. But I began from the concept affirmed in the judgment of fact and it is in the reflective "yes" that being is known as a matter of fact. Such *verba* are not uttered in the subjunctive mood, but in the declarative. The convertibility of the transcendentals constrains me to say that the will might come to act with regard to the goodness coterminously present in such a word so uttered. But if the "ought" that issues from the will in act pertains to that which already is, has this willing become superfluous or even futile on my model of the rational appetite? Not at all. I need only to distinguish the *desire* to realize some end in accord with the will's "ought" from the *love* one may have for some reality that similarly accords with the will's "ought." For there is no contradiction or futility in recognizing that what ought to be in fact is.

Of course, this resolves only the objective difficulty. The subjective question remains: is willing an already extant end manifest in the same manner as willing an end desired? Does love show itself immediately in a movement? And if the movement is to that which is and is precisely as in possession of its prior conditions, then is not this manifesting movement superfluous or futile? But the Thomist definition of love includes a hint to this conundrum. Love, on this view, is to will good to something. There is now not just the intentional

14 Lonergan, 299: "That which is good by reason of itself is an existing whole, that is, one, intelligible, complete, and existing."

object of love in the uttered word, the expressed concept, but there is also the substantial object of love to which the lover may be really related. Thus the originating movement of the will is analogous in the way detailed above to a judgment that, as a matter of fact, this extant being is good and it ought to be. Thus, the immanent *actus imperfecti* that follows from and is governed by the will's originating *actus perfecti* is not the hypothetical construction of means that would fulfill the end's prerequisite conditions but rather a kind of commitment, a readiness to serve and support, to contribute to and participate in, to cooperate with (insofar as I am able) the continued being of this being that ought to be.[15] Human loving is, in this way, a state of waiting-on the beloved, both in the sense of an attentive preparedness and in the sense of an other-oriented service. In this way, by love one wills a being's own goodness to it as both object-which is loved and the object-to-which the good is willed in love. I might say that such love, insofar as it is in accord with the autonomy of the will's "ought," ratifies the being of a being insofar as it is good.[16]

Free Human Actions

Human actions are free with a human freedom. It is a freedom to act or not to act. It is a freedom to determine which of a multiplicity of feasible means will determine one's course of action. It is, in this regard, a

---

15 This is an elaboration of what I take Lonergan to mean when he speaks of love as by nature uniting the mind affectively to the object loved. See Lonergan, *The Triune God: Systematics*, 679: "Second, it may seem as if the procession of Love, like the procession of the Word, is also a generation, since in both cases God proceeds from God. But against this is the fact that it is of the nature of generation that there not only proceeds that which is similar in nature [to its principle], but also that that which proceeds is similar by reason of the procession itself. Now, by its very nature the procession of an inner word is such that what is conceived in the word is the very same thing as what is understood by the intellect. But by its very nature the procession of love is such that it does not reproduce its object in the mind but rather that the mind joins and unites itself affectively with the object loved." See also *The Triune God: Systematics*, 675.

16 Of course, God does not will to produce creatures out of a desire predicated on a lack, but rather out of love, so that God's love for us causes us to be. See Lonergan, "God's Knowledge and Will," 313. See also Frederick E. Crowe, "Complacency and Concern in the Thought of St. Thomas Aquinas," *Theological Studies* 20 (1959): 1–39, 198–230, 343–95; David Burrell, *Aquinas: God and Action*, 3rd ed. (Eugene, OR: Wipf and Stock, 2016), 137–40.

freedom of independence. It is also a freedom governed by *velle*'s "ought," a law it properly produces for itself. Further, it is a freedom that proceeds rationally in accord with a borrowed intellectual law. Human freedom, in this regard, is a freedom of autonomy. This freedom proceeds both as *processio operationis* and *processio operati*, for *verba* produce the exercise of freedom as an operation in the will, but also as a product that above I have called "action-as-effect."

This has a perhaps startling implication. Where above human knowledge showed itself mediated by meaning through the integral process of conceptualization, here free human actions show themselves at once mediated by, but also fundamentally *constituted* by meaning. The key here is the subjunctive mood in which the *verba* initiating volitional process are "uttered" (*dicere*) in a judgment of value. These *verba* serve a mediating function in the exercise of human freedom, mediating between good apprehended and the deliberation about means, between the course of action as intelligently conceived and as substantially pursued. The *verba*, however, also serve a constitutive function. They are the agent object of volitional process. Their substance governs and so orders the series of acts in which the process consists. But what intelligibly orders a multiplicity into an identifiable whole ("this action") is the formal cause of that whole.

Finally, the substantial practical project that proceeds from a complete volitional process is governed by and so ordered to this meaning-constituted intention expressed by the *verba*. They function, then, as the essential *telos* of that project's being-toward essence, its *actus imperfecti*. For example, while fire depends as a natural effect on intelligible causal preconditions to come to act, the free human action called "arson" depends on a meaningful decision to come to act and so into being. In other words, arson *is* arson because of what the action-as-effect *means*. Human actions, then, are independent and autonomous, and so recognizably free. What I have labored to reveal above is the manner in which human actions are both mediated but also formally constituted by meanings and that these meanings emerge *poetically* no less than autonomously.

Human actions are carried rationally from motivation to reality by the mediating affirmations or negations uttered in judgments of value. But prior to this, they are founded upon the compound constructions of intellect and imagination that we affirm in judgments of fact and that express our insights into our experience. These constructions express a meant and express it rationally. Thus, insofar as the will is a rational appetite, the constitutive function of meaning in human actions is as integral to their freedom as conceptualization and rationality is to knowledge.

Articulating the Modern Problem of the Supernatural

At long last, the elements are assembled to articulate the modern problem of the supernatural adequately. Heretofore I have expressed the modern problem by the question, "What is God doing in free human action?" I have explored according to the logical techniques of metaphysics and the broadly phenomenological techniques of psychological description in both *"what God is doing …"* and *"… free human action."* I showed that what God is doing is governing human action by creation, conservation, and application. God operates our free agency as an instrument of his will. But still this did not reveal *what* God is accomplishing by this governance. Perhaps, though, my analysis of free human action provided a created analogue for God's uncreated free action? Could one not ask after God's intended end and motivation for which he acts through our actions? But God's end and motivation is His love for the divine goodness, which is *in se* ineffable and mysterious.[17] Could one get somewhere by asking after God's selected means to this transcendent end? I already showed the answer to this question: our free actions—in concert with the order of the universe as a whole—are God's selected means or, as I spoke of them so many chapters ago, "instruments." All of this I have in other ways asked and answered before. The modern problem cannot be solved by metaphysical analysis.

---

17 Lonergan, "God's Knowledge and Will," 309–11: "In God's single act of willing, the sole motive, the sole intended end or end of the agent, is the divine goodness itself. We, of course, can will means to the end not only for the sake of the end but also for their own sake. So, for example, we will to take a sweet-tasting medicine both for the sake of our health and also for its pleasant taste. This is possible because the goodness of the means adds to the goodness of the end. But divine goodness is the absolute good, and all other good things are good through participation in this absolute good. Since, therefore, divine goodness is the source of all other goodness, no other good can add any goodness to it, and since no other goodness adds to divine goodness, it is quite impossible that another goodness could provide any other motive whatsoever over and above the divine goodness itself." See also *Summa theologiae*, 1, q. 19, a. 2, ad 2m, 3m, 4m; a. 4, ad 3m; a. 5 c; q. 20, a. 2 c.

Fortunately, my analysis of free human action has shaken loose an additional element: those meanings formally constitutive of human actions. The constitutive function of meaning in free human action calls out for a technique I have not yet deployed. Metaphysical analysis only shows that the constituted acts are, are free, and are meaningful. Psychological description represents the experience of the various acts and their conscious qualities, sequences, and so forth. A technique specially suited for apprehending meanings immanent in the material artifacts of poetical process is needed. Human actions go forth in matter, marking the material with our intentions. Progress toward the modern problem of the supernatural, then, requires *hermeneutical* techniques of interpretation. But not just any hermeneutics will do. Human actions are not only mediated by acts of meaning but *constituted* by them. Furthermore, the effects of human actions are produced as compounds of the intelligibility meant by the action and the materiality in which it is expressed. Finally, but also most importantly, because human acts are not just formally, but also ontologically, existentially constituted by meaning, the entire field of human action and its effects is by extension produced by the constitutive function of those meanings. The field of the meaningful cannot be reduced to pure intelligibility, for that would sacrifice the very rationality on which theory depends. Nor can it be reduced to the material, for in the field of free human action, there are no purely material acts.[18] Consequently, the modern problem of the supernatural calls out for a radical and philosophical hermeneutics of the kind developed in what, following Frederick Lawrence and Lonergan, I have been calling the Second Enlightenment.

Still, the totality of human action is not synthesized into a single project and so no flatly general hermeneutics will do, no matter how radical or philosophical. There exists no kingdom of ends.[19] Human action is, rather, aggregated into enterprises at various scales and of various kinds, distributed across time and space. Of course, human action is subject also to the division sown by the surd of sin and evil that sunders human cooperation. But even if I bracket such failings and consider human cooperation only normatively,

---

18 See for example Paul Ricoeur, "Ideology and Utopia," in *From Text to Action: Essays in Hermeneutics II*, trans. Kathleen Blamey and John B. Thompson (Evanston, IL: Northwestern University Press, 2008), 300–316.

19 On a "kingdom of ends," see Immanuel Kant, *Groundwork for the Metaphysics of Morals*, ed. and trans. Mary Gregory and Jens Timmermann (Cambridge: Cambridge University Press, 2012), 41–46.

the basic material, temporal, and geographic divisions remain. Nonetheless, collective human enterprises at once give rise to and are founded upon common funds of meaning and value. But a community fund of meanings and values for an aggregate of persons is a culture.[20] As the practical projects of any one person are never hatched entirely *de novo*, but emerge in accord with available experiences, ideas, and on-going enterprises, so that person's actions arise in an intelligible nexus of these. Thus, free human actions are at once principally constitutive of cultures and also materially constituted by culture.

Whether in regard to my own actions, those of another person, or the aggregate whole of the human community, in order to answer the question that expresses the modern problem of the supernatural, "What is God doing in free human action?" there is required a *theological hermeneutics*, not in general, but *of culture* or, perhaps more precisely, of *cultures*, plural.[21] This prospective

20 "Besides the classicist, there also is the empirical notion of culture. It is the set of meanings and values that informs a way of life. It may remain unchanged for ages. It may be in process of slow development or rapid dissolution" (Lonergan, *Method*, 4). "More generally, human community is a matter of a common field of experience, a common mode of understanding, a common measure of judgment, and a common consent. Such community is the possibility, the source, the ground of common meaning; and it is this common meaning that is the form and act that finds expression in family and polity, in the legal and economic system, in customary morals and educational arrangements, in language and literature, art and religion, philosophy, science, and the writing of history. Still, community itself is not a necessity of nature but an achievement of man. Without a common field of experience people get out of touch. Without a common mode of understanding, there arise misunderstanding, distrust, suspicion, fear, hostility, factions. Without a common measure of judgment people live in different worlds. Without common consent they operate at cross-purposes. Then common meaning is replaced by different and opposed meanings. A cohesion that once seemed automatic has to be bolstered by the pressures, the threats, the force that secure a passing semblance of unity but may prepare a lasting resentment and a smoldering rebellion" (Bernard Lonergan, "Natural Right and Historical Mindedness," in *A Third Collection*, 2nd ed., ed. Robert M. Doran and John D. Dadosky, CWL 16 [Toronto: University of Toronto Press, 2017], 164–65).

21 To forestall a potential misunderstanding, I should note that the "theological hermeneutics of culture" envisioned here is theological insofar as it keeps transcendent agency and so the potential for transcendent acts of meaning in the frame while interpreting cultures. It is not meant to suggest an analogue to what has come to be known as the "theological interpretation of scripture," which takes a particular dogmatic context and content as the hermeneutical key for interpreting scripture. The theological hermeneutics of culture envisioned here would, for example, view

technique is theological insofar as makes the quiddity of divine meaning in history the object of its investigation. It is a hermeneutical technique insofar as it aims not at elucidating the conditions of the factual, nor describing the experience of the material, but interpreting the significance of the expressed, the meaningfully accomplished. Finally, it is "of culture" in that it centers culture as the matter, the "text" in which the cooperation of divine and human meaning immanently resides, but also as the reality accomplished.

Of course, matter is a principle of individuation. Cultures are, as expression of aggregate human communities, *de facto* multiple. At the same time, the divine *concursus* is universal. Thus, I alight upon that which makes this problem of interpreting divine meaning expressed in the concrete multiplicity of human cultures *modern*. The classical ideal of science, that would reduce the contingent to the necessary, suits a classical notion of culture. If there is one normative culture, then in human matters one could reduce the contingent variations (and "deficiencies") to their necessary principles (or failures of their efficacy). But the products of human freedom are necessary only on the presupposition of themselves. They are contingent, and moreover contingent upon something that contingently moves itself to act. So too are the meanings that formally constitute freedom's expression. As I have already shown, a metaphysical reduction will over and over again fail to gain traction on the part of the problem that is of the greatest consequence: *meaning*. What does God mean by the meaning-constituted actions, effects, and products of human agents?

The modern ideal of science, however, accords with our basic medieval commitment to God's transcendent causality. Modern science in the broad sense speaks only of verified possibilities, eschewing the antique division of the cosmos into necessary and contingent.[22] This, in turn, accords with the empirical notion of culture at the core of the problem here articulated. To ask what God is doing in free human action in this modern, radically hermeneutical way—the only way that can get any traction—is to ask after the divine meaning expressed in *every* human culture in a field extending indefinitely through time and across geography. The technique proportionate

---

dogmatic definitions as the expressions of a cultural milieu without remainder, but not on that basis foreclose the possibility that divine meanings are nonetheless genuinely disclosed thereby.

22 See Bernard Lonergan, "Dimensions of Meaning," in *Collection*, ed. Frederick E. Crowe and Robert M. Doran, CWL 4 (Toronto: University of Toronto Press, 1988), 232–45.

to this problem—a theological hermeneutics of culture(s)—cannot produce a synchronic theory to resolve, once and for all, the modern problem as posed. Nor can it settle for a phenomenology of religious experience or the like. Rather, its task is irreducibly diachronic, going on as long as human history does. But it is a matter of fact that intelligence intends unity. How can this technique address the modern problem of the supernatural in a manner that gives rise to more than a mere catalogue of differences? In the subsequent, eleventh, and final chapter, I briefly suggest how, by reflecting upon its own unfolding procedure, a theological hermeneutics of culture(s) might generate and refine a *method* that will order the series of scholarly acts in which any effort to address the modern problem will recurrently consist.

Conclusion

Perhaps it is clearer now why I gave such short shrift to the more obvious, putatively modern form of the problem of the supernatural in chapter 8: the question of the natural desire to know God. That specific metaphysical problem and the medieval, metaphysical solutions put forward to address it can do no more than restate the genuinely modern problem of the supernatural. How are we to discern what God is up to in free human action and in its cultural and historical products? Indeed, I pushed the metaphysical restatements of this question as far as they would go. I considered divine governance of human action and found that the question remained. I considered the nature of those free acts of the will on which free human actions rest and considered too the rationality on which volitional acts rest. I showed again that the question remained: what is God doing in free human actions? And this question can only be answered by discerning what divine meanings pertain to those actions and the human meanings that constitute them.

Pushing these restatements, however, was not an act of stubborn futility, nor a *reductio ad absurdum*. It revealed within the metaphysical efforts to address the problems of the supernatural, of God's *ad extra* agency in free human action, a residue of a higher problem. This residue I uncovered in the function of meaning within the rational and volitional processes on which free human action rests. Because meaning has an integral, mediating, and constitutive function in the prerequisite processes of free human action, it is at last visible how I made good on my promise to demonstrate that the modern problem of the supernatural is diachronic and radically hermeneutical. Moreover, I was able to discern on the basis of this diachronic hermeneutical residue some determinations by which to anticipate the solution to the modern problem. A diachronic and radically hermeneutical problem calls out for a diachronic and radically hermeneutical solution. So I proposed a theological hermeneutics of culture(s) that is irreducible to either metaphysical analysis or phenomenological description and that in fact must consist in the on-going, cumulative, progressive, and critical application of an intellectual technique, which is to say of a scholarly *method*. I turn in the next, indeed final chapter to a brief sketch of such a method's criteria for adequacy.

THE THEOLOGICAL HERMENEUTICS OF CULTURE(S)

Up to now I have accumulated a number of problems, distinctions, theorems, solutions, mentalities, ambiguities, and techniques. It is time to review these and how they coalesce to complete my final constructive proposal. There are two problems of the supernatural and the second, modern, diachronic, and hermeneutical problem is irreducible to the first, medieval, metaphysical problem. Moreover, whether these problems would be resolved by recourse to a negative or a positive solution depends on how one responds to the ambiguities of being. That is to say it depends on what prephilosophical posture of human freedom one takes before the problems themselves. Thomas Aquinas's solution to the medieval problem (mediated here by Bernard Lonergan's retrieval) rests upon the decision to construe the world as fundamentally susceptible to explanation. Blondel and Sartre showed two ways in which the modern philosophical mentality helped to make this decision explicit rather than tacit. The irreducibility of the modern problem to the medieval solution rested as well on a commitment to the complete explicability of being, but viewed through the lens of Thomas's affirmation that created causes universally cooperate with God's *ad extra* agency. From this vantage, I showed that interpreting "what God is doing in human action" requires explaining the data on God's work in history. Moreover, because human action is formally constituted by meaning, the data on God's work in history will be data on the meaningful products of human agency—namely, our culture(s). To this end, I suggested the development of a *theological hermeneutics of culture(s)* that would investigate what human action has concretely meant in its cooperation with God.

Admittedly, my notion of a theological hermeneutics of culture amounts to no more than a heuristic indication of the technique required. I distinguished the modern problem from the medieval problem and solution on the grounds that the former must be diachronic and hermeneutical, but the latter is synchronic and theoretical or metaphysical. But there are many theologies, many hermeneutics, and many cultures. Indeed, my focus on the exercise of freedom antecedent to the practice of philosophy implies the way in which all theologies, philosophies in general, and any philosophical hermeneutics in particular are themselves cultural products. Consequently, these basic determinations (diachronicity and hermeneuticality) are not of themselves adequate criteria for the technique by which to address the modern problem of the supernatural. Some further determinations are needed to guide in the development of this technique from anticipation to reality. In other words, a more developed heuristic is needed. After a brief review of the ground already covered, my task in this short final chapter will be developing such a heuristic. My controlling image for this heuristic consists in three Cartesian planes, intersecting as a Y-, an X-, and a Z-axis. Along the Y-axis one would plot theories of transcendence. Along the X-axis, one would plot differences of traditional/cultural context. Along the Z-axis one would plot axiologial transformations of intellectual, moral, religious, and theological authenticity and so the dynamics of what Lonergan has called progress, decline, and redemption.[1]

---

1 Lonergan explains these "differentials" with an analogy from Newton's planetary theory: "It was about 1937-38 that I became interested in a theoretical analysis of history. I worked out an analysis on the model of a threefold approximation. Newton's planetary theory had a first approximation in the first law of motion: bodies move in a straight line with constant velocity unless some force intervenes. There was a second approximation when the addition of the law of gravity between the sun and the planet yielded an elliptical orbit for the planet. A third approximation was reached when the influence of the gravity of the planets on one another is taken into account to reveal the perturbed ellipses in which the planets actually move. The point to this model is, of course, that in the intellectual construction of reality it is not any of the earlier stages of the construction but only the final product that actually exists. Planets do not move in straight lines nor in properly elliptical orbits; but these conceptions are needed to arrive at the perturbed ellipses in which they actually do move. In my rather theological analysis of human history, my first approximation was the assumption that men always do what is intelligent and reasonable, and its implication was an ever increasing progress. The second approximation was the radical inverse insight that men can be biased, and so unintelligent and unreasonable in their choices and decisions. The third approximation was the redemptive process resulting from God's gift of his grace to individuals and from the manifestation of his love in Christ Jesus. The whole idea

The notion of a theological hermeneutics of culture(s) addressed the subjective determinations of the modern problem, insofar as free human actions issue from a rational process that is mediated and constituted by meaning. These three axes serve to indicate and organize the objective data to which a theological hermeneutics of culture will be applied. The scale of the task posed by integrating these three axes into the unity of adequate understanding suggests that the development and application of this technique will have to be cooperative. Furthermore, the application of this technique will also have to be adaptive to the concreteness of its object. However, because the application of the technique will have to be cooperative and adaptive, but also because this cooperation and adaptation is to be effected by free human agents, there will be needed some reflection on the relative successes and failures of the technique and its application. Finally, the products of this reflection will need to be cooperatively and adaptively applied to the cumulative and progressive application of the technique to the data. Scholars will need to evaluate whether their efforts are producing cumulative and progressive results or not and cumulatively and progressively refine their methods. Thus, the theological hermeneutics of culture will also need to be a critical, cooperative, and methodical theology, whether in its full sense as applied to the data on divine self-communication or in a methodologically restricted philosophical mode.

The theology indicated by these heuristic determinations constitutes the only viable genre of response to the modern problem of the supernatural. Insofar as it is critical, it can be at home in the modern philosophical mentality and its demand for *via inventionis* validation. Insofar as it is adaptive and methodical, it is open in principle to scholarly reflection upon any and every culture. The nature of my integrating "Cartesian" scheme does not just allow for, but positively calls for the scholarly coordination of inquiries

---

was presented in chapter twenty of *Insight*. The sundry forms of bias were presented in chapters six and seven on common sense. The notion of moral impotence, which I had studied in some detail when working on Aquinas' notion of *gratia operans* in my dissertation, was worked out in chapter eighteen on the possibility of ethics" (Bernard Lonergan, "*Insight* Revisited," in *A Second Collection*, 2nd ed., ed. Robert M. Doran and John D. Dadosky, CWL 13 [Toronto: University of Toronto Press, 2016], 228–29; see also Bernard Lonergan, "The Human Good as Object: Differentials and Integration," in *Topics in Education: The Cincinnati Lectures of 1959 on the Philosophy of Education*, ed. Robert M. Doran and Frederick E. Crowe, CWL 10– [Toronto: University of Toronto Press, 1993], 49–79).

into multiple traditions/cultures insofar as they generate reflections on what God has done (and is doing) in history. This is true on the side of the object(s) under scholarly investigation, but it is also true on the side of the theologizing subject. Dealing with the data that raise the modern problem of the supernatural on the modern problem's terms poses a theological task that, even if we could freeze time and turn off the tap of history, fairly drowns the scholarly imagination. Thus, the theological hermeneutics of culture must also become a cooperative theology. But before investigating more thoroughly the consequences of integrating theology's three axes, I will review how I came to the precipice of a modern solution to the modern problem of the supernatural.

Summary of the Foregoing Constructive Proposal

In part 1, I jumped into the controversy over the supernatural as it was revived in the twenty-first century. This revival, unfortunately, occurred in much the same terms as the mid-twentieth century controversy. By drawing a parallel between the argumentative strategies deployed in the 1940s and in the early decades of this century, I tried to show that the debate is if not per se intractable, then de facto at a stalemate. In response to this intractability, I proposed that part of the problem with the problem of the supernatural is that it consists not in a single, but a *pair* of theological issues. The first is a long-standing medieval metaphysical quandary about how divine and human agency can both be at work in creation without crowding each other out. I have called this the medieval problem of the supernatural. The second problem asks how this cooperation between human beings and God can be discerned not in synchronic metaphysical terms but in the existential subject, in historical process, and in the kaleidoscopic panoply of human cultures across both time and geography. I contended, against the overwhelming tendency of the literature on the contemporary controversy, that the modern problem is irreducible to the medieval one. Consequently, possessing a solution to the latter does not of itself grant one an adequate solution to the former. I also argued that in order to address the modern problem adequately, one cannot simply dismiss the medieval problem. A mistaken position on the metaphysics of cooperation between human beings and God will set inquiry into the modern problem off on a goose chase for divine action unsullied by human taint, setting human autonomy in competition with God's universally efficacious agency. This in turn eventually leads some to the skeptical conclusion that God's agency in history cannot be known, because everywhere one looks there are only human meanings. And so both mid-century and contemporary Thomists are correct with regard to the indispensability of the Thomist metaphysical achievement, but the adherents of the *Nouvelle théologie* and their neo–de Lubacian inheritors are also correct that this achievement is ultimately insufficient to address problems of "our age."

Having construed the medieval problem in terms of operation, of action, and so as a theological problem of divine and human cooperation, in the chapters that make up part 2 I engaged in a lengthy retrieval of Lonergan's interpretation of St. Thomas on God's *ad extra* agency. I considered Thomas's theory of cooperation in general, with special reference to the problematics of grace that occasioned Aquinas's breakthroughs and to the synthetic position on divine and human cooperation it implies. Lonergan showed us how the advent of the theorem of the supernatural elucidated a need for grace beyond changes in the states of human nature vis-à-vis sin. Human beings have an ontologically fundamental need for grace to make us proportionate to acts meriting eternal life, whether we are under sin's law of death or not. This theorem demonstrates its mobility, however, insofar as it also indicates the compatibility of this need for grace with the integrity of our created freedom. It makes a general theory of *concursus* possible by which one can say how free human action cooperates with God's providential action without being denatured. The theorem of the supernatural also makes a special theory of cooperative grace possible as well. By the latter one can say how it is that human beings cooperate with God in habits and actions beyond the proportion of our created powers without impinging on the integrity of our freedom either. Furthermore, I showed how the notion of "entitative disproportion" at the heart of the theorem of the supernatural also distinguishes the general case of *concursus* from the specific instance of cooperative grace.

In part 3, I showed how the general—which is to say, the *philosophical*—application of the theorem of the supernatural suggests what I have called the medieval ambiguity of being. By divine *concursus* every created cause is caused as to its existence by God, for only God is proportionate to existence as an effect. But this invites one of two basic attitudes with regard to the divine causality: either it makes the greatest possible difference (for without it, there would be nothing at all) or it makes no difference at all (for everything that is exists). One can quite easily take existence for granted—that is, take it as a mere matter of fact—and set about investigating the world of finite beings entirely without reference to a transcendent agent. One can come to think that the question of fundamental explanation is not a question worth asking at all. This decision with regard to the meaningfulness of the question of being reflects back upon itself. One is invited to read the task of investigating the explicability of finite being as but one more merely factual being in the universe for which it is meaningless to demand a fundamental explanation. Alternately, one can take a more mystical posture with regard to human inquiry, setting it (and all other human action with it) within a cosmos whose ultimate explanation (and so purpose) is at once preeminently real but also ultimately hidden in the mystery of God's transcendent self-knowledge. Because both of these postures concern the meaningfulness and worthwhileness of asking and answering questions at all, adopting one or the other is necessarily a prephilosophical exercise of freedom.

Just because the medieval ambiguities of being became possible with the appearance of Thomas's theory of *concursus* in the thirteenth century did not mean that cognizance of it became probable straight away. I argued that a modern philosophical mentality came onto the scene, raising the likelihood anyone might actually advert to the medieval ambiguities. This mentality is marked by its insistence on a separated rather than subordinated philosophy and the elevation of its *via inventionis* to a criterion of validity for its conclusions. Within this mentality, I turned to two examples of how, according to each pole of the ambiguity, the modern philosophical mentality would come to articulate the ambiguities of being. In Maurice Blondel I showed a cumulative and progressive analysis of the explanatory role that God's *ad extra* agency would play if it were not excluded by the modern philosophical mentality's method of immanence. This explanatory lacuna persists, Blondel showed us, in every possible arena of phenomenological examination and yet cannot be closed except by a prephilosophical exercise of freedom— namely, a commitment to the transcendent, supernatural explicability of being in general and in human action specifically. Sartre, by contrast, begins from an opposed prephilosophical commitment that being simply is and so (as being) admits no explanation. Free human action likewise is and so then is also explained by nothing, such that any kind of rationalization of our actions proves a bad faith avoidance of responsibility. The explanation of our actions is simply that we freely chose to act. With Blondel, I acknowledged holding to the basic, if transcendent, explicability of being and human action. Thus I could indicate by contrast that Sartre's philosophy is a philosophy in bad faith insofar as it offers philosophical justifications for its basic commitment, even though it rests on a prephilosophic act of freedom. This does not render the prephilosophical choice posed by the medieval ambiguity of being philosophically decidable. However, it does unmask the pretension of existentialist atheism to establish itself as the only rational philosophy of action or foreclose the affirmation of transcendent meaningfulness as a good faith exercise of human freedom.

Before turning to part 4, I briefly considered the perhaps-more-familiar candidate for the modern problem of the supernatural, the question of the natural desire to know God. Quickly, however, I set out to show that the genuinely modern problem of the supernatural is in fact insusceptible to the techniques of metaphysical analysis. Moreover, I argued that aiming to address the question of what God is doing in human action by means of such metaphysical techniques would only succeed in restating the problem itself, rather than answering it. I turned this apparent dead-end to my advantage by developing some determinations of the modern problem from these metaphysical restatements, training my metaphysical analysis on human action itself, determining that, as free and human, it issues from acts of the will. I then considered the will in detail as "rational appetite," first by a lengthy excursus on the intellectual process of rationality itself and then the rationality of free human acts by extension. I offered something of an uncanny discovery in this process: human rationality, in its most fundamental form, is mediated by meaning. Further, we found that acts of the rational appetite are not just mediated but also constituted by meaning, for they proceed in the first place from a word, a *verbum*.

The constitutive function of meaning in human action proved the key to articulating the modern problem of the supernatural. Human action is historical. It emerges as meaningful from a diachronic process. Moreover, it emerges from a world of meaning that also has emerged from a meaning-mediated, meaning-constituted diachronic process. Free human agents are formed and constrained by the horizon set out in the aggregation of these actions and their products. The shared horizon of a community of free human agents is a culture, and so it is in cultures that the evidence on what God is doing in free human action coalesces into its matrices of relevance. However, cultures are many and explanation is unitary. How then can there be any solution to the modern problem of the supernatural? I indicated heuristically a technique for investigating these networks of data on the modern problem of the supernatural. I·called this technique a "theological hermeneutics of culture(s)." But the unity of a shared technique is not enough, for that is only a subjective unity. There is needed also a unity of results. For this, the technique must be developed, through reflection and refinement, into a method that yields cumulative and progressive results. What remains is to indicate the criteria for any methodical solution to the modern problem of the supernatural.

The Axes of Critical Cooperative Methodical Theology

With the above freshly in mind, I turn now to this final task: spelling out the significance of my heuristic scheme for applying a theological hermeneutics of culture(s) to the data on the modern problem of the supernatural. Any theology that would meet the modern problem of the supernatural should be coordinated across three axes. I will imagine them intersecting in the manner of Cartesian planes. First, such a theology must include at least an implicitly operative notion by which to speak of God. For this, I imagine a Y-axis on which to plot notions of transcendence.[2] Second, if a theology would resist charges of naïveté, chauvinism, parochialism, or special pleading, it must further make the critical step of understanding, evaluating, and discerning the principle of differences between itself and its others. For this, I imagine an X-axis on which to plot cultural, horizonal, or "contextual" differences. Third, a critical theology is not yet a methodical theology. A methodical theology takes stock of the conditions under which theologies have made progress and/or suffered decline, aiming to regularize the conditions of progress in pursuit of cumulative results.[3] A methodical theology has a theory of the dynamics of its own intellectual history and aims at taking the relevant

---

2 That the Y-axis is for plotting notions of transcendence does not prejudge whether theologies will affirm a strong or weak transcendence or deny divine transcendence altogether. However, insofar as the exigence for this scheme rests on Thomas's medieval solution to the medieval problem of the supernatural—namely, a strong theory of divine transcendence—it unavoidably presupposes that other doctrines of God will be coordinated with reference to it.

3 The manner in which I have built the modern problem of the supernatural atop Lonergan's characterization of Thomas's solution to the medieval problem of the supernatural would be one example of such speculative accumulation.

conditions in hand to guide the process into the future. For this, I imagine a Z-axis on which to plot genetic developments according to the differential transformations of progress, decline, and redemption. Coordinated across these three axes, a critical methodical theology can take shape. I will take each axis in turn, and then conclude by discussing why this scheme calls out for an unprecedented scholarly cooperation in stern and vertiginous terms.

Transcendence

For a time, the tendency to think of God as a being among beings stymied St. Augustine's inarguably powerful theological mind.[4] Still, his breakthrough unto the eternality and immateriality of God took a nascent form, operating as a basic doctrinal commitment controlled by an operative grammar.[5] His apprehension of God's transcendence meant that certain ways of speaking were inadmissible both as dogmatic formulation and speculative construction. Still, we can surmise that Augustine was not thereby able to articulate a speculative theorem that allowed the cascade of corresponding speculative theological problems to be resolved. Recall from chapter 3 how Augustine posits the distinction between operative and cooperative grace without explaining precisely how it answered the speculative difficulty driving denial of the gratuity of grace and/or the reality of human freedom. It was not until the medieval theorem of the supernatural came on the scene with Albert the Great, Philip the Chancellor, and Thomas Aquinas that these difficulties could be faced head on. A more adequate theory of transcendence allowed whole areas of theological inquiry to fall into a single

---

4 For Augustine's first-person account of this struggle, see St. Augustine, *The Confessions of St. Augustine,* trans. John K. Ryan (New York: Image, 2014).

5 By "grammar" here I mean something like what Kathryn Tanner calls "ruled structures of theological talk and their function." For Tanner, "theological statements work to establish Christian vocabularies and the usage rules appropriate for those expressions. In doing so, frameworks for discourse are constituted within which it makes sense to talk *about* God and try to conform one's self to Christian truths." Though Tanner does consider speculative questions of divine agency, she does so in accord with the Anglo-American analytic and pragmatist traditions of deriving theorematic content from the relationships among signs in a discourse, rather than by a more empirico-inductive path of analogy proper to the Aristotelian and Thomist tradition of metaphysical reasoning. See Kathryn Tanner, *God and Creation in Christian Theology: Tyranny or Empowerment?* (Oxford: Basil Blackwell, 1988), 10–13.

view—and, indeed, within the purview of a series of sufficiently diligent and prolific geniuses.

One may note several such figures who tip Christian theology into new epochs by the force of their commitment to a central, organizing theory of transcendence. Schleiermarcher's insight that the absolute transcendence of God, thought within the horizon of philosophical romanticism and idealism, suggested that the absolute dependence of creatures could itself be an (albeit indeterminate) state of consciousness (*Gefühl*). The miraculous perfection of this *Gefühl* in Christ controlled Schleiermacher's entire speculative response to the traditional *loci* of Christian theology in his *Glaubenslehre*.[6] In this fashion, he was able to produce what is among the most genuinely *systematic* Christian systematic theologies, controlled throughout by a single notion. But even when they are rather less systematic in structure, all theologies require at least an implied, controlling position along this "Y-axis" concerning transcendence. This is no less true if that position involves a denial of transcendence (Feuerbach) or radical modification of the notion (Process Theology). Moreover, all theologies necessarily benefit from that controlling principle of grammatical control finding theoretical elaboration, as one can see in the development between Schleiermacher's speeches and *Christian Faith*.

Context

Any "great man" theory of theological development raises the problem of adjudicating between the speculative visions of various theological schools and their masters. There arises the intellectual gridlock by which adherents of one system level extrinsic critiques at the adherents of another system for violations of their inherited first principles. When one speaks of "decadent scholasticism," one element of the imputed decadence consists in this deductive intractability. Recall, for example, Descartes's annoyance at philosophies of mere "plausibility." Moreover, responsible scholarship anymore recognizes that one ought not anachronistically or a-contextually hold the systems of major figures up to one another for brute comparison. Rather, one should make theoretical evaluations in light of the cultural circumstances under which their thought was developed and set down. This,

---

6 See Friedrich Schleiermacher, *Christian Faith*, ed. Catherine L. Kelsey and Terrance N. Tice, trans. Terrance N. Tice, Catherine L. Kelsey, and Edwina Lawler (Louisville, KY: Westminster John Knox Press, 2016).

at first blush, seems to bring in the question of history, but in fact such considerations pertain more properly to questions of what we might call "context" or culture.

Note, for example, how Thomas's moral theory is conditioned (though not determined) by its contemporary controversies in ways that make it only comparable by analogy to, for example, Kant's moral philosophy and its contemporary debates.[7] There are genuine points of contact, but substantive, even essential differences must be surveyed and controlled for. What goes for the agents of a theology goes too for its object(s). Indeed, this is the very heart of the modern problem of the supernatural: that God's work is manifest in the artifacts of cultural making precisely *as* cultural artifacts and in the making *qua* making. Thus, accounts of what God wrought in first-century Palestine can be compared and contrasted with what God has done, say, on the Indian subcontinent certainly, but only in terms of the cultural artifacts that persist in our world from theirs. This brings challenges, though they do not at all constitute an impossibility. Still, a certain analogical heuristic has to be followed lest the worst sins of interreligious polemics go uncritically repeated.[8]

These differences in context—whether individuated by historical epoch, geographical distance, or simply subcultural/demographic divisions—can be coordinated. Because they have a unitary principle (that is, the dynamism of human cognitive and volitional being) functioning as the variable from which their variations originate, to the extent that they emerge authentically and are intelligible, they possess a necessarily analogical relationship with one another. However, in chapter 10 I argued that theology cannot answer the modern problem of the supernatural by reducing these differences to their principle of variation and that they cannot be bracketed metaphysically. As a result, such artifacts must be investigated according to their place in the concrete

---

7 See for example Jean Porter's retrieval of the scholastic concept of the natural law and its relationship to modern and contemporary approaches thereto (*Nature as Reason: A Thomistic Theory of the Natural Law* [Grand Rapids, MI: Eerdmans, 2005], 1–52); see also Susan Neiman's account in *Evil in Modern Thought* of the moral theological debates into which Kant's moral theory emerged (*Evil in Modern Thought: An Alternative History of Philosophy* [Princeton, NJ: Princeton University Press, 2015], 14–83).

8 And, after Vatican II, a Roman Catholic theology is certainly not permitted to repeat them. See *Nostra Aetate*, October 28, 1965, http://www.vatican.va/archive/hist_councils/ii_vatican_council/documents/vatii_decl_19651028_nostra-aetate_en.html.

social, cultural, interpersonal, or religious order in which they are situated, which is itself constituted by human meanings, values, and actions.

To represent this vector of investigation, I have imagined the corresponding "X-axis." Along this axis, differences internal to a religious or theological tradition/culture would be at turns distinguished and catalogued, but also correlated. At the same time, each religious or theological tradition/culture would maintain a view to the investigation of parallel or adjacent religious or theological traditions/cultures occurring alongside. One may see an example of one such tandem investigation in David Burrell's *Towards a Jewish-Christian-Muslim Theology*.[9] Though the Jewish, Christian, and Muslim tracks converge on the work of Thomas Aquinas, Burrell is able to show how consonant but as-yet-incompatible positions developed under rather different religious and cultural pressures. Thus, he avoids the temptation to read later synthesis and development back through the traditions, imposing an occlusive sameness upon them. In this way, analogous positions can be given their due in terms of both similarity and difference, and a properly theoretical approach to theology can be wedded to a critical and historically conscious theology.

I should further note that Burrell's project does not only coordinate these investigations according to their socio-cultural similarities and differences. To do so would reduce theologians to sociologists of knowledge. It is not enough to take cognizance of this horizontal, X-axis of religious thought and practice. Its coordinates need to be at the same time correlated, as in Burrell, according to the theorematic positions on transcendence along the Y-axis. Theology cannot forget to speak explicitly of what God has done and is doing in the world, even when it recognizes that it always at once speaks *of* and *from* diverse human worlds. Conversely, if I note that the failure to take theology's X-axis into account risks naïveté, chauvinism, parochialism, or special pleading, I still leave out the arguably more serious critiques of power that mobilize so many "contextual" theologies, but that topic is more apropos of the Z-axis to which I turn now.

History

One might be tempted to identify the X-axis with contemporaneous differences of context and the Z-axis with historically discrete differences of context, and so the X-axis with geography and the Z-axis with "history."

---

9 David Burrell, *Towards a Jewish-Christian-Muslim Theology* (Malden, MA: Wiley-Blackwell, 2011).

This should be avoided. First, digital globalization has put to the sword the idea that cultural communities are identifiable with geographical proximities. Second, history is not strictly speaking reducible to temporal succession but is constituted by meanings and values that are always susceptible to configuration and reconfiguration.[10] Thus, the X-axis covers both of these kinds of differences, the temporal and the geographic. As mere differences in time and place do not make a difference in the applicability of classical physical laws, so mere differences of time and place do not make a difference in the explanatory power of well-wrought theological speculation. The rather-late centering of Thomas Aquinas's philosophy and theology in Catholic thought provides compelling evidence that his thought has relevance beyond Paris and the thirteenth century—even if it was shaped by historical, cultural, philosophical, and theological conditions at play there and then. This is precisely the point. The differences that make a difference are not those of mere time and place, but differences in the substantial meanings and values constituting the cultural world in which God has been at work in the religious life of a community and the reflection of its theologians. Consequently, these differences may fall along a single axis.

What *does* the Z-axis coordinate? Though theologies can be coordinated according to both theorematic and contextual differences, they can also be related as genetic stages of historical process. As such, they may be evaluated according to whether they amount to progress or decline or redemption. Religions, like any element of a culture, can flourish or they can fester, can grow or stagnate or recover anew, can emerge or collapse or rebuild. For Lonergan, theology becomes methodical when it can yield cumulative and progressive results. Thus, a theology needs to take stock of religious development and decline and redemption, plotting it along this Z-axis. Moreover, a theology must also appropriate its own historical trajectory, working to contribute to the accumulation and development and, as often as not, recovery and reconfiguration of theological understanding to clarify theological confusion. In this way, a theology needs to take a stand on the relative authenticity of religious practice and understanding but also on the authenticity of past scholarly reflection thereupon, to say

---

10 For a theological theory of history informed by Lonergan and Blondel but also sensitive to the impact of colonialism and race on our own cultural context, see Anne M. Carpenter, *Nothing Gained Is Eternal: A Theology of Tradition* (Minneapolis: Fortress Press, 2022).

nothing of scholars in their cooperation with God's grace. This facet of the theological task amounts to a "dialectical traditionalism" that appropriates its historical position in a religious and/or theological tradition but also inveighs "yes" or "no" as to whether elements therein ought to be carried forward or repudiated or remade. The concrete value of these decisions within a tradition constitute the inertial transformations in which progress or decline or redemption consist. Methodical theologians should not avoid coordinating their evaluations along this Z-axis, and they certainly cannot avoid having their evaluations coordinated by both contemporary and subsequent theologians in turn. The risk shared by every theology is that these judgments may be mistaken and so themselves contribute to a trajectory of decline. But if they are correct, resting upon intelligent inquiry, reasonable reflection, responsible deliberation, and a loving commitment to the good and its transcendent source, they contribute to the flourishing, the development, perhaps the recovery of a theological tradition and those "others" with which may be in dialogue.

The Demand and Challenge of Theological Cooperation

Once the theoretical (Y-axis), critical (X-axis) and the methodical (Z-axis) exigencies have been introduced to the theological task by the modern problem of the supernatural, the "great man" theory of theological advancement is no longer viable. Theology as a discipline has to transcend, through the generation of cumulative and progressive results, the historicity that conditions the individual theologians who produce it. To address the modern problem of the supernatural, it has to take stock of the work of God in the worlds of human culture across geography, society, and history. Moreover, recognizing now that the theorems guiding theological speculation are themselves the product of cultural process, theology cannot settle within a single theoretical horizon. It has to coordinate and analogically communicate between a diversity of theoretical horizons. Our task demands a "speculative pluralism."[11] Moreover, theology has to wrangle with the work above and its voluminous data in a way that does not simply catalogue what has gone

11 For an extended development of "speculative pluralism," see Ryan Hemmer, *The Death and Life of Speculative Theology: A Lonergan Idea* (Lanham, MD: Lexington Books/Fortress Academic, 2023).

before, but also takes its own stand on which new questions need answering, what old answers need revision, and which accomplishments—past and present—call out for continued attention, appropriation, and development.

On the other hand, "theology" cannot perform the above tasks, but only theologians—theologians who pray, read, study, think, and write from their concrete horizons. Consequently, no single theologian can perform the whole of the theological task. Indeed, no theologian (even as inestimable a theologian as St. Thomas Aquinas) can provide a unitary horizon in which all other theologians can then work with the force of his or her genius at their collective backs. No, theology at the level of our time can only be done in a decentered way, mediating between a religion and its cultural matrix while at the same time mediating between cultural matrices and evaluating from its vantage the relative authenticity of the religion, the cultural matrices, and the theologies at play in both its contemporary scene and that scene's effective history.[12] If nothing else, the billowing clauses of the above sentence should give some sense of the unwieldiness of this task and the need for a massive, intercultural, intergenerational, interdisciplinary cooperation in theology. This need is at once essential to theology's self-realization and also rather extravagantly beyond its present means.

Consequently, theologians face the temptation to define their task down by excising one or more of theology's axes. Perhaps one could forgo the existential risk of normative evaluation and only concern ourselves with disclosing the decenteredness of culturally and historically conscious theology? If theology lightens its load in this manner, one might expect to encounter a certain decadent postmodern theology that, if it theorizes at all, theorizes exclusively about the absolute alterity of God and the relative, but still impenetrable alterity between cultures, times, and even persons. Alternatively, perhaps theologians can find some refuge from the staggering expanse of cultural particularity in the logical inferences of theological speculation, laying down evaluations insofar as they accord with or contradict our theoretical formulations? But if the weight of history is removed from the theologian, the dual circumscription of a speculative theology's abstractive viewpoint is removed. The material circumscription of theology's cultural

---

12 This language, of theology mediating between a religion and a culture and its place in the matrix of that culture, is taken from the opening pages of Bernard Lonergan, *Method in Theology*, 2nd ed., ed. Robert M. Doran and John D. Dadosky, CWL 14 (Toronto: University of Toronto Press, 2017), 3.

horizon is occluded, but also the formal circumscription constituted by the particular valence of its questions. Theological answers become orphaned from their source in the light of agent intellect. Thus, one encounters a decadent scholasticism that assumes reality can be rendered entirely transparent by any adequately wrought metaphysics. But if metaphysics seems, in its airy speculation, too impractical an approach for theology to put front and center, perhaps theology can put ethics and moral theory in its place. Perhaps theology can content itself to inveigh for and against religions and theologies as they accord with or contradict our convictions about what constitutes moral thought or practice, foregoing the self-doubt that afflicts a liberal preoccupation with pluralism or the self-indulgent fastidiousness of metaphysical speculation. Such a theology, however, cannot but face the charge of idolatry, having decided for itself which God seems fit to worship, begging the question, "Whence these moral intuitions and their criteria?" No doubt readers can call to mind for themselves theologies embodying any one or more of these strategies for lightening theology's load. They may have some opinion about which are more forgivable, which more derisible. I exhort us, instead, to face the task in its full dimension and, as ever, do what we can with what we have, having faith that all these things will be added unto us. Recognizing the need and scope of a theological hermeneutics of culture(s) is trouble enough for today.

BIBLIOGRAPHY

Aquinas, St. Thomas. *Commentaria in Octo Libros Physicorum.* Translated by Richard J. Blackwell, Richard J. Spath, W. Edmund Thirlkel, and Pierre H. Conway. New Haven, CT: Yale, 1963.

———. *De Substantiis Separatis.* Translated by Francis J. Lescoe. West Hartford, CT: St. Joseph College, 1959.

———. *Expositio Libri Posteriorum Analyticorum.* Translated by Fabian R. Larcher. Albany, NY: Magi Books, 1950.

———. *In Librum De Causis Expositio.* Turin: Marietti, 1955.

———. *Quaestiones Disputatae de Potentia Dei.* Translated by the English Dominican Fathers. 1932. Reprint, Westminster, MD: Newman Press, 1952.

———. *Quaestiones Disputatae de Veritate.* Translated by Robert W. Mulligan, James V. McGlynn, and Robert W. Schmidt. Chicago: Henry Regnery, 1952–54.

———. *Quaestiones Quodlibetales.* Turin: Marietti, 1949.

———. *Scriptum Super Libros Sententiarum Magistri Petri Lombardi Episcopi Parisiensis.* 4 vols. Paris: Lethielleux, 1929–47.

———. *Sententia Libri De Anima.* Translated by Kenelm Foster and Sylvester Humphries. New Haven, CT: Yale University Press, 1951.

———. *Sententia Libri Metaphysicae.* Translated by John P. Rowan. Chicago: Henry Regnery, 1961.

———. *Summa Contra Gentiles.* Translated by Anton C. Pegis, James F. Anderson, Vernon J. Bourke, and Charles J. O'Neil. New York: Hanover House, 1955–57.

———. *Summa Theologiae.* Translated by Fathers of the English Dominican Province. New York: Benzinger Bros., 1947.

Aristotle. *The Basic Works of Aristotle.* Translated by C. D. C. Reeve. 1946. Reprint, New York: Modern Library, 2001.

———. *De Anima: Books II and III with Passages from Book I.* Translated by D. W. Hamlyn. Oxford: Oxford University Press, 1993.

St. Augustine of Hippo. *The Confessions of St. Augustine.* Translated by John K. Ryan. New York: Image, 2014.

———. *De Correptione et Gratia.* In *S. Aurelii Augustini Opera Omnia (Latin Edition)*, PL 44. Accessed March 14, 2019. http://www.augustinus. it/latino/correzione_grazia/index.htm.

———. *De Gratia et Libero Arbitrio.* In *S. Aurelii Augustini Opera Omnia (Latin Edition)*, PL 44. Accessed March 14, 2019. http://www.augustinus.it/ latino/grazia_libero_arbitrio/index.htm.

Bernardi, Peter J. *Maurice Blondel, Social Catholicism, and Action Française: The Clash over the Church's Role in Society during the Modernist Era.* Washington, DC: The Catholic University of America Press, 2009.

Blondel, Maurice. *Action (1893): Essay on a Critique of Life and a Science of Practice.* Translated by Oliva Blanchette. Notre Dame, IN: University of Notre Dame Press, 1984.

———. *Une Alliance Contre Nature, Catholicisme et Intégrisme: La Semaine Sociale de Bordeaux, 1910.* Reprint, Bruxelles: Éditions Lessius, 2000.

———. *The Letter on Apologetics and History and Dogma.* Translated by Alexander Dru and Illtyd Trethowan. Grand Rapids, MI: Eerdmans, 1994.

Boersma, Hans. "Sacramental Ontology: Nature and the Supernatural in the Ecclesiology of Henri de Lubac." *New Blackfriars* 88, no. 1015 (2007): 242–73.

Braine, David. "The Debate between Henri de Lubac and His Critics." *Nova et Vetera (English Edition)* 6, no. 3 (Summer 2008): 543–89.

Brotherton, Joshua R. "The Integrity of Nature in the Grace-Freedom Dynamic: Lonergan's Critique of Bàñezian Thomism." *Theological Studies* 75, no. 3 (2014): 537–63.

Burrell, David B. *Aquinas: God and Action.* 3rd ed. Eugene, OR: Wipf and Stock, 2016.

———. "On Thomas Joseph White's Wisdom in the Face of Modernity." *Nova et Vetera (English Edition)* 10, no. 2 (Spring 2012): 531–37.

———. *Towards a Jewish-Christian-Muslim Theology.* Malden, MA: Wiley-Blackwell, 2011.

Byrne, Patrick H. "God and the Statistical Universe." *Zygon: Journal of Religion & Science* 16, no. 4 (1981): 345–63.

Carpenter, Anne M. *Nothing Gained Is Eternal: A Theology of Tradition.* Minneapolis: Fortress Press, 2022.

Coakley, Sarah. *God, Sexuality, and the Self: An Essay 'On the Trinity.'* Cambridge: Cambridge University Press, 2013.

Colberg, Shawn M. "Aquinas and the Grace of Auxilium." *Modern Theology* 32, no. 2 (2016): 187–210.

Conway, Michael A. *The Science of Life: Maurice Blondel's Philosophy of Action and the Scientific Method.* Frankfurt am Main: Peter Lang, 2000.

Crowe, Frederick E. "Complacency and Concern in the Thought of St. Thomas Aquinas." *Theological Studies* 20 (1959): 1–39, 198–230, 343–95.

Cullen, Christopher M. "The Natural Desire for God and Pure Nature: A Debate Renewed." *American Catholic Philosophical Quarterly* 86, no. 4 (Fall 2012): 705–30.

Cunningham, Conor. "*Natura Pura*, the Invention of the Anti-Christ: A Week with No Sabbath." *Communio* 37, no. 2 (2010): 243–54.

De Lubac, Henri. *A Brief Catechesis on Nature and Grace.* Translated by Richard Anandez. San Francisco: Ignatius Press, 1984.

———. *The Drama of Atheist Humanism.* Translated by Mark Sebanc. San Francisco: Ignatius Press, 1995.

———. *The Mystery of the Supernatural.* Translated by Rosemary Sheed. New York: Herder and Herder, 1998.

———. "On Christian Philosophy." *Communio* 19 (Fall 1992): 478–506.

———. "*Remarques Sur L'histoire Du Mot 'Surnaturel'.*" *Nouvelle Revue Théologique* 61 (1934): 225–49, 350–70.

———. *Surnaturel: Études Historiques.* Paris: Aubier, 1946.

Descartes, René. *A Discourse on the Method of Correctly Conducting One's Reason and Seeking Truth in the Sciences.* Translated by Ian Maclean. Oxford: Oxford University Press, 2006.

Dupré, Louis K. *Passage to Modernity: An Essay in the Hermeneutics of Nature and Culture.* New Haven, CT: Yale University Press, 1993.

Feingold, Lawrence. *The Natural Desire to See God according to St. Thomas Aquinas and His Interpreters.* 1st ed. Naples, FL: Sapientia Press, 2004.

———. *The Natural Desire to See God according to St. Thomas Aquinas and His Interpreters.* 2nd ed. Naples, FL: Sapientia Press, 2010.

Gallagher, David M. "Thomas Aquinas on the Will as Rational Appetite." *Journal of the History of Philosophy* 29, no. 4 (October 1991): 559–84.

Gendlin, Eugene. *Experiencing and the Creation of Meaning.* Evanston, IL: Northwestern University Press, 1997.

Grumett, David. "De Lubac, Grace, and the Pure Nature Debate." *Modern Theology* 31, no. 1 (January 2015): 123–46.

Hart, David Bentley. *You Are Gods: On Nature and Supernature*. Notre Dame, IN: University of Notre Dame Press, 2022.

Healy, Nicholas J. "Henri de Lubac on Nature and Grace: A Note on Some Recent Contributions to the Debate." *Communio* 35, no. 4 (Winter 2008): 535–64.

Hemmer, Ryan. *The Death and Life of Speculative Theology: A Lonergan Idea*. Lanham, MD: Lexington Books/Fortress Academic, 2023.

Hütter, Reinhard. "Aquinas on the Natural Desire for the Vision of God: A Relecture of *Summa contra Gentiles* III, c. 25, *après* Henri de Lubac." *The Thomist* 73, no. 4 (2009): 523–91.

———. "*Desiderium Naturale Visionis Dei—Est Autem Duplex Hominis Beatitudo Sive Felicitas*: Some Observations about Lawrence Feingold's and John Milbank's Recent Interventions in the Debate over the Natural Desire to See God." *Nova et Vetera (English Edition)* 5, no. 1 (2007): 81–131.

———. *Dust Bound for Heaven: Explorations in the Theology of Thomas Aquinas*. Grand Rapids, MI: Eerdmans, 2012.

Kant, Immanuel. *Groundwork for the Metaphysics of Morals*. Edited and translated by Mary Gregory and Jens Timmermann. Cambridge: Cambridge University Press, 2012.

Lamb, Matthew L. "Fr. Bernard J. F. Lonergan, S.J.: The Gregorian Years." In *Lonergan's Anthropology Revisited: The Next Fifty Years of Vatican II*, edited by Gerald Whelan, 57–80. Rome: G & B Press, 2015.

Landgraf, Artur Michael. *Dogmengeschichte der Frühscholastik*. Regensburg, Germany: Verlag Friedrich Pustet, 1952.

Larsen, Sean. "The Politics of Desire: Two Readings of Henri de Lubac on Nature and Grace." *Modern Theology* 29, no. 3 (July 2013): 279–310.

Lawrence, Frederick. "'The Modern Philosophic Differentiation of Consciousness' or What Is the Enlightenment?" In *Lonergan Workshop*, vol. 2, edited by Fred Lawrence, 231–79. Chico, CA: Scholars Press, 1981.

Le Grys, James. "The Christianization of Modern Philosophy according to Maurice Blondel." *Theological Studies* 54, no. 3 (September 1993): 455–84.

Lombard, Peter. *Libri IV Sententiarum*. Florence: Ad Claras Aquas, 1916.

Lonergan, Bernard. *Collection*. 2nd ed. Edited by Frederick E. Crowe and Robert M. Doran. CWL 4. Toronto: University of Toronto Press, 1988.

————. *"De Ente Supernaturali."* In *Early Latin Theology*, edited by Robert M. Doran and H. Daniel Monsour, translated by Michael G. Shields, CWL 19, 52–255. Toronto: University of Toronto Press, 2011.

————. *"De Scientia Atque Voluntate Dei."* In *Early Latin Theology*, edited by Robert M. Doran and H. Daniel Monsour, translated by Michael G. Shields, CWL 19, 256–411. Toronto: University of Toronto Press, 2011.

————. *Grace and Freedom: Operative Grace in the Thought of St. Thomas Aquinas.* Edited by Frederick E. Crowe and Robert M. Doran. CWL 1. Toronto: University of Toronto Press, 2000.

————. *Insight: A Study of Human Understanding.* 5th ed. Edited by Frederick E. Crowe and Robert M. Doran. CWL 3. Toronto: University of Toronto Press, 1992.

————. *Method in Theology.* 2nd ed. Edited by Robert M. Doran and John D. Dadosky. CWL 14. Toronto: University of Toronto Press, 2017.

————. *A Second Collection.* 2nd ed. Edited by Robert M. Doran and John D. Dadosky. CWL 13. Toronto: University of Toronto Press, 2016.

————. *A Third Collection.* 2nd ed. Edited by Robert M. Doran and John D. Dadosky. CWL 16. Toronto: University of Toronto Press, 2017.

————. *Topics in Education: The Cincinnati Lectures of 1959 on the Philosophy of Education.* Edited by Robert M. Doran and Frederick E. Crowe. CWL 10. Toronto: University of Toronto Press, 1993.

————. *The Triune God: Systematics.* Edited by Robert M. Doran and H. Daniel Monsour. Translated by Michael G. Shields. CWL 12. Toronto: University of Toronto Press, 2007.

————. *Verbum: Word and Idea in Aquinas.* Edited by Frederick E. Crowe and Robert M. Doran. CWL 2. Toronto: University of Toronto Press, 1997.

Long, D. Stephen. Review of *Natura Pura: On the Recovery of Nature in the Doctrine of Grace*, by Steven A. Long. *Modern Theology* 27, no. 4 (2011): 695–98.

Long, Steven A. *Natura Pura: On the Recovery of Nature in the Doctrine of Grace.* New York: Fordham University Press, 2010.

————. "On the Loss, and the Recovery, of Nature as a Theonomic Principle: Reflections on the Nature/Grace Controversy." *Nova et Vetera (English Edition)* 5, no. 1 (2007): 133–83.

————. "On the Possibility of a Purely Natural End for Man." *The Thomist* 64, no. 1 (2000): 211–37.

Malloy, Christopher J. "De Lubac on Natural Desire: Difficulties and Antitheses." *Nova et Vetera (English Edition)* 9, no. 3 (2011): 567–624.

Mansini, Guy. "The Abiding Theological Significance of Henri de Lubac's *Surnaturel.*" *The Thomist* 73, no. 4 (2009): 593–619.

———. "Henri de Lubac, the Natural Desire to See God, and Pure Nature." *Gregorianum* 83, no. 1 (2002): 89–109.

Matava, Robert Joseph. *Divine Causality and Human Free Choice: Domingo Báñez, Physical Premotion, and the Controversy de Auxiliis Revisited.* Boston: Brill Academic, 2016.

Milbank, John. *The Suspended Middle: Henri de Lubac and the Debate concerning the Supernatural.* 1st ed. Grand Rapids, MI: Eerdmans, 2005.

———. *The Suspended Middle: Henri de Lubac and the Renewed Split in Modern Catholic Theology.* 2nd ed. Grand Rapids, MI: Eerdmans, 2014.

———. *Theology and Social Theory: Beyond Secular Reason.* 2nd ed. Malden, MA: Blackwell, 2006.

Misner, Paul. *Catholic Labor Movements in Europe: Social Thought and Action, 1914-1965.* Washington, DC: The Catholic University of America Press, 2015.

———. *Social Catholicism in Europe: From the Onset of Industrialization to the First World War.* New York: Crossroad, 1991.

Moloney, Raymond. "De Lubac and Lonergan on the Supernatural." *Theological Studies* 69, no. 3 (2008): 509–27.

Mulcahy, Bernard. *Aquinas's Notion of Pure Nature and the Christian Integralism of Henri de Lubac: Not Everything Is Grace.* New York: Peter Lang, 2011.

Neiman, Susan. *Evil in Modern Thought: An Alternative History of Philosophy.* Princeton, NJ: Princeton University Press, 2004.

Neville, Robert C. *God the Creator: On the Transcendence and Presence of God.* Albany: SUNY Press, 1992.

Nichols, Aidan. "Thomism and the *Nouvelle Théologie.*" *The Thomist* 64, no. 1 (2000): 1–19.

Oakes, Edward T. "Scheeben the Reconciler: Resolving the Nature-Grace Debate." *Nova et Vetera (English Edition)* 11, no. 2 (Spring 2013): 435–53.

———. "The Surnaturel Controversy: A Survey and a Response." *Nova et Vetera (English Edition)* 9, no. 3 (Summer 2011): 625–56.

Ormerod, Neil. "Addendum on the Grace-Nature Distinction." *Theological Studies* 75, no. 4 (2014): 890.

———. "The Grace-Nature Distinction and the Construction of a Systematic Theology." *Theological Studies* 75, no. 3 (2014): 515–36.

Osborne, Thomas M. "Natura Pura: Two Recent Works." *Nova et Vetera (English Edition)* 11, no. 1 (Winter 2013): 265–79.

Peirce, Charles Sanders. *The Essential Peirce: Selected Philosophical Writings.* Edited by Nathan Houser and Christian Kloesel. Vol. 1, *1867–1893*. Bloomington: Indiana University Press, 1992.

Pinckaers, Servais. "The Natural Desire to See God." *Nova et Vetera (English Edition)* 8, no. 3 (Summer 2010): 627–46.

Pius XII. *Humani Generis.* August 12, 1950. http://w2.vatican.va/content/pius-xii/en/encyclicals/documents/hf_p-xii_enc_12081950_humani-generis.html.

Porter, Jean. *Nature as Reason: A Thomistic Theory of the Natural Law.* Grand Rapids, MI: Eerdmans, 2005.

Ricoeur, Paul. "Ideology and Utopia." In *From Text to Action: Essays in Hermeneutics II*, translated by Kathleen Blamey and John B. Thompson, 300–316. Evanston, IL: Northwestern University Press, 2008.

———. *Time and Narrative.* Vol. 1. Translated by Kathleen McLaughlin and David Pellauer. Chicago: University of Chicago Press, 1984.

Rosenberg, Randall S. *The Givenness of Desire: Concrete Subjectivity and the Natural Desire to See God.* Toronto: University of Toronto Press, 2017.

Russell, Bertrand. *A History of Western Philosophy.* New York: Simon and Schuster, 1945.

Sadler, Gregory B. *Reason Fulfilled by Revelation: The 1930s Christian Philosophy Debates in France.* Washington, DC: The Catholic University of America Press, 2011.

Sartre, Jean-Paul. *Being and Nothingness: A Phenomenological Essay on Ontology.* Translated by Hazel Estella Barnes. New York: Pocket Books, 1966.

———. *Existentialism Is a Humanism.* Translated by Carol Macomber. New Haven, CT: Yale University Press, 2007.

Scheeben, Matthias Joseph. *Nature and Grace.* Translated by Cyril Vollert. St. Louis: B. Herder, 1954.

Schleiermacher, Friedrich. *Christian Faith*. Edited by Catherine L. Kelsey and Terrance N. Tice. Translated by Terrance N. Tice, Catherine L. Kelsey, and Edwina Lawler. Louisville, KY: Westminster John Knox Press, 2016.

Smith, Christopher. "*Surnaturel* Revisited: Henri De Lubac's Theology of the Supernatural in Contemporary Theology." PhD diss., Universidad de Navarra, 2013.

Sokolowski, Robert. "The Method of Philosophy: Making Distinctions." *Review of Metaphysics* 51, no. 3 (March 1998): 515–32.

Stebbins, J. Michael. *The Divine Initiative: Grace, World-Order, and Human Freedom in the Early Writings of Bernard Lonergan*. Toronto: University of Toronto Press, 1995.

Tanner, Kathryn. *God and Creation in Christian Theology: Tyranny or Empowerment?* Oxford: Basil Blackwell, 1988.

———. "Grace without Nature." In *Without Nature?: A New Condition for Theology*, edited by David Albertson and Cabell King, 363–75. New York: Fordham University Press, 2010.

Vatican Council II. *Gaudium et Spes*. December 7, 1965. http://www.vatican.va/archive/hist_councils/ii_vatican_council/documents/vat-ii_const_19651207_gaudium-et-spes_en.html.

White, Thomas Joseph. "Good Extrinsicism: Matthias Scheeben and the Ideal Paradigm of Nature-Grace Orthodoxy." *Nova et Vetera (English Edition)* 11, no. 2 (Spring 2013): 537–63.

———. "Imperfect Happiness and the Final End of Man: Thomas Aquinas and the Paradigm of Nature-Grace Orthodoxy." *The Thomist* 78, no. 2 (2014): 247–89.

———. "The 'Pure Nature' of Christology: Human Nature and *Gaudium et Spes* 22." *Nova et Vetera (English Edition)* 8, no. 2 (2010): 283–322.

———. *Wisdom in the Face of Modernity: A Study in Thomistic Natural Theology*. Ave Maria, FL: Sapientia Press, 2009.

Wittgenstein, Ludwig. *Philosophical Investigations*. Translated by G. E. M. Anscombe, P. M. S. Hacker, and Joachim Schulte. 4th ed. Malden, MA: Wiley-Blackwell, 2009.

Wood, Jacob W. *To Stir a Restless Heart: Thomas Aquinas and Henri de Lubac on Nature, Grace, and the Desire for God*. Washington, DC: The Catholic University of America Press, 2019.

SUBJECT INDEX

Controversy, 1, 31, 45, 56, 63, 156, 168,
184n20; *de auxiliis*, 3–4; *Surnaturel,*
4–5, 22; twentieth century, 4, 7, 14,
21–30, 214; twenty-first century, 5,
7, 13–30, 35–43, 53–54, 137, 159–60,
170, 214, 221
Cooperation, 43, 45–50, 54–59, 65,
67–69, 71, 78, 86–91, 99–108,
112–13, 117–19, 124, 141–46, 153,
203, 206, 208, 211, 213–15, 218–19,
224–25; *Concursus,* 3, 47, 55, 58, 69,
87, 88n55, 117, 169, 171–72, 208,
215–16; serial, 87–91, 100
Creation, 6, 18, 27, 41–44, 53, 59–62,
66–69, 72, 78, 79n31, 82–84, 86–91,
96–108, 112–14, 117–19, 124–25,
129, 137–38, 147–48, 155–56,
162–72, 203n16, 205, 211, 214–15,
220; doctrine of, 113, 119
Culture(s), 3, 17, 23, 26–27, 35, 39, 47,
108, 207, 211–14, 217, 220–25;
classical view of, 207n20, 208;
empirical view of, 207n20, 208;
modern, 31–33, 40, 48;
superstructure, 32; theological
hermeneutics of, 47, 207–12, 214,
218, 226

Decline, 3n7, 134, 212, 218–19, 223–24
Decision, 101, 113, 119–20, 170,
200–201, 204, 212n1, 224;
Pre-philosophical, 44, 49–50, 108,
115–16, 145–46, 148, 151–57,
168–69, 172, 211, 216–17
Desire, 56, 61, 83–84, 118–19, 137–38,
178, 200n11, 202, 203n16; for
God, 4, 14, 16, 18, 22, 27, 137–38,
160–69, 209, 217; to know, 145,
161–69, 178, 182, 185
Dialectic, 14–15, 24, 36, 48, 125, 136,
150, 152, 178; dialectical position,
55–58, 64; dialectical traditionalism,
224

Doctrine, 4, 17–18, 20, 23, 25, 28, 31,
55–58, 62, 65, 72, 75, 77–80, 108,
113, 119, 122–23, 125–30, 132–44,
155, 160, 162n7, 164, 200, 218n2, 219
Dogma, 42, 57, 63, 116, 124–25, 129,
134, 155, 207n21, 219
Dualism, 122, 129, 150

Empirical, 33, 37, 193, 207n20, 208,
219n5
Enlightenment, 33, 130; second,
33–34, 44, 46–47, 130, 170, 206
Essence, 28, 32, 34, 63, 66, 76, 89n61,
93, 99, 118–19, 128, 153, 156–57,
160–66, 169, 179–80, 191–92,
196–97, 198n7, 204, 221; essential
definition, 181, 182n2, 192–93;
beyond, 170
Existence, 81, 84, 88, 89, 91, 93–102,
105, 114–20, 128, 150–51, 154, 162n7,
164–65, 167–68, 172, 177n1, 187,
196n2, 200, 202, 206, 212n1, 215–16
Existential, 25, 30, 37–38, 45, 108,
112, 115–16, 120–21, 129, 141, 146,
151–52, 154, 168, 214, 217, 225

Freedom (see Liberty), 3, 8, 35, 44–45,
47, 55–58, 60–61, 64, 66, 71, 81, 91,
100, 102–3, 107–8, 114, 119–20,
132, 141, 143, 146, 152–57, 160,
172, 195–96, 200–205, 208, 211–12,
215–17, 219

Gaudium et Spes, 5, 29–30
Gift, 6, 25–26, 41, 56, 60, 62–63, 66,
98, 106, 144, 147, 172
Grace, 1–2, 4, 7, 24, 39, 47, 49, 54–68,
71, 73n5, 81, 86, 97–98, 101, 107,
112, 127, 156, 162, 164, 168, 172,
212n1, 224; nature and, 1–2, 4, 7,
14, 17–20, 25, 30, 35–37, 41–43, 53;
(co)operative, 54, 65, 67–68, 215, 54,
56, 67–68, 87, 215, 219